Home Money

HOW TO SAVE ENERGY AND DOLLARS IN YOUR HOME

BY
Richard Heede
WITH
Owen Bailey, Linda Baynham, David Bill,
Maureen Cureton, and Daniel Yoon

FOREWORD BY
Amory & Hunter Lovins

Rocky Mountain Institute
SNOWMASS • COLORADO

Brick House Publishing Company
AMHERST • NEW HAMPSHIRE

Rocky Mountain Institute
1739 Snowmass Creek Road
Snowmass, CO 81654-9199

Phone (303) 927-3851. Fax (303) 927-3420. E-mail: orders@rmi.org
Starting 2 April 1995: (970) 927-3851 and (970) 927-3420

Rocky Mountain Institute is an independent, nonprofit research and educational foundation whose goal is to foster the efficient and sustainable use of resources as a path to global security.

Please note that Rocky Mountain Institute does not endorse or warrant the businesses and products listed herein. We encourage you to shop around and compare, ask questions, and decide for yourself what is best for your home or business. We have made every attempt to be as complete and accurate as possible. While the resource sections at the end of each chapter list numerous manufacturers and organizations as a service to our readers, space limitations made it impossible to include all of the thousands of makers of efficient equipment or materials.

Please feel free to let us know how we can improve this book by writing us at the address above.

Portions of this book were previously published in *Practical Home Energy Savings*, Rocky Mountain Institute, 1991.

A Good Idea Book from Rocky Mountain Institute

What do we want the Earth to be like fifty years from now? Let's do a little dreaming and then see that this dream is not cut off at the pass. A future by design, not default. Aim high! Navigators have aimed at the stars for centuries. They haven't hit one yet, but because they aimed high they found their way.

—David Brower

Contents

Introduction

"What's the use of a house if you haven't got a tolerable planet to put it on?"
                                                    —Henry David Thoreau

Homemade Money sets before you a spread of cost-effective things you can do to make your home use energy and water more efficiently. None of the projects in this book requires a degree in rocket science. Some projects require just a phone call, some will send you to the hardware store, and others will induce you to put on the overalls, take the phone off the hook, and unholster that caulk gun.

The emphasis in this book is on suggestions that make economic sense, though they will undoubtedly also improve your comfort. Some measures cost nothing, many others will pay for themselves in less than one year, most of the rest in two to five years. After a project pays for itself, it will then be earning money for you. Energy and water efficiency won't be just a free lunch, but a lunch you're paid to eat.

As you leaf through these pages, check out the many low-cost or no-cost opportunities you can seize. As you'll see, in many cases it will be the easiest projects that make the biggest dents in your energy and water bills.

We can't say exactly how much you'll save by following the recommendations in this book—housing types, climates, and opportunities vary too much. But if your energy bills are high, you should be able to cut them by 20 to 30 percent without breaking a sweat. That's worth several hundred dollars per year, every year, in lower energy bills. You can save much more if you get serious about cost-effective ways to save energy. Use the discussion on priorities in Chapter 1 to guide your decision-making process.

Homemade Money is a tool to help you get involved. As you go through the book, don't be dismayed by the sheer number of suggestions. You can implement all of them or start with just one.

To help you decide what to do first, in *Part One* we have listed, in order, the projects that cost the least and will cut your bills the most. We also suggest what you can do if you're a renter or live in a mobile home, and tell you how you can seek financial assistance for energy improvements.

Part Two describes how to save energy in the heating and cooling of your home—everything from weatherstripping and insulation to advanced window glazings and high-efficiency furnaces.

Part Three looks at a variety of energy uses—water heating, appliances, lighting—and is similarly comprehensive in its suggestions for efficiency.

Part Four is for those who are designing and building a super-efficient house from the ground up. (In each chapter we've included checklists of energy-saving practices.)

In the *Appendix* we list whom you can call for information and supplies, and what resources you can use to go even further.

Foreword

People and nations behave wisely—once they have exhausted all other alternatives. —Abba Eban, Israeli diplomat and writer

Buildings aren't just a roof over our heads and where we spend upwards of 85% of our time. They also use a third of the energy and two-thirds of the electricity in the United States. Supplying energy to homes costs us over $110 billion a year. It costs our kids and the planet too. Making America's electricity, for example, converts a third of the nation's fuel resources into pollution, emitting a third of the carbon and nitrogen oxides and two-thirds of the sulfur oxides in the process.

Burning fuel in our homes or in the powerplants that keep the lights on and motors humming also imposes costs on others. The earth in Kentucky and Wyoming suffers when we dig up coal. Nuclear wastes provide an unwelcome kind of job security to those who must look after them for hundreds of thousands of years. Because we depend on other countries, often in unstable regions, for half our oil, our nation is less secure and less prosperous. Wastes from using energy pollutes our air, streams, forests, and oceans. Even the planet's climate may be in peril. How much of that depletion and pollution has your name on it?

Energy also consumes gigantic amounts of tax money. In recent decades, taxpayers have spent some $30–60 billion per year—the same as the total investment in durable-goods manufacturing industries—on subsidies to the energy sector. (It's hard to compete with other countries when we buy that much of the wrong stuff.)

Conversely, *saving* energy saves money, fuel, and pollution. It's typically cheaper to save fuel than to burn it, because it keeps the utility from having to build and run billion-dollar powerplants. Substituting energy efficiency for this fuel prevents pollution, not at a cost but at a profit.

The leverage is biggest in saving electricity. Since three or four units of fuel must be burned to make one unit of electricity, *saving* one unit of electricity avoids burning those three or four units of fuel, mainly coal, at the powerplant. The resulting environmental leverage can be astonishing.

A single compact fluorescent lamp, for example, can save enough coal-fired electricity over its lifetime to keep a power plant from emitting three-quarters of a ton of carbon dioxide (which contributes to global warming) and fifteen pounds of sulfur dioxide (which causes acid rain). Yet far from paying extra to help the environment, that lamp saves tens of dollars more in replacement lamps, labor, and fuel than it costs. It also defers hundreds of dollars worth of utility investments, dollars that could be invested more productively in other industries. Far from making us sacrifice quality of life, the efficient lamp yields warm, naturally colored light, with instant start, no flicker or hum, less glare, and about one-thirteenth the maintenance of a regular bulb. That's not a hard choice for us or for the earth.

Years ago, when Bill Clinton was still Governor of Arkansas, he had us analyze some innovative energy-saving opportunities. In a typical existing house in Little Rock with a central air conditioner, we found that a carefully selected package of off-the-shelf techniques (many of which are discussed in the following pages) could save three-fourths of the house's annual and over four-fifths of its summer-peak use of electricity. Its gas use would also fall by three-fifths without even improving the gas appliances. All the measures would pay for themselves in three years. Many were conventional: better insulation, weatherstripping, and caulking, and more efficient lights and appliances. (We also left out a few good ideas now better understood, such as a light-colored roof and more shade trees.)

Most important, though, were high-performance windows, installed right over the existing clear single glazings, and designed to let in light while reflecting heat away. The windows seemed expensive, but they cut the summer cooling loads so dramatically that they were largely responsible for eventually replacing the air conditioner with one two-thirds smaller than the old one. Because the next air conditioner was smaller, it was also cheaper; the saved money virtually paid the extra cost of getting a unit that was twice as efficient and three times as effective in dehumidification. Those improvements in turn saved a lot more energy. In all, those expensive windows made it possible to double the energy savings at one-third lower cost.

Today's technologies are even better. In 1992, Pacific Gas & Electric Company's Advanced Customer Technology Test for Maximum Energy Efficiency commissioned Davis Energy Group to design an experimental tract house for Ridge Builders. This 1,672-square-foot house in Davis, California, where temperatures can exceed 110°F, achieves normal summer comfort levels *with no air conditioner*—just excellent passive-solar design. It uses only one-fifth as much energy as the nation's strictest energy building code allows for the five biggest uses—space and water heating, space cooling, refrigeration, and lighting. It's also attractive, conventional-looking, and readily marketable.

The best news of all is that this innovative design, if widely practiced, would cost $1,800 *less* to build than a regular house, because eliminating its air conditioner, furnace, and ductwork more than pay for the energy savings that make them unnecessary. Similarly, maintenance costs, expressed in a lump sum in today's dollars, are $1,600 less.

The opportunities for saving energy in existing houses are often different, but they follow the same general principles: do the cheapest things first to wring more work from the energy you're already using. Let improvements do multiple duty. Start at the end of the application that you use, like the showerhead or faucet, and work back upstream toward the energy supply system like the water heater. Avoid losses in between and you can make the supply device smaller, simpler, and cheaper. Let the improvements cut the loads on your heating, cooling, and water heating equipment so that when those eventually need replacement, you can consider making the new ones smaller and using their downsizing to pay for making them even more efficient. Let the money saved by one measure pay for the next.

Your forays with a caulk gun and duct tape may seem small, but collectively, millions of such tiny savings now give our country two-fifths more energy than does the entire domestic oil industry. Added up, those little actions bring enormous national benefits. We can only spend a dollar on one thing at a time: if we spend it on oil ($50-billion a year imported, and $1 trillion already sent abroad to pay OPEC for the oil we blow out our tailpipes and chimneys), we can't spend it on books or computers. If we send it to a utility to turn coal into global warming, we can't spend it on public transit or on rebuilding our cities.

If we have trouble borrowing money to buy a house, maybe it's because on a larger scale too much of society's savings have been unwisely invested in other things. As a nation, we make such mistakes often: for example, $1 billion might be invested in an offshore oil rig rather than $10 million on a super-window coating machine that would save as much energy as the oil well would extract. Or maybe we spent $1 billion building part of a powerplant instead of $10 million on a machine to make compact fluorescent lamps of equivalent energy value, all because builders and householders bought the wrong light bulbs.

Efficiency, like charity, begins at home. In this second edition of our best-selling *Practical Home Energy Savings,* now updated, expanded, and renamed as *Homemade Money,* our colleagues at Rocky Mountain Institute try to anticipate and answer the questions we're asked most often about how to use household energy in a way that saves money, pollution, and hassle. This book provides practical hints and information sources that you can use to eliminate much of the resource use and pollution caused by your own home. By using resources more efficiently, your skill, imagination, and dedication to elegant frugality can truly help to build a better world—one house at a time.

—Amory and Hunter Lovins
Old Snowmass, Colorado
January 1995

Thank You!

Our gratitude and respect goes first and foremost to our colleagues who helped write parts of this book. David Bill, who is now building a co-housing community on Lopez Island in the maritimes of Puget Sound, Washington, wrote the original edition *(Practical Home Energy Savings)* of this book as a visiting researcher in 1990. Daniel Yoon, who is now with McKinsey & Co. in San Francisco, helped re-organize the book and wrote our chapter on windows. Linda Baynham, who is now at the University of Wisconsin, did much of the initial redrafting of the book's original chapters.

Richard Heede is the book's principal author and serves as RMI's Research Scholar. He has published widely on energy and climate policy, energy subsidies, and energy-efficient technology. He and his wife Susan Hassol recently designed and built a passive solar, superinsulated, rammed earth home near Rocky Mountain Institute.

Amory and Hunter Lovins co-founded Rocky Mountain Institute in 1982. They have published hundreds of articles and books on energy efficiency and policy over the years and have nurtured the Institute and its current staff of 40 individuals dedicated to fostering the efficient and sustainable use of resources. Amory invented most of the regulatory reforms that re-shaped the electric utility business in the 1980s and '90s. His major interest today is to transform transportation in the U.S.

similarly by re-thinking policy and land-use, and by encouraging the manufacture of safe, attractive four-passenger superefficient (150 to 400 mpg) hybrid-electric automobiles. Hunter is the President of RMI, supervises its Research Group, and does much of RMI's editing, including this book. We're grateful for Amory and Hunter's deep dedication to resource efficiency, and their exceptional ability to put a humanistic vision of a sustainable future into practice around the world and in their own lives.

Owen Bailey was an exceptional research assistant. Maureen Cureton kept a keen eye on accuracy and new products. Jeanette Darnauer managed the project and tirelessly edited the book. AJ Thompson and Richard Malik provided research and administrative support far beyond the call of duty. Our thanks go to our editor, Bob Runck of Brick House Publishing Company, for all his good advice and late nights. Many thanks to Jenifer Seal of RMI who drew or re-sketched most of the illustrations with a fine hand.

Thanks also to all of the experts who reviewed sections of this book for us: David Brook of the Oregon State University Extension Energy Service, Alex Wilson of *Environmental Building News*, Randy Udall of the Pitkin County Energy Office, Al Wasco and Don Jones of the Housing Resource Center, Ted Stedman of the Florida Solar Energy Center, Robert Sardinsky and Roger Leafgreen of Rising Sun Enterprises, Susan Reilly of EnerModal, Larry Weingarten of Elemental Enterprises, Bion Howard of The Alliance to Save Energy, Mona Newton of the Boulder Energy Conservation Center, Pat Huelman of the Cold Climate Housing Center, Steve Standiford of the Roaring Fork Energy Center, and Dennis Creech of Southface Energy Institute. Numerous others provided us with their expertise through telephone conversations and the written word.

We are especially grateful for funding from W. Alton Jones Foundation and The Educational Foundation of America.

Part One

A Formula for Saving Energy

Enough, if something from our hands has power
To live, and act, and serve the future hour.
—William Wordsworth

This book suggests hundreds of projects to make your home more resource efficient. Which ones make sense to do first? The answer is simple: do the easiest, most cost-effective measures first.

The following chapter will help you get started. You will also find three sets of prioritized measures, starting with the easiest, most cost-effective projects first, and ending with high-cost investments that may or may not make sense for your climate or situation. There is also a list of simple no-cost measures that make sense for nearly every homeowner or renter. Chapters 2 through 9 discuss all of these tips, and many more, in detail.

1

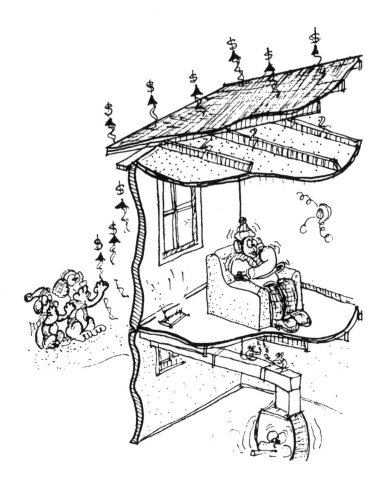

Energy efficiency doesn't mean you have to freeze in the dark. Adapted from an illustration by Saturn Resource Management, Helena, MT.

1

Priorities: What to Do First

Never doubt that a small group of thoughtful committed citizens can change the world. Indeed it's the only thing that ever has.
—Margaret Mead

Houses and apartments vary greatly in size, type of construction, age, solar exposure, insulation levels, previous weatherization, your climate, and so on. Despite this diversity, there are some likely best buys for your home listed below, and discussed more fully in following chapters.

The first chart, on the next page, shows the distribution of energy expenses for an average American household, which totals nearly $1,500. The second chart, on the following page, shows household energy consumption by region of the country. Few homes actually conform to these averages, however, and your bills may differ substantially. Use the charts only as a rough guide.

Getting started

1. Collect your fuel and electric bills for the last twelve months. Divide their total by the square footage of your home—but don't include garages and unheated basements. Most annual bills range from 60 to 90 cents per square foot. If your bills fall in this range, or are even higher, you have many cost-effective opportunities to dramatically reduce your bills. (Rocky Mountain Institute's bills are less than 10 cents per square foot per year.)

Average annual household energy expenditures in the U.S.

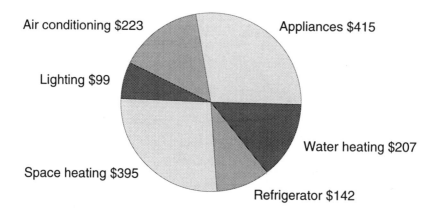

Air conditioning $223

Appliances $415

Lighting $99

Water heating $207

Space heating $395

Refrigerator $142

Statistics are for households of three to five occupants. Total expenditure averages $1,481. Adapted from Energy Information Administration (1993), *Household Energy Consumption and Expenditures, 1990*, p. 84, Washington, DC.

2. Measure the thickness of insulation in the attic, basement, and walls. Note the age and condition of your home's major heating and cooling equipment, appliances, the type of windows, and if your water heater is wrapped with an insulating jacket. How does your home feel? Is it drafty on windy days? Are you comfortable?

3. Call for help. Most State Energy Offices have useful consumer information booklets, and can refer you to local weatherization agencies and other energy experts who can help you
(telephone numbers are listed in the Appendix). Many electric
utilities offer free or discounted water heater blankets, new
showerheads, or compact fluorescent lamps; many also offer
financial incentives for the purchase of more efficient appliances or heat pumps.

**Typical household energy consumption in regions of the
U.S. (in million Btu per household per year)**

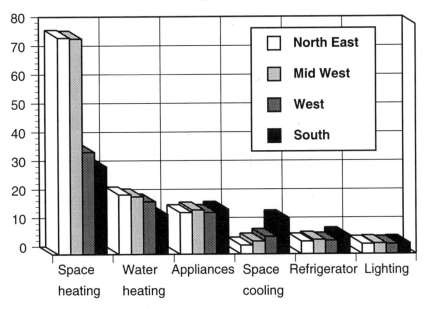

One Btu is roughly the amount of energy you'd get by burning one kitchen
match. Energy consumption is for energy used in the household only, and
does not include powerplant conversion and transmission losses. Adapted
from Energy Information Administration (1993), *Household Energy Consumption and Expenditures, 1990,* p. 54, Washington, DC.

4. You may want to have a comprehensive audit done on
your home, in which case the auditor should list, in order of

importance, what should be done. Many electric utilities and weatherization agencies will send an auditor to your home, often at no charge to you. Professional audits, including a blower door test, typically cost $50 to $150, but if your home energy bills are high it will most likely be worth it.

5. Make a plan of action. This book is full of cost-effective projects, and the following lists are a useful place to start. Feel free to substitute your own priorities, since only you, and the professionals who may be helping you, know your situation.

Priority lists

Free—things that cost nothing and save cash

√ Turn down water heater thermostat to 120°F.

√ Turn off lights when leaving a room.

√ Set thermostats to 68°F in winter when you're home, and down to 55°F when you go to bed or when you're away. Programmable thermostats are another option.

√ Use energy-saving settings on washing machines, clothes dryers, dishwashers, and refrigerators.

√ Wash clothes in cold water and only in full loads.

√ Don't waste water, hot or cold, inside or outside your home.

√ Clean your refrigerator's condenser coils once a year.

√ Air-dry your clothes.

√ Close heating vents in unused rooms.

√ Repair leaky faucets and toilets (5% of water "use" is leakage).

√ Close drapes (and windows) during sunny summer days and after sunset in the winter.

Simple and inexpensive—things that will pay for themselves in lower energy bills in less than one year

√   Install a water-saving 2.5 gallon per minute showerhead ($15).

√   Install water-efficient faucet heads for your kitchen and bathroom sinks ($2 each).

√   Install a programmable thermostat ($26).

√   In the attic and basement, plug the air leaks a cat could crawl through, and replace and reputty broken window panes ($\approx$ $20).

√   Clean or change air filter on your warm-air heating system during winter and on air conditioning units in the summer ($2).

√   Install an R-7 or R-11 water heater wrap ($12).

√   Insulate the first three feet of hot and inlet cold water pipes ($6).

√   Install a compact fluorescent light bulb in the fixture you use the most ($15).

Getting serious—measures that collectively will cost up to $500 and have paybacks of one to three years

√   Get a comprehensive energy audit, including a blower door test, to identify sources of air infiltration.

√   Caulk and weatherize all leaks identified by the test. Start with the attic and basement first (especially around plumbing and electrical penetrations, and around the framing that rests on the foundation), then weatherize windows and doors.

√   Seal and insulate warm-air heating (or cooling) ducts.

√   Have heating and cooling systems tuned up every year or two.

√   Install additional faucet aerators, showerheads, and
     programmable thermostats.

√   Make insulating shades for your windows, or:

√   Add insulating storm windows (or shade sunny win-
     dows or add solar gain control films in southern
     states).

√   Insulate hot water pipes in unheated basements or
     crawlspaces.

Going all the way—measures that will save a lot of energy and money, but will take three to fifteen years to pay for themselves

√   Foundation: insulate inside rim joist and down the
     foundation wall to below frostline to *at least* R-19 in
     cold climates and to R-11 or better in moderate
     climates. Remember to caulk first.

√   Basement: insulate the ceiling above crawlspaces or
     unheated basements to at least R-19 in cold climates.
     If your basement is heated, insulate the inside of base-
     ment walls instead to R-19 or more above grade and
     to R-11 or more below grade. Basement or found-
     ation insulation is usually not needed in hot climates.

√   Attic: increase attic insulation to R-50 in the northern
     U.S., R-38 in milder climates, and R-30 plus a radiant
     barrier in hot climates.

√   Walls: adding wall insulation is more difficult and
     expensive, but may be cost-effective if your house is
     uncomfortable. See the *Insulation* chapter for details.

√   Install more compact fluorescent bulbs. Put them in
     your most frequently used fixtures, including those
     outdoors.

√ Replace exterior incandescent lights with compact fluorescents and put them on a timer or motion sensor if they're on more than a couple of hours a night.

√ Install a radiant barrier in your attic if you live in the Sunbelt states.

√ Convert to solar water heating, and perhaps also supplementary solar space heating.

√ Upgrade your water heater, furnace, boiler, air conditioners, and refrigerator to more efficient models. Newer units are far more efficient. Upgrading is often cost-effective, and definitely cost-effective if you need to replace failing units anyway. Also, if you have weatherized and insulated, you will be able to downsize the heating and cooling system.

√ Upgrade to superinsulating or at least low-e windows in cold climates, or low solar transmittance windows in the southern U.S., if replacement is needed.

√ Replace high-flow toilets with modern water-efficient toilets that use 50% to 80% less water.

√ Install awnings or build removable trellises over windows that overheat your home in the summer.

√ Plant a tree to shade your largest west window in summer. You won't save any money for years, but you'll get an A+ for long-range vision.

Hundreds of other measures are discussed in this book. Some have quick paybacks, others may be lengthy. You may want to do some things regardless of their return on investment, just because your home will be more comfortable or because you'll sleep better knowing you prevented additional pollution.

Watt's a kill-a-watt hour anyway?

You really wouldn't want to kill a watt-hour even if you were a gun-toting cowboy, 'cause there isn't a lot of meat on one watt. You can just barely cook a pot of rice with a *thousand* watts if you leave it on the stove for a whole hour. And that is a "kilowatt-hour" (kWh) of electricity. Using it will cost about eight cents on average (though rates around the country range from 4.5 to 17 cents per kWh).

Watts x hours = watt-hours

1,000 watt-hours = 1 kilowatt-hour (kWh)

kWh use per year x $ per kWh = $ household electricity cost per year

For example: To find out how much it will cost to run a 60-watt porch light for 11 hours every night for a year when electricity costs $0.083 per kWh:

60 watts x11 hours/day = 660 watt-hours/day

660 Wh/d x 365 days/year = 240,900 Wh/year

240.9 kWh/year x $0.083/kWh = $20

(And this doesn't count the cost of having to replace the incandescent lightbulb five times during the year.)

For more information on how electricity, natural gas, and heat are measured, please see "How Energy Is Measured" in the Appendix.

How much does energy cost?

The efficiency with which different fuels are used matters greatly. For instance, while electricity is very expensive, its conversion efficiency *at your house* is near 100%, whereas 5% to 35% of the energy in natural gas escapes up the flue, depending on the efficiency of, say, the boiler or water heater. Even so, when energy cost and conversion efficiency are combined, gas water heating is the better buy—and better for the environment, too—than heating water with electricity.

Two-thirds of the energy in electricity is lost as heat to the environment before it gets to your house (these conversion and transmission losses account for the high cost of electricity versus other fuels in the table below). From the perspectives of cost, whole-system efficiency, and environmental impact, the use of electricity should be limited to its most important applications: lights, many appliances, air conditioning, computers, electronics, motors, and so on. If you already use electricity for less optimal uses such as space and water heating, it may be cost-effective to switch to solar, natural gas, or propane. If fuel-switching is not practical, this book contains lots of good tips for reducing your use of electricity.

The average cost of fuels and electricity in the U.S.			
Energy source	Cost per unit	Dollars per million Btu	Thousand Btu per dollar
Hardwood	$100 per cord	$4.65	215
Natural gas	$0.58 per therm	$5.80	172
Heating oil	$1.03 per gallon	$7.43	135
Propane	$0.74 per gallon	$8.10	123
Electricity	at 8.3 cents/kWh	$24.33	41
Electricity	at 12 cents/kWh	$35.17	28

Energy prices in 1992. Btus and therms are energy units; see the Appendix.

How much does energy *really* cost?

What's that question supposed to mean? Doesn't the sum of our energy bills indicate our total energy costs? Not exactly. In fact, it's not even close. On a national level, we pay many additional energy costs through Federal subsidies and environmental impacts that don't appear on our electric or heating oil bills. Through Federal taxes we each subsidize energy supply: we pay for research and development in the nuclear power industry, for oil and gas exploration, and even a small (but

growing) amount for renewable energy. These subsidies—
which were estimated to cost taxpayers $36 billion in 1989 (or
$390 per household)—do not show up in the prices we pay for
energy: they show up in our taxes. The deficit would be
smaller and the economy stronger if the Federal government
thoughtfully removed the vast majority of subsidies.

The environmental costs of using energy don't show up on our
bills either. These costs include: urban smog, global warming,
polluted groundwater, oil spills in once-pristine areas, acidi-
fied lakes, and so on. We can't easily quantify such costs, but
we *do* know how we've each been affected by them. We may
not see such environmental costs every day, but they are real.

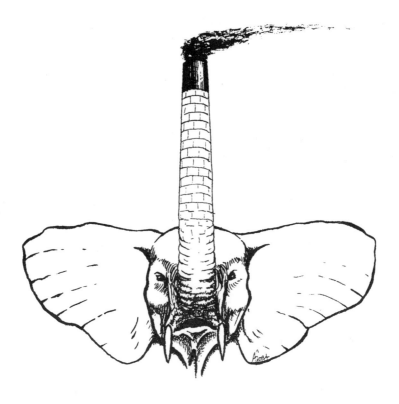

Concerted action by homeowners and renters across the land can eliminate
the need for new "white elephant" powerplants.

Life-cycle energy costs

The cost to buy energy-efficient appliances can be deceptive if you do not consider the cost over its life-cycle. For example, a 100-watt lightbulb seems cheap at the store, but keep it lit for 10,000 hours and it will cost you about $97 for electricity and a dozen replacement bulbs. To get the same illumination from a compact fluorescent bulb will cost about $49—*including the high-priced $25 bulb*—over the same 10,000 hours. When buying energy-using appliances and equipment, always consider the life-cycle cost. In some parts of this book we've made these calculations for you. They are easy to do for any appliance, and it's worth your while to make this kind of comparison. If you need a good discussion of how to do such computations, see Alex Wilson's and John Morrill's *Consumer Guide to Home Energy Savings*, listed in the Appendix.

Renters' options

We hear it again and again: "But I rent!" Of course you're not going to use your next paycheck to put wall insulation or storm windows into the apartment your landlord owns. But ask yourself, "Who's paying the utility bills and who has to live with the drafts and the frost on the inside of the windows?" Inefficient and wasteful housing hurts you too. If the landlord buys the cheapest water heater available, which is likely to be the least efficient, you may have to pay the electric bills ever after. Break the cycle. You do have a stake in efficient housing. So does your landlord, who'll find it easier to rent a cozier, energy-efficient apartment.

A number of our recommendations have such a rapid payback (the time it takes for your savings to equal your investment in efficiency) that you should do them regardless of your landlord's support. Install compact fluorescent bulbs in your most-often used lamps. Caulk, weatherstrip, wrap your hot water tank, tape air gap films on your windows, and install water-efficient showerheads and faucet aerators. These inexpensive solutions offer such cost-effective energy savings that you'll come out ahead, even if you live there for just one winter. And don't forget—you can take the water-efficient showerhead and efficient lights with you when you move.

Involve your landlord too. A landlord may be willing to pay you by the hour, or at least buy the materials, so you can carry out many of the measures in this book. And when your refrigerator, furnace, or any other major appliance dies, ask your landlord to replace it with an efficient model.

Also ask your State Energy Office, your utility, or your state's Department of Social Services if there are programs to help improve the efficiency of your apartment.

Financial assistance
for low-income owners and renters

The Weatherization Assistance Program—run by the U.S. Departments of Energy and Housing and Urban Development—helps lower-income homeowners, apartment dwellers, and renters pay for weatherization and energy improvements to their homes. If you qualify for such assistance, weatherization agencies will often do the work for you. Call your State Energy Office (telephone numbers are listed in the Appendix) for information on the local organizations who run the Weatherization Assistance Program.

Many utilities offer free or low-cost audits of your home, helping you identify the best opportunities for reducing your utility bills, and they frequently offer financial incentives for buying more efficient lights, refrigerators, showerheads, and heating and cooling equipment. Regional non-profit energy and weatherization groups can also assist you with information.

Mobile home dwellers

More than 14 million Americans live in mobile homes and manufactured housing. Over 60% of these homes were built in the 1960s and 1970s. Even though the U.S. Department of Housing and Urban Development set stricter energy codes in 1976 (requiring a minimum of R-7.9 insulation in most frost-belt states), most are underinsulated and drafty and have poorly insulated water heaters, no duct insulation, and single-pane windows.

Consequently, a great many of the recommendations discussed in this book apply to mobile homes. In cold climates, interior storm windows, blown-in roof and belly insulation, air sealing, and duct repair have proven particularly cost-effective. In hot and humid climates, roof insulation, weatherstripping and caulking and duct repair are the most important measures for increasing comfort and reducing energy bills. Of course, lots of additional measures, such as installing efficient showerheads, faucet heads, water heater wraps, lights, and appliances are usually cost-effective no matter what type of housing you live in.

Selling or buying a house?

Energy efficiency improvements are among the most worthwhile investments you can make in your home. Not only will you reap the benefits of lower utility bills as long as you live there, but you'll recoup an estimated 70 to 90% of the investment in increased equity (typically a better return than remodeling a kitchen). The house may also sell faster, as many buyers are reluctant to buy an energy hog.

An increasing number of states are debating legislation to require the seller to upgrade the home to conform to higher efficiency standards before the house can be sold. Some states, backed by Federal lending guidelines, are encouraging banks to include the cost of efficiency improvements in the mortgage. Typically, a homeowner, or new home buyer, can finance substantial energy upgrades and still see an increase in spendable income, since the higher mortgage payments plus the lower utility bills will be less than the previous smaller mortgage payments and high utility bills. Such Energy Efficient Mortgage (EEM) programs benefit the current and future owners of the home, the lenders, the environment, and the community.

Many states are also promoting Home Energy Rating Systems (HERS) in an effort to inform potential home buyers about energy costs and specifics such as insulation levels, window types, and heating systems, for example.

If you are buying a house in a state that has not adopted an energy rating system, it is worth your while to carefully consider the home's annual energy bills (ask the sellers for copies). Let your agent know that you value energy efficiency, and that you'd be more interested in seeing homes that met your standards. It is also a good idea to give the house an energy audit before you buy; house doctors and energy professionals are usually listed under "energy management" in the phone book.

Where to find

energy programs for low-income homeowners & renters

First, call your State Energy Office for information on programs in your state, eligibility requirements, and so on (see the Appendix for telephone numbers). The Federal government also helps low-income families pay utility bills through the Low-Income Home Energy Assistance Program (LIHEAP); inquire with your county's Department of Social Services or with the State Energy Office. You may also want to call your electric utility about weatherization programs, financial assistance, and other information.

HUD User, Department of Housing and Urban Development, Rockville, MD, (800) 245-2691.

Weatherization Assistance Program, U.S. Department of Housing and Urban Development, 451 7th Street SW, Washington, DC 20410, (202) 708-2720.

mobile home information

Since mobile homes are built differently, and the cost-effectiveness of various measures differ somewhat from conventional housing, we suggest that you get a copy of one of the following resources:

Your Mobile Home Energy and Repair Guide, by John Krigger, is available from Saturn Resource Management, 324 Fuller Avenue, Helena, MT 59601-9984; (406) 443-3433. $15.95.

Making Your Mobile Home Energy Efficient, by the North Carolina Alternative Energy Corporation, PO Box 12699, Research Triangle Park, NC 27709; (919) 361-8000, is a step-by-step guide for retrofitting mobile homes in moderate climates. $5.

New Mexico Cooperative Extension Service has a video on mobile home energy retrofits; PO Box 3AE, New Mexico State University, Las Cruces, NM 88003; (505) 646-3425.

energy efficient mortgages and home energy rating systems

If you qualify for a Federal Housing Administration or Veterans' Affairs loan, or are approved by FreddieMac or FannieMae (Federal loan guarantee programs), you may be able to include the cost of energy efficiency improvements to the home you are buying in the home's mortgage. Inquire with your lender or with your State Energy Office to see if energy mortgages are available, or whether your state has a HERS program.

California Home Energy Rating System, 1700 Adams Avenue, Suite 102, Costa Mesa, CA 92626, (714) 540-0501.

Energy Rated Homes of America, 100 Main Street, Little Rock, AR 72201, (501) 374-7827.

Home Energy Rating Systems Council, 1300 Spring Street, Silver Spring, MD 20910, (301) 565-2691.

National Association of Energy Efficient Mortgage Service Companies, 3121 David Avenue, Palo Alto, CA 94303, (415) 858-0890.

National Conference of State Legislatures, 1560 Broadway, Suite 700, Denver, CO 80202, (303) 830-2200, *State Legislative Report*, vol. 18(10), September 1993, discusses the status of HERS programs around the U.S.

Office of Single Family Housing, Federal Housing Administration, U.S. Department of Housing and Urban Development, 451 7th Street SW, Washington, DC 20410, (202) 708-2720.

Part Two

Staying Warm and Keeping Cool

If a house isn't resource-efficient, it isn't beautiful.

—Amory Lovins

On average, heating and cooling a home costs well over six hundred dollars a year, which is over forty percent of the average family's energy bill. That's a princely sum, and no doubt it could be better spent on such things as a vacation, new toys, or the movies. Fortunately, it is not difficult to cut our space heating and cooling bills dramatically with a judicious mixture of weatherization, additional insulation, heating system and air conditioner improvements, and window upgrades.

These improvements to your building envelope and space conditioning systems are the subject of the following chapters, which also include discussions on how to manage moisture issues and avoid indoor air quality problems.

Think of your home as having four components to its heating system: 1) solar and internal heat gain (see the *Windows, Lighting*, and *Appliances* chapters), 2) heat loss through the building shell (see the *Weatherization, Insulation,* and *Windows* chapters), 3) furnace, boiler, woodstove, or other *heating plant*, and 4) heat *distribution* system (see the *Heating* chapter). All of these components must be systematically considered if you want to make truly cost-effective energy investments. It doesn't make much sense, for example, to replace the furnace without first assessing how to reduce the home's heat loss through weatherization and insulation and how to improve the efficiency of the furnace's heat distribution system.

The chapters are not only sequenced in terms of cost-effectiveness, but also in order of what should logically be done first: you should seal air leaks in the attic before adding insulation, for instance, and you'd want to weatherize and insulate before buying a new furnace, because you may well be able to buy a smaller heating system if it needs replacement. But first, let's discuss how your home loses heat (or gains unwanted heat in air conditioning climates).

How your home loses heat

Heat flows from warmer objects to cooler ones in nature's attempt to make everything the same temperature. For buildings, this heat flow occurs in three basic ways:

Radiation

Radiant heat moves from a warm object, like the inside of your house, to a cold object, like the coldness outside. You can feel radiant energy by holding your hand near a heated cast-iron pan: the hot pan will radiate energy at you even after the flame has been turned off. People, being warm, will radiate heat to an uninsulated wall or window in the winter. The wall will essentially pull heat from you if you're sitting nearby. As a consequence, we feel colder sitting next to a wall in an uninsulated building than next to a wall in a well-insulated house *even if the inside air temperature in the two houses is exactly the same.* To compensate for the discomfort caused by this radiant heat loss, it's likely we'll turn up the thermostat, wasting energy and money. Conversely, a dark roof in a hot and sunny climate will get hot enough to cook an egg, and much of this heat will be radiated into your house or attic, adding to your air conditioning bills.

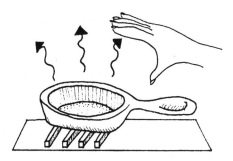

You can feel heat radiating from a warm cast-iron pan. This same type of infrared radiation is emitted by the surface of your house and passes directly through normal windows. Adapted from Reader's Digest *Home Improvements Manual* (1982), p. 352.

Air Leakage

Cold or hot air enters or escapes through cracks in the shell of your home, including around windows and doors, fireplace damper, recessed light fixtures, and so on. A thorough job of sealing attic and foundation air leaks and caulking and weatherstripping will reduce this leakage. Upward movement of heated air—convection—is the engine driving air leakage into your attic, or through the chimney when you're using the fireplace. This pulls cold air into the house from the basement, or around windows and doors, and can even pull radon gas through the slab or crawlspace into your home.

Conduction

Heat can pass directly through any material. The difference between materials is merely the *rate* of heat conduction. Glass and metal are excellent conductors of heat, whereas fiberglass or foam insulation are poor conductors, and therefore good insulators. R-value is a measure of a material's resistance to heat transfer by conduction. Insulation is measured by R-value; the higher the value, the more insulating the material. A single-pane window has an R-value of slightly less than 1. For comparison, five and one-half inches of fiberglass has an R-value of 19. Windows are sometimes not rated by R-value, but by U-value, which measures heat *conductance* rather than resistance. The *lower* the U-value, the more insulating the window.

Heat movement and heat loss

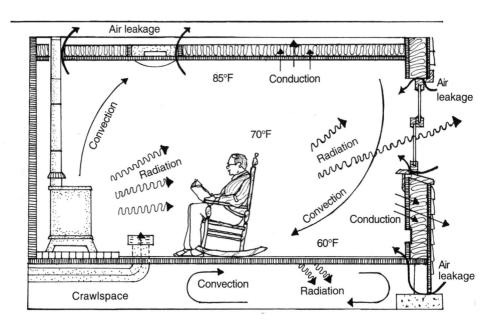

Buildings lose energy by exfiltration of heated or cooled room air (and infiltration of outside air), and radiation and conduction through windows and the building's shell. Adapted from Reader's Digest *New Complete Do-it-yourself Manual* (1991), p. 456, Pleasantville, NY.

2

Weatherization

Each year in the U.S. about $13 billion worth of energy—in the form of heated or cooled air—or $150 per household escapes through holes and cracks in residential buildings.
    —American Council for an Energy-Efficient Economy

An average unweatherized house in the U.S. loses the same amount of air through leaks it would lose through a four-foot-square hole in the wall. This accounts for 25–40% or more of heating and cooling bills. Even in tighter homes, air leaks account for 15–25% of heat loss in winter or unwanted heat gain in summer. Plugging these leaks is one of the most cost-effective energy saving measures you can do. Average space heating and cooling costs total over $600 yearly (much more in some places), and weatherizing a drafty house can easily save $100–$150 or more on your annual heating bill. As one expert put it, "Unless you print your own money, weatherizing and adding insulation are your best bets for fattening your wallet."

The chart below shows air infiltration sources in an ordinary house (which vary greatly, so use this chart as a baseline only).

Air infiltration sources

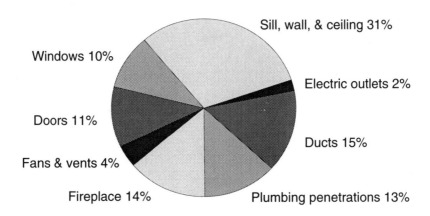

Air infiltration sources in a typical house with a fireplace. Adapted from Reinhold and Sonderegger, *Component Leakage Areas in Residential Buildings* (1983), Lawrence Berkeley Laboratory, Berkeley, CA.

Where to begin: find and plug leaks

Before suiting up in overalls and getting grubby, you *might* consider calling your local utility for an energy audit on your home, which would show where and how big your air leaks are. Getting audited—by a "house doctor," not the IRS—is a great way to find hidden air leaks and overlooked places to weatherize.

Although many utilities offer no- or low-cost home audits (some will even give you an energy conservation kit), it is often worth the $50–$150 cost to have an audit done by a home energy professional, who will look aggressively for savings, even if you plan to do most of the improvements yourself.

Your State Energy Office may also be able to refer you to private businesses that perform these audits. Such businesses might be found under "Energy Conservation" in your phone book. Some insulation contractors also provide weatherization and audit services.

A good energy audit will include what's called a "blower door" test. A blower door is a large fan that fits tightly into a doorway in your home. It depressurizes the space inside your home, which then causes air to flow in through the cracks. You or the energy auditor can then walk around and tell where the leaks are by feeling for air flow with your hand or by using a "smoke pencil" and noting where the smoke is blown.

The blower door test

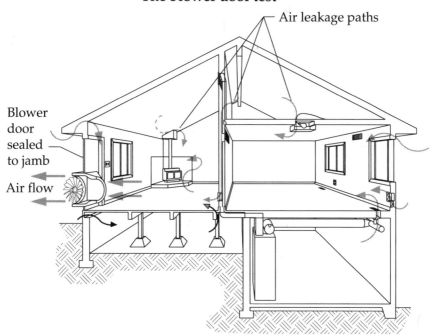

The blower door is sealed to the frame of your home's entry door. When windows, fireplace dampers, and ventilation openings are closed, the fan on the blower door creates a partial vacuum by sucking air out, and sources of air infiltration or exfiltration are noted and sealed. Illustration courtesy of Bonneville Power Administration (1992), *Builder's Field Guide to Energy Efficient Construction*, p. 147, Portland, OR.

You can also perform a blower door test by yourself by closing all the windows and doors in your home and turning on a whole-house fan or a large portable fan temporarily sealed in an open window. Be sure to seal off the sides with cardboard and tape. (This simple test does not substitute for a professional audit, since that includes better equipment and methods to find all the places worth sealing.)

While up in the attic, you may also be able to spot places where air is leaking from your living space into the attic by locating gray smudges on the insulation. Chances are that air has been filtering through these spots for some time.

Once you've located the air leaks in your home, you are ready to start plugging them. *First, go after holes a cat could crawl through.* These are often tucked away in unlikely spots: a chimney with an open or missing damper, around the drain under the bathtub, in the basement, in the attic where vent pipes run through interior walls and then into the attic, around the dryer exhaust vent, and behind drop ceilings. (Check also for pet doors that don't shut properly.)

A good rule of thumb is to "seal the high and low air leaks first"—namely your home's attic floor and crawlspace or basement ceiling and walls, especially around the sillplate and rimjoist (these rest on the foundation wall), since a lot of air can leak in around this framing. Use the checklist at the end of this section as a guide.

Selecting caulk

Caulk is your best bet for cracks thinner than a pencil. Buy it in a cylindrical tube designed to be used with a caulking gun (you'll have to pick up the gun too—it's lots of fun to use). Caulk comes in clear or paintable white and colors.

Caulks—what they can do

Type	Cost	Life in years	Ease of application	Interior/ Exterior	Wx & UV resistance
Oil	Low	1–5	Messy	Interior	Poor
Latex	Low/ medium	2–5	Easy	Interior	Medium
Butyl	Medium	10–15	Slightly difficult	Interior or shaded exterior	Good Wx, poor UV resistance
Acrylic-latex	Medium	10 interior, 3–5 exterior	Easy	Interior (recom.)	Fair
Acrylic–solvent	Low	20	Difficult	Exterior	Good UV resistance
Silicone	High	20+	Easy	Mainly exterior, also interior	Excellent
Co-polymers	Medium/ high	20	Easy	Interior/ exterior, out of sun	Good
Poly-urethane	Medium/ high	20	Relatively easy	Interior, exterior	Good
Foam	Medium/ high	20	Messy, difficult	Interior, & exterior if caulked	No UV resistance
Poly-sulfide	High	20	Difficult	Interior, shaded exterior	Moderate UV and Wx

Note: "Wx" means weatherability—ability to weather the ravages of time.

Adapted from Tang & Obst, "Getting a Bead on Caulks: How to Choose the Right Kind," *Home Energy*, March/April 1991, p. 37-43. Great article on selecting caulks.

Adhesion to surfaces and flexibility is key to caulk's effectiveness at stopping leaks. If the caulked material moves or shifts, however, it can lose its seal, letting air through.

Caulking can be a little messy, and it's a sure bet that your neighbor won't come over and say: "Whoa, that's a nice caulk job there, buddy." But do it nonetheless, if not for fun, then for the environment and your wallet.

Make sure the type of caulk you choose works on the materials you wish to seal. As there are many varieties on the market, it is wise to read labels carefully. Spend a couple of extra dollars on higher grades of caulk with high flexibility that can last up to 20 years longer than a cheaper type. Good preparation (such as wire brushing, cleaning, and drying) of the surfaces to be sealed is also important for a long-lasting air seal.

With a little practice (perhaps in the basement first) you'll be able to apply a nice, even bead. Hint: apply a small bead, and smooth it out with a moistened finger as you work.

Caulk gun in action

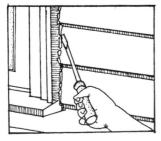 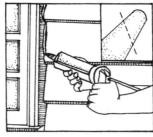 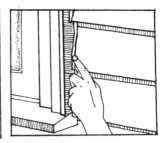

A caulk gun is easy to use, and sealing air and moisture leaks is well worth your while. Adapted from Reader's Digest (1982), *Home Improvements Manual*, p. 364, Pleasantville, NY.

Silicone and siliconized caulks

Silicone caulk has high moisture resistance, lasts a long time, and remains flexible over its lifetime, but cannot be painted over. It is often used to seal plumbing penetrations that are hidden from view. If the caulk is going to be exposed to a great deal of moisture, make sure it is treated with a fungicide, or else the caulk will turn black with fungal growth.

When silicone is added to acrylic latex caulk the result is a "siliconized" product that lasts longer, adheres better, and has more flexibility than normal acrylic caulk. It isn't as flexible as silicone caulk, but it is paintable. Among builders and weatherization professionals, siliconized caulk is easily the most popular variety.

Other types of caulk, such as high-temperature silicone caulk, have special applications: your hardware store or home center will be able to tell you more about their specific uses.

Rope caulk

This should be used for windows and other places you'll want to be able to open up again come summertime. This gray, putty-like material comes in long strips or rolls and can either be round or flat. It is easy to work with, remains flexible, and is easy to remove when the weather turns warm. Don't expect it to last longer than a year, though.

Other crack fillers

Expanding foam

This is great for filling voids up to a couple inches. It comes in aerosol cans and takes about fifteen minutes to cure. You'll want to wear your grubbiest work clothes and put down a damp cloth when you use this stuff. It's messy, and you'll need to scramble around under the house and in a dusty attic.

Spraying a little water mist from a "spritzer" bottle will reduce the stickiness of the surface of the foam, but a good rule to remember is: you touch it, you wear it.

Stuff for big voids

Foil-Ray™, Reflectix™, or other foil-faced bubble wrap (available at hardware stores) attached with silicone caulk is great for sealing gaps too wide for foam. For really big holes, cut sections of rigid foam insulation to fit and glue into place with expanding foam.

Weatherstripping

Weatherstripping is used to reduce leakage around the top and sides of doors and windows you want to be able to open year round. Like caulk and foam, it's available from any hardware or building-supply store. It may come with an adhesive backing and is fairly simple to install (instructions should be on the package).

Common weatherstripping materials and door sweeps

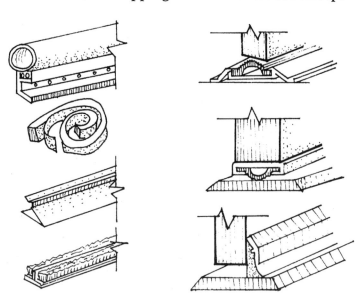

On left, from top: rolled vinyl with rigid metal backing, foam rubber, thin spring metal, fin seal. On right: vinyl bulb threshhold, door shoe, door sweep. Adapted from an illustration by New Mexico State University Cooperative Extension Service, *Saving Energy in Your Mobile Home.*

Compression seal weatherstripping is composed of a wood or preferably aluminum strip with foam, vinyl, or rubber attached to it. In very cold climates, "silicone bulb," a compression weatherstripping, is recommended because it remains flexible in cold weather.

Another common, and often preferred, type of weatherstripping is V-tape, made of spring-metal or plastic, folded to seal the edge around windows and doors. These are also available in long-lasting, but harder-to-install spring-metal strips.

Door sweeps

These are great for stopping drafts and keeping bugs out. These devices fit on the bottom of doors and prevent warm air from leaking out and cold air from coming in. Recommended types use felt strips or plastic bristles instead of flaps. An automatic door sweep works best but costs more: it lifts up when the door is opened, preventing wear.

Another good option is to replace your old door threshold with a new vinyl or wood threshold that makes a tight seal with the door. Many doors once had a vinyl bulb weatherstrip built in. In such cases, replacing missing or worn-out weatherstripping is usually better than adding new products.

Foam rubber gaskets

These are used behind outlets and switch-plates located on exterior walls.

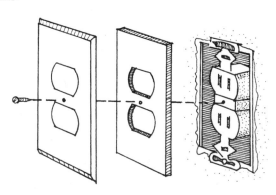

Where to weatherize

√ In the attic

- Weatherstrip and insulate the attic access door.

- Seal around the outside of the chimney with metal flashing and high temperature sealant such as flue caulk or muffler cement.

- Seal around plumbing stacks, both in the attic floor and in the roof. Check roof flashing.

- Seal the top of interior walls on pre-1950s houses where you can peer down into the wall. Use strips of rigid board insulation and seal the edges with silicone caulk.

- Stuff strips of fiberglass insulation around electrical wire penetrations at the top of interior walls and where wires enter ceiling fixtures (but not around recessed light fixtures unless the fixtures are rated IC—insulation contact).

- Seal all other holes between the heated space and the attic.

√ In the basement or crawlspace

- Seal and insulate around accessible forced-air heating and central air conditioning ducts, both in the basement and the attic. (See the *Insulation* chapter for more information.)

- Seal any holes that allow air to rise from the basement or crawlspace directly into the living space above. Check where your bathtub drainpipe, your chimney, and any other plumbing or electrical penetrations come down through the floor above.

- Caulk around basement window frames.

- Seal holes in the foundation wall as well as gaps between where the concrete foundation ends and wood structure begins (that is, at the sillplate and rim joist). Use caulk or foam sealant.

√ Around windows and doors

- Replace broken glass and reputty loose panes. (See the *Windows* chapter for upgrading to better windows.)

- Install new sash locks, or adjust existing ones, on double-hung and slider windows.

- Caulk on the inside around window and door trim, sealing where the frame meets the wall and all other window-woodwork joints.

- Weatherstrip exterior doors, including those opening into garages and porches.

- For windows that will be opened, use weatherstripping or temporary flexible rope caulk.

Air leakage around a window frame

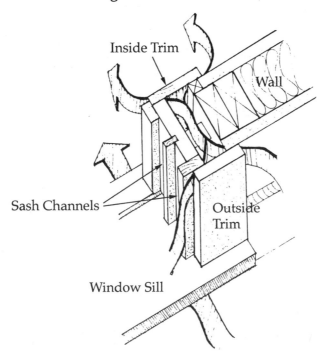

Adapted from City of Oakland (1983), *Retrofit Right: How to Make Your Old House Energy Efficient*, Oakland, CA, p. 93.

Air leakage sites

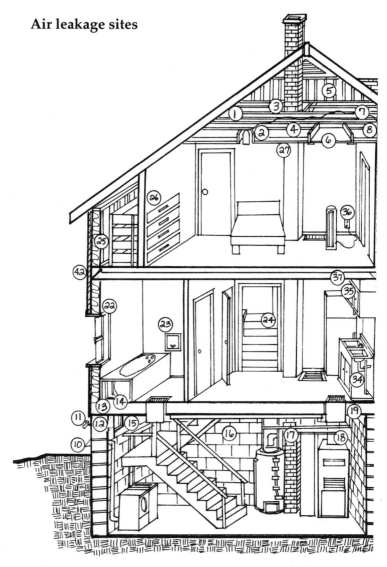

Attic:
1 Dropped ceiling
2 Recessed light
3 Chimney chase
4 Electric wires and box
5 Balloon wall
6 Attic entrance
7 Partition wall top plate
8 Plumbing vent chase
9 Exhaust fan

Basement and crawlspace:
10 Dryer vent
11 Plumbing/utility penetrations
12 Sill plate
13 Rim joist
14 Bathtub drain penetration
15 Basement windows and doors
16 Block wall cavities
17 Water heater and furnace flues
18 Warm-air ducts

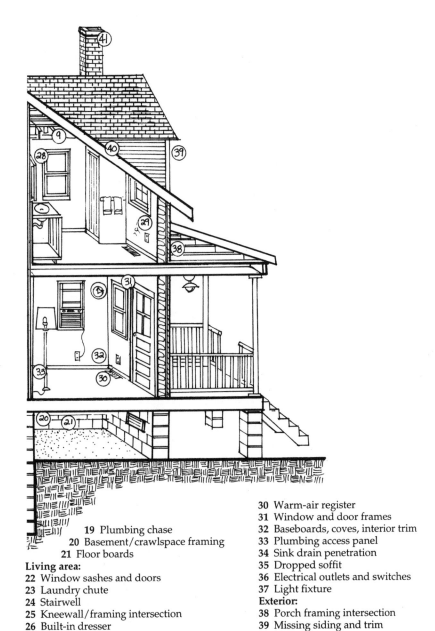

19 Plumbing chase
20 Basement/crawlspace framing
21 Floor boards
Living area:
22 Window sashes and doors
23 Laundry chute
24 Stairwell
25 Kneewall/framing intersection
26 Built-in dresser
27 Chimney penetration
28 Built-in cabinet
29 Cracks in drywall
30 Warm-air register
31 Window and door frames
32 Baseboards, coves, interior trim
33 Plumbing access panel
34 Sink drain penetration
35 Dropped soffit
36 Electrical outlets and switches
37 Light fixture
Exterior:
38 Porch framing intersection
39 Missing siding and trim
40 Additions, dormers, overhangs
41 Unused chimney
42 Floor joist

Adapted from an illustration by Conservation Connection, Fairchild, WI.

√ In living areas

- Install foam-rubber gaskets behind outlets and switch plates on exterior walls to reduce air leaks.
- Stuff IC (insulation contact)-rated fiberglass insulation above and around the rim of recessed ceiling light fixtures if there's a gap between the fixture's rim and the sheetrock.
- Use paintable, clear, or colored caulk around bath and kitchen cabinets on exterior walls.
- Use fiberglass insulation, caulk, or expanding foam around all bath and sink drains and water pipes—even those that penetrate exterior walls, and especially those coming up from the basement or crawlspace.
- Install timer switches ($10) on bathroom exhaust fans. If you are replacing an exhaust fan, get a quiet model with "sone level" (noise-level rating, on the package) of 1.5 to 2.5 for bathrooms and 4.5 to 5 for the kitchen.
- Caulk any cracks where the floor meets exterior walls. Such cracks are often hidden behind the edge of the carpet.
- Caulk around baseboard molding.
- Got a fireplace? Make sure your damper closes tightly when you don't have a fire burning. If your fireplace doesn't have a damper, repair it, or install a chimney-top model or a door on the fireplace. See the chapter on heating for more tips on improving fireplace efficiency.

√ On the exterior

- Caulk around all penetrations where electrical, telephone, cable, gas, dryer vents, and water faucets enter the house. You may want to stuff some fiberglass insulation in the larger gaps first. Expanding foam can also be used, but only in places you'll never need access to again. Don't foam in the telephone wire, for example, in case you might need to add a wire. Instead, stuff a little fiberglass in the hole.

- Caulk around all sides of window and door frames to keep out the rain and to reduce air infiltration.

- Check your dryer exhaust vent hood. If it is missing the flapper or it doesn't close easily, replace it with a tight-fitting model.

- Remove window air conditioners in winter; or at the very least cover them, use rope caulk around them, and make insulating covers for the flimsy side panels.

- Caulk any cracks in overhangs of cantilevered bays and chimney chases.

√ In mobile homes

Most of the tips listed above apply equally well to mobile homes, even though mobile homes are built differently. Older mobile homes are often quite drafty, and draft-proofing measures can be very cost-effective. Blower-door tests are useful in identifying air leaks.

- Seal around flues and ventilators.

- Seal forced-air heating and cooling supply ducts (including crossover ducts in double-wide mobile homes).

- Caulk around cabinets.

- Seal around plumbing and electrical penetrations.

- Seal around windows and doors.

For more specific how-to and step-by-step information, get a copy of John Krigger's *Your Mobile Home Energy and Repair Guide*, available from Saturn Resource Management, 324 Fuller Avenue, Helena, MT 59601-9984, (800) 735-0577 or (406) 443-3433. Other resources are listed in the mobile home section at the end of Chapter 1.

Indoor air pollution

Once you've weatherized your home and plugged the air leaks, compounds such as radon, formaldehyde, cigarette smoke, carbon monoxide from ranges, fireplaces, and heating systems, and organic chemicals used in furnishings and building products may be present in unacceptably high concentrations. Should you worry about the quality of the air you've kept in? Not necessarily. A tight house with controlled ventilation is far safer than a drafty house with uncontrolled ventilation.

The most important way to maintain indoor air quality is to choose carefully the materials—drapery, cleansers, carpets, paints, even furniture, and so on—that go into your home to begin with. You should also make sure that combustion appliances such as gas water heaters, oil heating systems, and wood stoves are properly vented and that combustion or make-up air is ducted from the outside directly to the appliance. Gas-fired ranges should always have a ventilator that exhausts to the outside.

In these ways you'll minimize or eliminate the sources of pollutants rather than spending money constantly cleaning or attempting to remove polluted air. The pollutants themselves, not the ventilation rate, cause the indoor air quality problem.

√ Radon

Radon is a heavier-than-air gas resulting from the decay of uranium. It is present in soils under much of the U.S. (see the radon map on page 40). The U.S. Environmental Protection Agency estimates that one in fifteen houses has radon concentrations above the "recommended action level" of 4 picocuries per liter (pCi/l) of indoor air, and radon is estimated to cause 14,000 cases of lung cancer every year.

Sources of some common indoor air quality problems

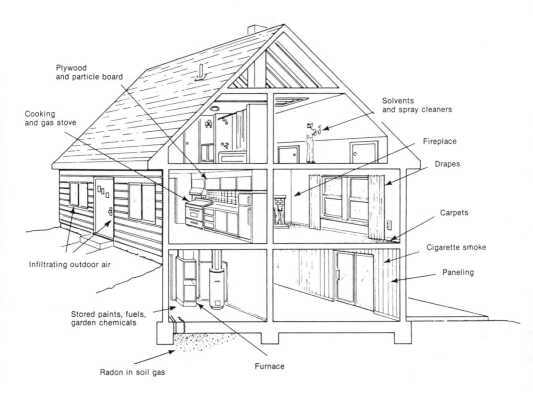

In addition to the sources depicted above, car exhaust fumes, paints and chemicals stored in your garage are hazardous, radon is present in some water supplies, lead is present in old paints and plumbing solder, and asbestos is still found as insulation around old boilers. Illustration courtesy of U.S. Congress, Office of Technology Assessment (1992), *Building Energy Efficiency,* OTA E-518, p. 47, Washington, DC.

Radon is sometimes dissolved in water. If your water comes from a well, the radon will come out when you shower, but the amount of radon released into a home has been shown to be insignificant compared to other sources—even with high radon levels in the water.

Homes with full basements or a slab floor lying directly on the soil are especially susceptible to radon intrusion. If you're in an area of high radon concentration—your local or state environmental office can advise—then test your home. Even if you aren't, it's still a good idea to test. You can buy radon testing kits for $15 to $30 at hardware stores.

Potential radon areas in the United States

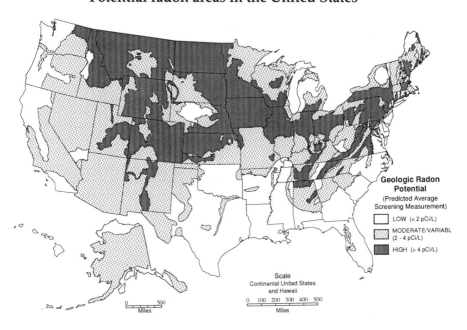

Geologic Radon
Potential
(Predicted Average
Screening Measurement)

LOW (< 2 pCi/L)

MODERATE/VARIABL
(2 - 4 pCi/L)

HIGH (> 4 pCi/L)

Scale
Continental United States
and Hawaii

0   100 200 300 400 500
Miles

0   500
Miles

While the darker areas have a probability of higher soil radon, all homes should be tested. Illustration courtesy of the U.S. Geological Survey, Washington, DC, based on data from the U.S. Environmental Protection Agency.

Covering your crawlspace with a heavy polyethylene or EPDM barrier sealed carefully to the stem wall will reduce radon migration. In serious cases, you can lay a grid of PVC pipe with half-inch holes drilled every six inches into a layer of washed gravel and/or 3-inch rock, cover the gravel with a barrier, and suction the radon out with a fan connected to the pipe. In new construction, such a system is also effective under concrete slabs and full basements. An alternative method is to pressurize the house slightly with a mechanical ventilation system.

Depending on the seriousness of the problem, mitigation can be simple and easy, or it can cost $2,000 to $5,000. See the resource box at the end of this section for more information.

Radon mitigation in a house with a crawlspace

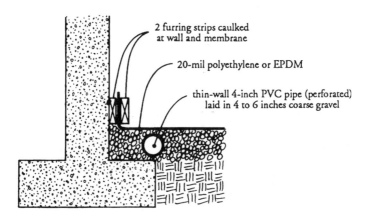

Illustration courtesy Montana Department of Natural Resources and Conservation (1990), *This New House: Crafting Houses for Comfort and Savings in Montana*, p. 24, Helena, MT.

√ Asbestos

Asbestos is now a proven carcinogen, but was used extensively in homes and public buildings from the 1950s to the 1970s as insulation around steam pipes and boilers, as wall and duct insulation, as a soundproofing material, and in such products as vinyl flooring, textured coatings, and exterior shingles.

Asbestos was banned by the EPA in the 1970s for use in buildings, though it is still being used in brakes and some sealed appliances and other equipment. An estimated one-quarter of American homes and apartments still contain asbestos products. Normally, asbestos will only be a health hazard if the fibers are released into the air, but this can readily happen as the material frays, corrodes, or ages.

What should you do if you suspect asbestos in your home? Contact your State Energy Office, environmental health department, or the EPA lab listed at the end of this chapter. *Do not handle suspected asbestos materials yourself.*

√ Volatile organic compounds

Chemicals are part of most modern carpets, cabinets, and furniture. Volatile organic compounds (VOCs), like formaldehyde, are present in paints and cleaning fluids, and adhesives in wood, furniture, and plastics. New building materials and furnishings release VOCs into your home, creating a health hazard. Now a number of companies are manufacturing building adhesives, laminated woods, paints, and furnishings with less or no VOC content.

Removing the worst chemicals from the living space is one obvious step to reduce air quality problems. Another option is to buy used building materials and furnishings, because most of the hazardous compounds will have disappeared. Airing out a new carpet for a week or two (in a separate, well-ventilated area such as a garage, if possible) will also help. Paint with water-based or VOC-free paints.

√ Combustion gases

One of the more dangerous gases that you'll find in your home is cigarette smoke. You might want to ask people to go outside if they must light up.

Dangerous gases like carbon monoxide or nitrogen dioxide can build up inside the house if combustion gases are not vented properly—and occasionally even when they are. Providing combustion air from the outside to appliances that use oil, gas, or wood is important for both energy efficiency and air quality reasons. It is a good precaution to have your fuel-using appliances checked by a heating or energy contractor every year or two to ensure they are venting properly.

When exhaust gases go up the flue or chimney, that air must be replaced somehow: either through air leaks in the shell of the house, or through a duct specifically providing an outside source of combustion air. If you have tightened your home, or have no combustion air, the negative air pressure inside the house can cause the fireplace, woodstove, or heating system to backdraft and smoke up your house—or worse, suffocate you with odorless and invisible carbon monoxide.

Adequate ventilation, as described below, is the answer, plus one or more carbon monoxide alarms. Be sure, however, that air intakes to a house are not located next to some other source of pollution, such as a driveway or garage where cars may idle while being warmed up. Sealing the floor or wall between the living space and the garage will reduce the infiltration of automobile fumes. Leaky ductwork in homes can also draw in vapors, soil gases, airborne particles, and fumes from combustion appliances and then distribute them throughout the home.

√ Mighty mites, molds, and mildew

Dust mites are another source of indoor air pollution. Although these occur naturally, dirt and high humidity create conditions for dust mites and other tiny critters that pollute living spaces. Regular vacuuming or cleaning is usually sufficient unless you have particular allergies.

Molds and mildew are other natural pollutants that can be avoided in part by ventilating properly and by eliminating standing water and dampness in basements. Molds are occasionally a problem in the ducts of central air conditioning systems or when attics aren't properly vented.

Ventilation systems

If you have an indoor air quality problem, a ventilation system will remove stale air while providing a controlled amount of fresh air to your home. A balanced ventilation system, in which separate fans bring equal amounts of air into and out of the home, reduces the chance that the ventilation system will make indoor air pollution, cold air drafts, and other problems *worse*. The challenge, of course, is to ventilate the home without losing too much heat in winter and cool air in summer.

House ventilation and pressure

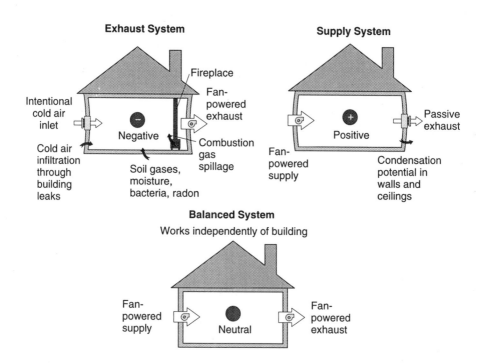

Exhaust and supply systems create pressure differences which may cause problems. Balanced systems avoid pressure-related problems. Illustration courtesy E SOURCE (1993), *Space Heating Technology Atlas*, p. 132, Boulder, CO.

Heat recovery ventilators (sometimes called air-to-air heat exchangers) are designed with this challenge in mind. These are exhaust fans that warm the incoming air with the heat from the outgoing air, recovering about 50–70% of the energy. In hot climates, the function is reversed: the cooler inside air passes by the incoming hot air and reduces its temperature.

The heat recovery ventilator

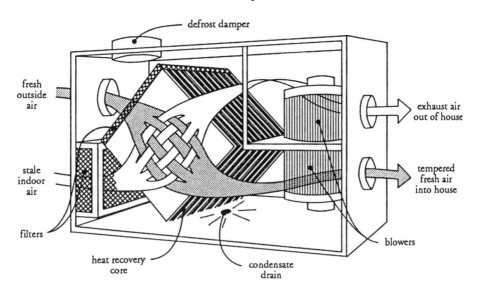

A heat recovery ventilator's heat exchanger transfers 50–70% of the heat from the exhaust air to the intake air. Illustration courtesy of Montana Department of Natural Resources and Conservation, *op. cit.*, p. 40.

These clever inventions can save a lot on your heating or cooling costs, but are most cost-effective in cold climates. They must be properly installed, however, or they won't do much good. It's best to install air-to-air heat exchangers in new construction since retrofits can be difficult and expensive. (Also, unless a home is fairly airtight, a heat recovery ventilator may not do much good, though it won't do any harm either.) You can get units for individual rooms or whole-house systems. Check the "Where to find" section for HRV sources, and the

Heating and *Hot Water* chapters for related equipment. Heat-recovery ventilation systems are also available that use exhaust air to heat water before it is vented to the outside.

"Air-cleaning" devices and filters in existing ventilating systems are useful for people with allergies caused by indoor air pollutants.

Moisture problems

A word to the wise: if you are buttoning up your house by weatherizing and adding insulation, be sure to assess moisture problems first, and use this guide to fix them by installing vapor barriers *before* you insulate.

Moisture degrades the performance of insulation, encourages the growth of unhealthy fungi and molds, and increases the danger of rot in wood. It enters through cracks in walls and ceilings (and, to a smaller extent, diffuses through plaster or drywall) during the winter as warm, moist air condenses in the colder insulation. In warm, humid climates, moist air can condense within the wall cavity on its way into an air conditioned house. Showers, cooking, plants, human breathing (a family of four will put nearly two gallons of water into the air daily), heating systems, and poorly drained foundations can all bring interior humidity levels past the recommended range of 30–50% in the winter and 40–60% in the summer. In addition to water vapor and condensation problems, more obvious water problems—such as roof leaks, foundation leaks, plugged roof gutters and downspouts, and site drainage problems—also damage structures and reduce insulation performance. Fix these problems first.

Look for excessive condensation on windows and in bathrooms, wet insulation in the attic, over-damp basements or crawlspaces, or smells of molds and mildews in some places.

To remove moisture before it becomes a problem, use bathroom and kitchen exhaust fans. (Make sure fans are actually vented outside; sometimes they're vented into the crawlspace or attic!) Use a dial timer so the fan continues to remove moisture and shuts itself off after you have left, and install a quiet fan so that people will use it. Moisture sensitive fans are available; please see the end of this section for information.

Additional mechanical ventilation is another good solution. It may be cost-effective to install a heat-recovery ventilator, though they are expensive. If you don't have the money to install one, have the house tested with a blower door after you have sealed most of the obvious sources of air infiltration. An air exchange rate of 0.25 ACH (air changes per hour) or higher will provide your home with a safe level of natural ventilation.

√ In the living space

Unless you are planning a major remodel, the only practical way of retrofitting a vapor retarder on your walls is to use a vapor retarding paint. Installing gaskets behind electric outlets and caulking around window and door trim and baseboard molding will also reduce diffusion of moist air and its condensation in walls.

If you are remodeling or building a new house, the vapor barrier should be on the interior (warm) side of the insulation in most parts of the United States. (If you live in a hot, humid area, call your State Energy Office for advice on vapor barriers.)

√ In the basement or crawlspace

If you have a crawlspace, a 6- or 10-mil polyethylene vapor barrier placed right over the ground will help keep the moisture from sneaking up from the earth. Lay it on top of the footer, too, and place a few bricks on it to keep it in place. Where you have joints, leave a good foot of overlap.

Fix drainage problems around the exterior of the basement walls if necessary by sloping dirt away from the house, especially where gutters and leaders drain the roof.

Vapor barrier installed in a crawlspace

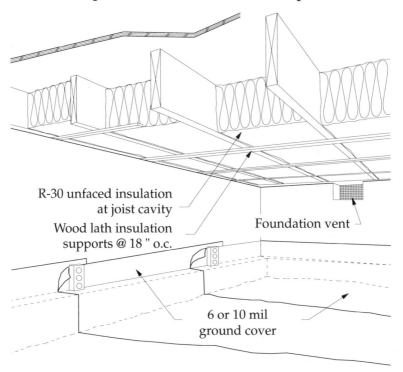

R-30 unfaced insulation at joist cavity

Wood lath insulation supports @ 18 " o.c.

Foundation vent

6 or 10 mil ground cover

A vapor barrier on the dirt will help prevent moisture problems in your crawlspace. If you have a radon problem, additional precautions must be taken. Illustration courtesy of Bonneville Power Administration (1992), *Builder's Field Guide to Energy Efficient Construction*, p. 172, Portland, OR.

If drainage is a serious problem and you are digging up around the foundation walls anyway, by all means damp-proof the foundation wall and add rigid foam board insulation on the exterior.

If you are planning to insulate the interior of an unfinished basement, it's probably best to not add a vapor barrier so you don't trap moisture in the insulation.

If you are insulating the crawlspace or basement ceiling, and no insulation is in place, install a vapor barrier on the bottom of the floor decking, between the joists. Cut strips of polyethylene sheet about six inches wider than the joist space so you can staple the plastic barrier to the decking; leave the joists themselves uncovered, and don't staple the barrier to the bottom of the joists, as this would trap moisture.

√ In the attic

By far the greatest amount of moisture entering your attic is through the huge holes that often exist between the attic and the living space below. Seal all holes around plumbing and electrical penetrations first (also the top of open-topped partition walls, if your house has them, and around chimney chases, plumbing vents, and heating or cooling ducts) with rigid or expanding foam or plastic bags filled with fiberglass or cellulose. Caulk the smaller cracks and holes. If you do a good job of sealing air (and moisture) leaks, you can probably skip the vapor barrier in the attic.

With respect to new construction, opinions differ about whether top floor ceiling vapor barriers are a good idea or not; check with local experts first. In existing homes, if your attic floor has no insulation, it is easy, inexpensive, and probably worthwhile to add a vapor barrier. Cut the polyethylene vapor barrier into strips and install the strips on top of the ceiling decking (between the joists) before insulating (just like you did—upside down—in the basement). Most likely, though, you already have insulation in the attic, so skip the vapor barrier, as you don't want moisture to condense between the layers of insulation.

Air barriers are quite different from vapor barriers. Air barriers stop wind from blowing through the wall but let moisture through. Like a windbreaker over a sweater, an air barrier helps keep wind from disturbing the still air that provides the insulating value.

Where to find

weatherization materials

Most weatherization materials can be purchased at your hardware store. When purchasing caulk, pay attention to expected lifetime, ease of clean-up, paintability, shrinkage, and long-term flexibility. Start with a half-dozen tubes, though you'll need at least a dozen tubes if you are going to get serious about thoroughly sealing an un-weatherized house.

Energy Federation, Inc., 14 Tech Circle, Natick, MA, 01760, (800) 876-0660, has a full line of weatherization products, rope caulk, weatherstripping, caulk, expanding foam, and heat-recovery ventilators.

Enviro-Energy, 6601 East Mill Plane Blvd, Vancouver, WA 98661, (800) 263-3674, sells the DraftStopper for chimneys.

weatherization information

In addition to your local utility, local library, State Energy Office, and private energy auditor, you may want to call one of the regional non-profit energy or housing groups listed in the Appendix. Also, many regional non-profit groups perform house audits and provide weath-erization measures for low-income homeowners and renters. Many such organizations are listed in the Appendix.

Energy Efficiency & Renewable Energy Clearinghouse, PO Box 3048, Merrifield, VA, 22116; (800) DOE EREC and (800) 523-2929 has several useful information packets on weatherization and re-lated topics.

Massachusetts Audubon Society, 208 South Great Road, Lincoln, MA 01773, (617) 259-9500, has pamphlets ($3) on weatherization techniques entitled *Weatherize Your Home or Apartment* and *Contractor's Guide to Finding and Sealing Hidden Air Leaks.*

ventilation equipment

To find local vendors of heat-recovery ventilators, and other ventilation systems, check your phone book under air cleaning & purifying equipment, and heating, ventilating, and air conditioning specialists.

Energy Federation, Inc., 14 Tech Circle, Natick, MA, 01760, (800) 876-0660, sells several brands of heat-recovery ventilators.

W. W. Grainger has a large catalog and a wide selection of fans, ventilation systems, hoods, ducting, etc. (Check your local listing or call Grainger in Lincolnshire, IL, (708) 913-7058.)

See **Home Ventilating Institute's** *Certified Products Directory,* listed below, and *Energy Source Directory: A Guide to Products Used in Energy-Efficient Residential Buildings*, by **Iris Communications,** 258 East 10th Avenue, Suite E, Eugene, OR 97401, (800) 346-0104.

The following companies manufacture heat-recovery ventilators:

Altech Energy, 7009 Graywood Road, Madison, WI 53713, (608) 221-4499.

Broan Manufacturing Company, PO Box 140 , Hartford, WI 53027-0140, (800) 637-1453.

Conservation Energy Systems, PO Box 10416, Minneapolis, MN 55440, (800) 667-3717.

Honeywell, Inc., 1985 Douglas Drive North, Golden Valley, MN 55422, (612) 542-3356.

Lennox Industries, PO Box 799900, Dallas, TX 75379-9900, (214) 497-5000.

Research Products Corporation, PO Box 1467, Madison, WI 53701, (800) 334-6011.

indoor air quality information

Your State Energy Office, County Health Department, State Department of Environmental Quality, or the U.S. Environmental Protection Agency may be able to answer your indoor air quality questions.

EPA has several excellent publications on abating indoor air pollution. Local information sources and services can be found by looking under Radon Mitigation, Radon Testing, and Environmental and Ecological Services in your phone book.

Carpet and Rug Institute, 310 Holiday Drive, Dalton, GA 30720, (800) 882-8846. The Institute tests carpets and can provide test results on specific brands and types of carpets.

Energy Efficiency & Renewable Energy Clearinghouse, PO Box 3048, Merrifield, VA, 22116; (800) DOE EREC or (800) 523-2929 has a fact sheet (#FS 208) on indoor air quality issues.

Environmental Health Watch, 4115 Bridge Avenue, Room 104, Cleveland, OH 44113, (216) 961-4646, has information on all sorts of household hazardous materials. They also sell kits for testing radon and formaldehyde in your home and radon and lead in your drinking water.

Home Ventilating Institute, 30 West University Drive, Arlington Heights, IL 60004-1893, (708) 394-0150, has two publications of interest: *Home Ventilation Guide* and *Certified Products Directory.*

The U.S. Environmental Protection Agency (EPA) operates the **Indoor Air Quality Information Clearinghouse**, PO Box 37133, Washington, DC 20013, (800) 438-4318.

If you have or suspect you might have an asbestos problem, the EPA has a free list of certified asbestos-detection agencies available through the **National Voluntary Laboratory Accreditation Program,** Gaithersburg, MD (301) 975-4016.

EPA also has a **Toxic Substances Control Hotline**, Washington, DC (202) 554-1404 that can help you locate a testing laboratory to assess suspected asbestos substances.

Many states have offices devoted to helping citizens with radon problems; try your state's Department of Environmental Quality. If you do have a radon problem, make sure your radon abatement contractor has attended a certified radon mitigation course.

The U.S. EPA has numerous free publications and other helpful assistance, and operates the **Radon Hotline**: (800) SOS -RADON.

Safe-Aire, PO Box 160, Canton, IL 61520; (800) 589-7233, sells radon mitigation equipment such as fans, sealing compounds, etc.

Sun Nuclear, 425-A Pineda Court, Melbourne, FL 32940; (407) 254-7785, manufacturers continuous radon monitoring equipment.

Also check the following sources:

Advanced Air Sealing: Techniques for Air Leakage Control in Residential Buildings, is a builder's manual available from Iris Communications, Inc., 258 East 10th Avenue, Suite E, Eugene, OR 97401-3284; (503) 484-9353. ($15).

The Healthy Home: An Attic-to-Basement Guide to Toxin-Free Living, by Linda Mason Hunter, is available from Rodale Press, 33 East Miner Street, Emmaus, PA 18098-0099, (215) 967-5171. ($21.95).

Healthy House Building: A Design and Construction Guide, by John Bower, is available from **Healthy House Institute**, 7471 North Shiloh Road, Unionville, IN 47468, (812) 332-5073. ($21.95).

The Healthy House: How to Buy One, How to Cure a 'Sick' One, How to Build One, also by John Bower, is available from Carol Publishing, 120 Enterprise Avenue, Secaucus, NJ 07094, (201) 866-0490.

Indoor Air Quality and Human Health, by Isaac Turiel, is available from Stanford University Press, Stanford, CA 94305, (415) 723-9434. ($27.50).

Indoor Air Quality Publications, 4520 East-West Highway, Suite 610, Bethesda, MD 20814, (301) 913-0115; and *Indoor Air Quality Update,* Cutter Information Corporation, Arlington, MA 02174, (617) 648-8700; both publish newsletters and other materials.

Nontoxic, Natural & Earthwise and *The Non-Toxic Home and Office,* by Debra Lynn Dadd, are available from Jeremy P. Tarcher Inc., 5858 Wilshire Boulevard, Suite 200, Los Angeles, CA 90036, (800) 631-8571. ($12.95 and $10.95, respectively.)

moisture solutions

Energy Efficiency & Renewable Energy Clearinghouse, PO Box 3048, Merrifield, VA, 22116, (800) 523-2929, *Moisture Control in Homes*, Fact sheet #208.

National Center for Appropriate Technology (1983), *Moisture and Home Energy Conservation: How to Detect, Solve, and Avoid Related Problems*, Butte, MT 59702, (406) 494-4572. Available as report #061-000-00615-01 from the U.S. Government Printing Office (Washington, DC 20402, and regional GPO offices).

The Underground Space Center, 500 Pillsbury Drive SE, Minneapolis, MN 55455, (612) 624-0066, has publications on how to remedy or avoid foundation moisture problems.

Moisture Control for Homes, by Ned Nisson, is for home builders, renovators, and handy do-it-yourselfers. Available from Cutter Information, 37 Broadway, Suite 1, Arlington, MA 02174-5552, (800) 964-5118 or (617) 641-5118. 2 volumes, $70.

Moisture Control Handbook, by Joseph Lstiburek's and J. Carmody, is also for technical readers, 1991, Oak Ridge National Laboratory, Oak Ridge, TN. Available from the National Technical Information Service, 5285 Port Royal Road, Springfield, VA 22161, (703) 487-4650. ($36.50).

Broan sells a SensAir™ fan (for around $120) that senses changes in humidity, turns itself on, then shuts off automatically. This type of fan is excellent for remodeling or new construction. **Broan Mfg. Co.,** PO Box 140, Hartford, WI 53027-0140, (800) 637-1453.

Kanalflakt, NuTone, and Panasonic make very quiet bathroom fans (tested at 0.5 to 1.0 sones). **Kanalflakt, Inc.,** 1712 Northgate Boulevard, Sarasota, FL 34234, (813) 359-3267; **NuTone, Inc.,** Madison and Redbanks Road, Cincinnati, OH 45227; (800) 543-8687; **Panasonic/Matsushita Electric Corporation of America,** 1 Panasonic Way, Secaucus, NJ 07094; (201) 392-6442.

3

Insulation: Your Best
Security Blanket

*There is an old New England saying: "What with the high cost of
heating, the average icicle on a roof costs about five dollars a foot."*
—Eric Sloane, "Reverence for Wood," 1965

Half or more of an ordinary home's heat loss is through exterior walls, floors, and roofs. Along with draftproofing, good insulation is one of the keys to reducing this loss. New building codes recognize the importance of insulation and require several times the insulation levels commonly found in older buildings. New homes are roughly twice as well insulated as homes built in the early 1970s, and millions of homeowners have added insulation to older homes in recent years. Yet an estimated two-fifths of homes have no insulation in the walls, one-sixth have no insulation in the roof, and 95% of foundations lack insulation. A high fraction of homes that are insulated don't have enough. Fortunately, the insulation of floors and attics of most older homes can be boosted cheaply and easily since these areas are often accessible, and it is usually a good investment to do so. Insulating exterior walls, however, is more difficult unless you're building a new home or doing a major remodel and will most likely require you to hire a contractor to do the work for you. How much insulation to add will depend on your existing insulation, your climate, and your finances. This chapter serves as a guide for what to insulate first, and which insulation materials to use.

Some insulation myths

MYTH: Heat rises, so a well-insulated attic means a well-insulated home.

FACT: Hot air does rise—that's why it's important to seal the air leaks between living spaces and the attic before insulating. Attic insulation is very important, but attic (and basement) air leakage control is just as important. Since houses have more heat-losing surface area of walls than of attic, a well-insulated home must also have its walls and basement insulated.

MYTH: Since my basement isn't heated and dirt is a good insulator, I don't need to worry about insulating my basement walls.

FACT: Dirt is not a good insulator—it slows heat flow but doesn't stop it. If your attic and walls are insulated, an uninsulated basement can account for one-third of your heating bill, whether you heat your basement or not. Your above-ground foundation walls have the same insulating value as a single-paned window—which isn't much.

Where to begin

If you are unsure whether or not to add insulation, it might make the most sense to have an energy auditor perform an audit on your home. An auditor can tell you where you need insulation, roughly how much it will cost, and how much money you're likely to save.

You can also call the Energy Efficiency and Renewable Energy Clearinghouse for a list of recommended minimum insulation levels listed by zip code areas of the country; see "Where to find" section at the end of this chapter. Keep in mind, though, that these are *minimum* recommended levels, and even though these are typically higher than most state or local building codes, you may want to go beyond those levels to optimize your insulation investment. If you are building a new house or doing an addition, consider 2x6 framing—which allows for higher insulation values while reducing lumber costs.

Once you know how much insulation you need and where to put it, you can choose which insulation jobs you want to do yourself and which you want an insulation contractor to do for you. For tricky jobs like insulating walls, they have equipment and expertise that you can't find in a hardware store.

Whether you are adding insulation or building a new house, it may be cost-effective to have an expert buy and install the insulation for you since his or her volume discounts may offset the labor costs. When comparing contractors' bids, be sure they are for the same insulating R-value (not just the same number of inches).

Check on experts' work: a sloppy insulation job can cut the insulating value in half. Make sure there aren't large voids between the batts of insulation, at the ends, or in tight places. Check that they actually install the amount of insulation they've charged you for.

Because loose insulation settles, the depth of the insulation at the time of installation may be misleading. If you are buying blown-in insulation, make sure the contractors are installing the number of bags of insulation needed for the square footage of your walls or attic as listed on the bags.

Insulation materials

Cellulose insulation

This is made of fire-resistant recycled newspaper, is great for retrofitting insulation into existing walls and attics, and has an insulating value of R-3.5 to R-3.8 per inch. Cellulose insulation, because of its density and greater coverage (especially when

Common insulation materials and their relative cost

FORM	TYPE	R-VALUE (approx.)	RELATIVE COST (per R per sq. ft.)
Batts Blankets	Fiberglass or Rock Wool	3½″ (R-11) 5½″ (R-19) 9½″ (R-30)	1.8¢ to 2.0¢
Loose Fill	Fiberglass or Rock Wool	R-2.7 per inch	1.8¢ to 2.0¢
	Cellulose	R-3.7 per inch	1.6¢ to 1.8¢
Rigid Board	Expanded Polystyrene (Beadboard)	R-4 per inch	3.6¢ to 4.8¢
	Extruded Polystyrene	R-5 per inch	4.8¢ to 7.2¢
	Polyurethane or Polyisocyanurate	R-7 to R-8 per inch	4.8¢ to 6.0¢
Foamed in Place	Polyurethane	R-7 to R-8 per inch	8.4¢ to 12.0¢

Illustration courtesy of New Mexico State University Cooperative Extension Service, *New Mexico Home Energy Guide*, p. 7, Las Cruces, NM.

wet-sprayed in place or when high-density dry cellulose is used), cuts air infiltration better than insulating with fiber-glass—but it's no replacement for caulking or foam.

Cellulose comes as loose material and can be poured dry onto the attic floor. It can also be mixed with water to form a spray for insulating walls and is best installed by an insulation con-tractor who has the special equipment necessary.

If you are doing the insulation work yourself—in the attic, for instance—cellulose will cost about half as much per square foot as fiberglass. Adding R-22 of extra cellulose will cost about 10 cents per square foot of attic area. If you cannot find cellulose locally, call one of the manufacturers listed in the "Where to find" section at the end to the chapter.

Fiberglass insulation

This is another cheap and easy form of insulation to use. Fiberglass is made from sand, and some manufacturers use up to 30% recycled glass. Fiberglass has an insulating value of R-3.2 to R-3.7 per inch, depending on density.

It is available in pre-formed batts or blankets and as loose-fill for blowing into the attic or walls. (Rigid fiberglass boards are available in Canada, but are not widely available in the U.S.) Use fiberglass in walls, roofs, attics, in the floor above an un-heated crawlspace or garage, and inside foundation rim joists.

The glass fibers can get into your skin and itch fiercely; pro-longed exposure can irritate your lungs, too. There has been some concern in recent years about the health effects of breath-ing small glass fibers (fiberglass is a suspected carcinogen to unprotected insulation contractors), particularly since some manufacturers are increasing the small-fiber content of fiber-glass, so be sure to use a respirator when handling these ma-terials. A hat, gloves, and a long-sleeved shirt will protect against skin contact and irritation during installation.

Rockwool

This is a recycled material similar to fiberglass (made from basalt or other rock, or made from steel mill waste materials) and used for blown-in applications. A new kind of semi-rigid rockwool batt is now available in Canada (from Roxul, Inc.), and may soon be available in the U.S.

Air Krete

This is a new type of blown-in insulation that looks like foam-ed cement, is made from silicates and magnesium oxide from seawater, and has an R-value of 3.9 per inch.

Insul-Cot

This is a cotton/polyester material made from denim recycled from blue jean and other denim mills, and has an R-value of 3.2 per inch.

Cork

Some builders are experimenting with cork insulation materials (cork is a renewable resource, as only the bark of the cork trees are "harvested," and the bark regenerates every seven years or so).

Expanded polystyrene (EPS)

Also called white "beadboard," this does not contain HCFCs and instead is manufactured with pentane and steam. It has an R-value around 3.6 per inch. For below-grade outdoor applications where moisture resistance is important, high-density expanded polystyrene is the best choice. A termite-resistant variety is available in some parts of the country.

Extruded polystyrene (XPS)

Also commonly called "blueboard" or "pinkboard," XPS has good moisture resistance and is used primarily in below-ground and under-slab applications. It has an insulating value of R-5 per inch. These qualities are achieved using HCFCs, which are less ozone-damaging versions of chlorofluoro-carbons (CFCs) but are still very potent greenhouse gases.

Polyisocyanurate

This is a widely used rigid foam board that boasts a high insu-lating value of around R-7.5 per inch, obtained using HCFCs (CFCs were prohibited after December 31, 1993, except for the sale of existing inventories). This insulation comes with a foil facing that serves as a radiant barrier if installed correctly. Because XPS and "polyiso" pose a threat to the Earth's ozone layer and climatic stability, they should only be used where thin, high R-value insulation is necessary.

Insulating structural materials

Several other insulation materials are on the market—**stress-skin panels, foam blocks, and insulated concrete blocks**, for example—but these are more appropriate for new construc-tion. If you are planning a major reconstruction or a new addi-tion to your house, by all means look into using these insulat-ing structural materials. Some manufacturers use recycled plastics, and many of the panels and blocks are expanded with pentane and steam rather than HCFCs.

Radiant barriers

The radiant-barrier foil (or foil coating on bubblepack insula-tion) reflects heat, or infrared, radiation. It is light-weight, easy to use, and contains no HCFCs. Radiant barriers for attics are becoming widely used to keep houses cool in the southern part of the U.S. (See the *Cooling* chapter for more information on radiant barriers.) Installed vertically, such as around a wa-ter heater, the foil has an R-9.8 value for a 3⁄8 in. sheet. For its reflective properties to work properly, this material needs a dead air space between the foil and the insulated surface (in other words, if the reflective material is in direct contact with the surface to be insulated it won't function properly). It can also be applied underneath and on the sides of waterbeds, on the inside of garage doors, and around water heaters.

Harmful effects of CFCs and HCFCs

International agreements have been signed to protect the Earth's ozone layer from being depleted by chemical reactions caused by industrial gases such as CFCs. This agreement, the Montreal Protocol, has moved manufacturers of rigid foam insulation boards to find less harmful alternatives. Various HCFC compounds are now used as "blowing agents" instead of CFCs to expand the foam into its finished form.

While HCFC leakage out of the insulation boards is slow, the manufacturing process itself releases some of the chemicals into the atmosphere. In addition, houses are eventually demolished and the wreckage hauled off to the dump where the CFC molecules in pre1994 foams will escape into the atmosphere.

HCFCs are the principal alternative blowing agents now being used, and while they are far less harmful to the ozone layer, HCFCs and CFCs share another important environmental impact: they are both very strong greenhouse gases. As a greenhouse gas, CFC-11 is 1,600 times more powerful per unit weight than CO_2.

What this translates to is that a typical new house using one inch of polyisocyanurate board on the exterior walls will contribute the equivalent of 22 *tons* of carbon dioxide into the atmosphere. That's twice as much CO_2 as the average house emits in a year. Consequently, we encourage homeowners and builders to use non-CFC and non-HCFC insulation materials such as expanded polystyrene, cellulose, fiberglass, and other alternatives.

Where to insulate

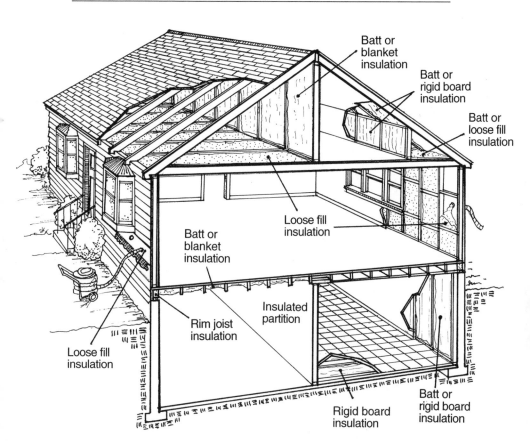

Illustration adapted from Reader's Digest (1982), *Home Improvements Manual*, p. 360, Pleasantville, NY.

√ In the attic

In an unfinished attic, insulation will be right on the attic floor, in between the ceiling joists. (A finished attic is a different story, since the insulation, if any, will be above you, between the rafters, which are covered by drywall.) If the existing insulation is visible, crawl up there with a ruler and measure how thick it is. In all but the mildest climates (warm winters and cool summers), there should be 8 to 16 inches of it. (For more information on minimum recommended insulation levels for your climate, contact the Energy and Renewable Energy Clearinghouse, listed at the end of the chapter.)

In an unheated attic, lay fiberglass batts or blankets between the floor joists (or across the joists if you're adding insulation on top), or pour cellulose between or above the joists. If the joist spaces are already insulated but you want to add more insulation, lay the new insulation *across* the joists. Do not cover recessed lights or vents. If the attic has floorboards, loosen a few boards and blow insulation between the joists.

In a finished attic, insulate kneewalls and sidewalls with batts or cellulose, and insulate between roof rafters with rigid boards or fiberglass batts. You will have to remove the drywall. Leave at least a one inch space between the insulation and the underside of the roof decking for ventilation. Before you actually start insulating, however, there are a few details to handle.

Attic air bypasses should be weatherized and sealed *before* laying down batts or cellulose. Attic air bypasses allow air to flow from the heated part of the house into the attic, resulting in energy loss. For example, a wall that is not sealed at the top will allow air to flow from below up into the attic. Attic air bypasses result from oversight during construction. Be certain that all the studwall cavities and plumbing stacks are sealed before you begin: heat mustn't escape up the walls around the edge of the attic-floor insulation. Sealing these holes will make the insulation much more effective. If a contractor is doing the work for you, make sure he or she is doing this work properly.

Before you go to the building supply store for the insulation, determine the precise dimensions of your attic and the distance between the ceiling joists so you can buy insulation in the appropriate width. The distance between joists is usually 14.5 or 22.5 inches.

Be careful to keep the insulation away from any heat-generating light fixtures, exhaust flues, and attic ventilators. Consider replacing ordinary recessed fixtures with IC-rated recessed cans made for contact with insulation. Some brands reduce air (and moisture) leakage from your living space into the attic.

Attic air sealing and insulation

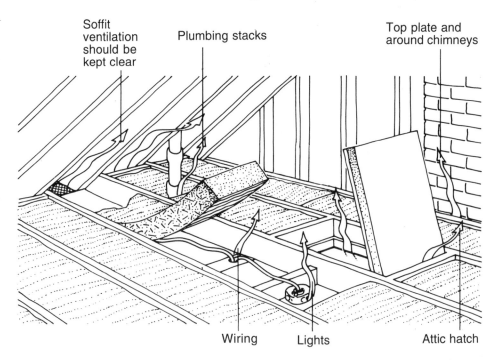

Soffit ventilation should be kept clear · Plumbing stacks · Top plate and around chimneys · Wiring · Lights · Attic hatch

Seal air leakage around wiring, plumbing, recessed light fixtures, attic hatch, and chimney before adding cellulose or fiberglass insulation. Illustration courtesy of Ontario Ministry of Energy (1989), *Consumer's Guide to Buying Energy-Efficient Resale Homes*, p. 12, Toronto, Canada.

While you are crawling around in the attic, check for attic vents. Proper attic ventilation keeps your house warmer in the winter and cooler in the summer by keeping your insulation dry and allowing the hot air to escape in the summer. If you don't see where air can circulate from outside, you should probably have a carpenter install ventilating screens.

It would be worth investigating moisture problems; see the section on "Moisture Issues" in the *Weatherization* chapter. If you're adding insulation over existing insulation, *don't* buy insulation with a vapor barrier, as that will trap moisture in the insulation below. Unfaced fiberglass is cheaper and avoids vapor barrier problems.

A good solution for hot climates is to install unfaced batts or rolls and staple a radiant barrier to the roof rafters. That way dust won't accumulate on the radiant barrier, reducing its performance. See the *Cooling* chapter for additional discussion of radiant barriers.

As a last word, don't forget to weatherstrip and insulate the attic access door on your way out.

√ In the basement

Uninsulated basements can account for as much as 25–30% of a home's total heat loss. Since only one in twenty foundations is insulated, there's a good chance that yours could use an inspection.

Where and how to insulate a basement depends on what type of foundation your home has. For an unheated basement or crawlspace, your simplest solution is to attach radiant-barrier bubblepack insulation to the bottom of the floor joists. Another good option, though a little more expensive, is to insulate between the floor joists of the floor above with at least 5.5-inch (R-19) fiberglass batts (less in milder climates). The insulation should be tight against the floor, but don't compress it because that reduces its R-value.

In both crawlspaces and basements, seal the air leaks around the rim joist and sill before you insulate the rim joist. Then lay down a 6- or 10-mil polyethylene vapor barrier on the ground to reduce moisture levels in the crawlspace. Tape it to the stem wall 6 inches up from the footer (or lay bricks around the perimeter) to hold the plastic in place. Then insulate the walls of the crawlspace with rigid and/or fiberglass insulation.

While you're down there be sure to insulate the hot water pipes—especially the pipes hanging below the now-insulated joists. This isn't likely to be cost-effective, but it will save water and energy, keep the water warmer between uses, and possibly prevent a frozen pipe.

Two ways to insulate crawlspace walls

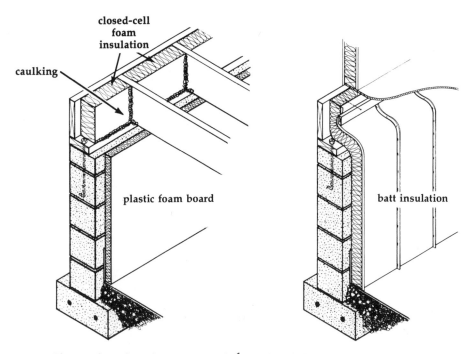

If using foam boards, cut strips of $1\,^1/_2$-inch board for the top of the stem wall and inside the sillplate. If using fiberglass batts, screw the wood lath loosely to the rim joist to avoid compressing the insulation. Illustration courtesy of Illinois Department of Energy and Natural Resources (1987), *more for your money ... Home Energy Savings,* p. 4-14, Springfield, IL.

(Note: if you have a radon problem, you must take better care to seal the vapor barrier seams and edges, and perhaps even install a ventilation system in the dirt or gravel beneath the vapor barrier. The *Energy Source Directory* lists sources for such materials; see the "Where to find" lists at the end of this and the *Weatherization* chapters.)

The best insulation option for a heated basement or a basement you'd like to finish is to "furr out" the inside of the walls with 2x4s, insulate between the studs with fiberglass insulation, and hang drywall onto the furring strips. This retrofit has a long payback—in the range of 15 years or more—but may well be an attractive option as it also gives you a finished workshop or play area.

Retrofit insulation for a full basement wall

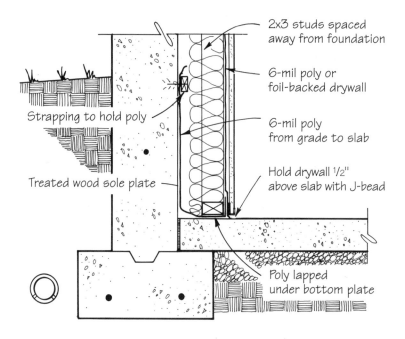

Build a 2x3 frame wall on a 2x4 or 2x6 bottom plate (not shown) to provide an air space behind the wall. Nail a 1x to the masonry wall above the exterior grade to fasten the vapor barrier that will help prevent moisture damage. Insulate with fiberglass batts and finish with drywall. Illustration courtesy of Ned Nisson of *Energy Design Update* and *The Journal of Light Construction*, February, 1992, p. 34, Richmond, VT.

To protect the fiberglass from moisture penetrating the masonry wall, provide an air space between the wall and the insulation. Seal cracks around the perimeter of the room before installing insulation. If faced fiberglass batts are used, the facing should be toward the room (warm) side. A rigid foam basement insulation system (Wallmate™ from Dow Chemical) is now on the market that incorporates furring strips for hanging drywall (see "Where to find insulation materials" section at the end of the chapter).

√ In the exterior walls

If your house was built before 1960, you can bet your walls are poorly insulated. If you haven't had an energy audit done yet, you can check the insulation by turning off the power at the service panel or fuse box and by removing an electrical outlet cover plate on an exterior wall.

If you can't see any insulation behind or around the electrical box (or can't feel any by sticking a *plastic* knitting needle through the back or side of the box), you probably don't have any. You may have to drill a test hole or two in the wall to make sure. Your best option in this case is to have a contractor blow in cellulose insulation.

In exterior walls, cellulose insulation is blown in from the exterior by removing exterior planking or by drilling small holes in the exterior sheathing every foot and a half to get the insulation into the wall cavity. In homes with shingles or aluminum or vinyl siding, the siding can be removed before drilling so as not to leave visible marks.

Cellulose insulation costs about 65 cents per square foot of 2 x 4 ft wall area for materials and labor. That works out to $500 to $1,200 for an average house. It might also be useful to have an independent or utility auditor appraise how cost-effective this would be.

√ Around air ducts

Air leaks in heating ducts can be a bigger waste of energy than most people realize, especially in cases where they pass through unheated spaces. It has been estimated that heating and cooling ducts often waste more energy than leaks through the building shell itself. Duct leaks can raise a typical home's heating and cooling costs by 20 to 30% (up to twice as much in homes with uninsulated ducts).

Duct insulation

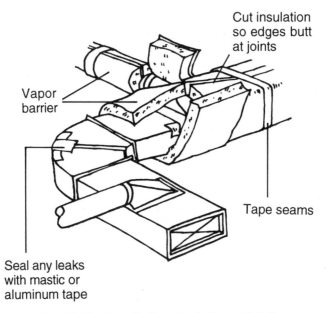

Re-tighten and seal leaky ducts before insulating with foil- or paper-faced batts. Tape seams with aluminum or duct tape. Illustration courtesy of Public Service Company of Colorado (1992), *Your Energy Guide to Heating, Cooling, and Home Appliances*, p. 21, Denver, CO.

Ducts can lose heat by conduction through the metal, by radiant heat loss to the surroundings, and by air leakage through gaps in the ductwork. Retighten all duct sections and plenum branches, screw together loose sections, and support ducts using plastic or metal straps where needed. Seal any leaks with special latex-based mastic or metal-backed tape (duct tape, despite its name, will harden and crack after being exposed to the duct's high temperature), then wrap the ducts with foil- or paper-faced fiberglass insulation.

Leave the foil or paper on the outside and tape the joints and any exposed fiberglass with duct tape. Or use high-temperature aluminum tape, available from a heating supplier; it is stickier and lasts longer. Be sure to seal return ducts, too, so you can stop breathing crawlspace air. If you are unsure how to seal ducts correctly, you may want to call a trained technician; otherwise, you can make the situation worse. Sealed ductwork should be tested for leaks to assure both improved energy efficiency and air quality.

√ In mobile homes

One of the main reasons the average utility bills of mobile home owners are nearly 50% higher per square foot of living area is that mobile homes are poorly insulated compared to site-built homes. Homes manufactured prior to 1976 often had little or no insulation. Even in chilly Alaska, the 1976 code only requires a minimum of R-9.6 insulation.

Most mobile homes, especially in cold climates, are good candidates for additional insulation in roof and wall cavities and under the belly. Heating ducts should be adequately sealed and insulated, too. It may not be cost-effective to add wall and belly insulation in warmer climates. Adding roof insulation is often worthwhile in any climate. New insulation—fiberglass, cellulose, or polystyrene beads—can be blown into roof cavities, or rigid foam boards can be laid onto the existing roof surface with a new rubber roof membrane applied on top. The latter option is not as cost-effective as adding blown-in insulation unless the existing roof needs extensive repairs anyway.

Where to find

insulation materials

Lumber yards and home building centers have many of the insulation materials discussed in this chapter. For below-ground applications, you may need to ask the lumber yard to special-order the high-density expanded polystyrene used as a good alternative to extruded polystyrene. Cellulose insulation is often available at lumber yards and home building centers. If not, call local insulation contractors and ask them for sources, or call one of the manufacturers.

Air Krete, Inc., PO Box 380, Weedsport, NY 13166, (315) 834-6609, makes "Air Krete" foamed-in-place insulation.

Ark-Seal International, 2190 South Klamath, Denver, CO 80223, (800) 525-8992, makes the "Blow-In-Blanket" insulation system combining a binder with fiberglass, rockwool, or cellulose.

BASF Wyandotte Corporation, 100 Cherry Hill Road, Parsippany, NJ 07054, (800) 526-1072, makes low and high density expanded polystyrene (EPS) insulation board.

CertainTeed Corporation, PO Box 860, Valley Forge, PA 19482, (800) 441-6720, makes fiberglass batts and blankets.

Cotton Unlimited, PO Box 760, Post, TX 79356, (806) 495-3511, makes "Insulcot" cotton insulation.

DFI Pultruded Composites, 1600 Dolwick Dr., Erlanger, KY 41018, (606) 282-7300, makes the "Insul-Guard" protection board for foundation insulation.

Dow Chemical Company, Construction Materials Group, 2020 Dow Center, Midland, MI 48674, (800) 232-2436, manufactures the "Wallmate" foam insulation system for basement walls.

Environmental Construction Outfitters, 44 Crosby Street, New York, NY 10012, (800) 238-5008 and (212) 334-9659, sells cork insulation in half- or one-inch sheets.

Flexible Air Movers, 2910 East Heaton Avenue, Fresno, CA 93721, (800) 456-1326, makes an R-11 flexible heating and cooling duct.

Kwik-R Systems, 6223 Middleton Springs Dr., Middleton, WI 53562, (800) 292-1228, makes EPS basement wall insulation boards.

Louisiana Pacific Corp., 2001 Hitzer Court, Fenton, MO 63026, (800) 467-7779, makes "Nature Guard" cellulose insulation.

NPS Corporation, PO Box 348, Perryville, MO 63775, (800) 888-2332, manufactures expanded polystyrene (EPS) exterior insulation.

Owens-Corning Fiberglas Corporation, Fiberglas Tower, Toledo, OH 43659, (800) 447-3759, makes batt and blanket insulation, including high density composite panels.

parPAC, PO Box 1504, Norfolk, NE 68702, (800) 228-0024 has a new dry blown-in cellulose product.

Perma Chink, 17639 NE 67th Court, Redmond, WA 98052, (800) 548-1231, makes "Stuc-O-Flex" foundation insulation protection coat.

Roxul, 551 Harrop Drive, Milton, Ontario L9T 3H3, (416) 878-8474, manufactures the "flexi-edge" rockwool available in Canada.

Schuller International, PO Box 5108, Denver, CO 80217, (800) 654-3103, makes the Manville line of fiberglass batt and blanket insulation, including high density.

Simplex Products Division, PO Box 10, Adrian, MI 49221-0010, (800) 545-6555, makes the "Finestone" EPS exterior insulation system.

Southern Cellulose, 4530 B Patton Drive, Atlanta, GA 30336, (404) 344-3590, makes cellulose insulation.

ThermoGuard Insulation, 452 Charles Street, Billings, MT 59101, (406) 252-1938, manufactures cellulose insulation.

information

Energy Efficiency and Renewable Energy Clearinghouse (EREC), PO Box 3048, Merrifield, VA, 22116, (800) DOE-EREC and (800) 523-2929, provides information on a wide array of energy issues, including insulation. Ask for their *Insulation Fact Sheet*. This recommends, using a zip-code reference system, minimum insulation R-values for walls, ceilings, floors, and crawlspaces for several climate regions and types of heating equipment.

Also check out the following sources:

"Environmental Aspects of Insulation Materials," by Alex Wilson, reprint available from *Environmental Building News*, RR1, Box 161, Brattleboro, VT 05301, (802) 257-7300.

All About Insulation is one in a series of low-cost booklets published by the Massachusetts Audubon Society, 208 South Great Road, Lincoln, MA 01773, (617) 259-9500.

Home Insulation by Harry Yost is a 138-page book published by Storey Communication, Inc., 105 Schoolhouse Road, Pownal, VT 05261, (802) 823-5811.

The Residential Energy Audit Manual has detailed technical information on insulation and moisture control written for auditors and house doctors, but is also useful for do-it-yourselfers. Fairmont Press, 700 Indian Trail, Lilburn, GA 30247, (404) 925-9388.

Energy Source Directory: A Guide to Products Used in Energy-Efficient Residential Buildings, Iris Communications, 258 East 10th Avenue, Suite E, Eugene, OR 97401-3284, (800) 346-0104.

Your Mobile Home Energy and Repair Guide, by John Krigger, is available from Saturn Resource Management, 324 Fuller Avenue, Helena, MT 59601-9984; (406) 443-3433. $15.95.

Making Your Mobile Home Energy Efficient, by the North Carolina Alternative Energy Corporation, PO Box 12699, Research Triangle Park, NC 27709; (919) 361-8000, is a step-by-step guide for retrofitting mobile homes in moderate climates. $5.

4

Fine-Tuning Your
Heating System

*Using electricity to heat your home is like using bottled water
on your lawn.*

By weatherizing and insulating your home, you've reduced
the amount of heat escaping through the walls and roof. It
now makes sense to look at how efficiently your heating system produces and delivers the heat that you have taken the
trouble to save. This chapter gives tips for making your existing heating system run more efficiently whether it is gas, electric, oil, wood, or solar powered. The suggestions given are
either relatively inexpensive or free. All are cost-effective.

For those of you in the market for a *new* furnace, boiler, heat
pump, or woodstove, there are some helpful ideas on which
kind of heating system will keep your house warm reliably for
the smallest life-cycle cash outlay. Modern heating systems
have seen dramatic efficiency gains over the past few years.

It probably won't be cost-effective based on fuel savings alone to replace a working heating system. But if the system appears close to a natural death, or its maintenance costs are high, it could well save you money to replace it. And if you do, buying a high-efficiency model—rather than an average one—will almost certainly be cost-effective. Remember that weatherizing and insulating your home will greatly reduce your heat losses, allowing you to reduce your capital outlay by buying a significantly smaller heating system.

Trends in the efficiency of natural gas furnaces

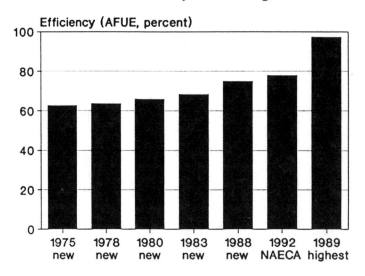

"New" means the shipment-weighted average of all units shipped in that year. "NAECA" is the Federal standard passed into law in the National Appliance Energy Conservation Act of 1992. "Highest" refers to the most efficient unit commercially available in 1989. Illustration courtesy of U.S. Congress, Office of Technology Assessment (1992), *Building Energy Efficiency*, OTA E-518, p. 38, Washington, DC.

For safety reasons, adjustments, tune-ups, and modifications to your heating system itself are best done by a heating system professional. Homeowners and renters can improve system performance by insulating ducts and pipes, cleaning registers, replacing filters, and installing programmable thermostats.

Furnaces and boilers

√ Heating system tune-ups

Gas furnaces and boilers should be tuned every two years while oil units should be tuned once a year. Your fuel supplier can recommend a qualified technician. Expect to pay $60–$150. It's money well spent. It's also a good idea to have the technician do a safety test to make sure the vent does not leak combustion products into the home. (You can do a simple test by extinguishing a match a couple of inches from the spill-over vent and ensuring that the smoke is drawn up the chimney.)

During a gas furnace tune-up, the technician should clean the furnace fan and its blades, correct the drive belt's tension, oil the fan and its motor bearings, clean or replace the filter, and help you seal ducts, if necessary. If the fan motor on the furnace's forced-air distribution system has failed, ask your technician to replace it with a more efficient motor.

√ Efficiency modifications

While the heating contractor is there to tune up your system, he or she may be able to recommend some modifications such as reducing the nozzle (oil) or orifice (gas) size, installing a new burner and an automatic, motorized flue damper, or replacing the pilot light on a natural gas furnace with an electronic (spark) ignition. If you have an older oil burner, installing a flame-retention burner head (which vaporizes the fuel and allows more complete combustion) will typically pay back your investment in 2 to 5 years.

√ Turn off the pilot light during the summer

This will save you about $2 to $4 per month. Do this only if you can safely light it again yourself, so you don't have to pay someone to do it. Be sure to solve any moisture problems in your basement so the pilot light doesn't rust when the flame is off. Federal regulations now require that new natural gas-fired boilers and furnaces be equipped with electronic ignition, saving $30 to $40 per year in gas bills. Propane-fired units cannot be sold without a pilot light and cannot be safely retrofitted with a spark ignitor unless you install expensive propane-sniffing equipment.

√ Insulate the supply and return pipes on steam and hot-water boilers

Use high-temperature pipe insulation such as fiberglass wrap for steam pipes. The lower temperatures of hydronic or hot water systems might allow you to use ordinary foam insulation, but this depends on your boiler's operating temperatures; check with your heating technician.

√ Clean or change the filter on a warm-air furnace

To new homeowners it may be a revelation that filters are made for more than coffee and cars. A clogged furnace filter impedes air flow, makes the fan work harder, and cuts overall efficiency. The hardest part of this maneuver will be turning into the hardware store parking lot. So while you're there, pick up several filters, since you'll want to replace the filter every month during the heating season. They'll set you back a buck or two apiece. For five bucks you can buy a reusable filter that will still need to be vacuumed clean every month, but will last a year or two.

√ Seal and insulate warm-air heating ducts

Losses from leaky, uninsulated ducts—especially those in unheated attics and basements—can reduce the efficiency of your heating system by as much as 30%. An estimated $10 billion worth of energy is lost through leaky and poorly insulated forced-air heating and air conditioning ducts per year. Accessible warm-air ducts should be sealed thoroughly with mastic before being insulated with fiberglass. See the *Insulation* and *Cooling* chapters for details on cutting this waste. In new construction, warm-air ducts should be run inside the thermal envelope of the house where possible and sealed and tested before being covered up with insulation or framing.

MYTH: Turning down your thermostat at night or when you're gone means you'll use more energy than you saved when you have to warm up the house again.

FACT: You always save by turning down your thermostat no matter how long you're gone. The one exception is older electric heat pumps.

MYTH: You can warm up your house faster if you turn the thermostat up to 90°F initially.

FACT: Most heating systems have only one "speed." They're either on or off. The house warms up at the same rate no matter what temperature you set the thermostat. Setting it higher only causes the furnace to overshoot the desired temperature, wasting energy.

Radiators and heat registers

√ Vacuum the cobwebs out of your warm-air registers

√ Reflect the heat from your radiator

You can make foil reflectors by taping aluminum foil to cardboard. Place them behind radiators on exterior walls, with the shiny side facing the room. A piece of half-inch foil-faced rigid insulation or foil-faced bubble wrap works well for this, too.

√ **Vacuum the connector fins on baseboard heaters**

Keeping furniture and drapes out of the way also improves air flow from the radiator.

√ **Install or replace improperly functioning air vents on steam radiators**

√ **Bleed the air out of hot-water radiators**

Trapped air in radiators keeps them from filling with hot water and thus reduces their heating capacity. Doing this should also quiet down clanging radiators. You can buy a radiator key at the hardware store. Hold a cup or a pan under the valve as you slowly open it with the key. Close the valve when all the air has escaped and only water comes out. If it turns out that you have to do this more than once a month, have your system inspected by a heating contractor.

Thermostats

√ **Install a programmable thermostat**

One-half of homeowners turn down their heat at night and save roughly 6% to 16% of heating energy. A programmable or clock thermostat can automatically do this chore for you, and in addition to lowering room temperatures while you sleep, it will also raise temperatures again before you get out from under the covers. Sound good? It's cost-effective too. Some folks use such a thermostat to warm up the house before they get home from work. *Home Energy* magazine reports savings in excess of 20% with two eight-hour, 10F° setbacks.

Electronic thermostats are available for $25 to $150 at hardware and heating supply stores. You can install one yourself, but make sure you turn off the power to the furnace or boiler before you begin. If connecting wires makes you jittery, have an electrician or heating system technician perform the service for you. If you have a heat pump or central air conditioning, be sure the thermostat is designed for your system.

Programmable thermostat

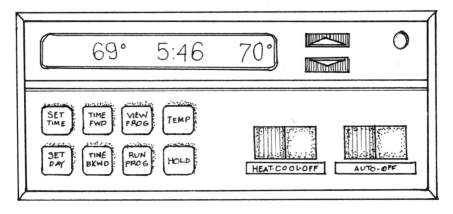

Replace your old mercury thermostat with an electronic, setback, clock, or programmable thermostat. It's easy to do.

Heat pumps

√ Change or clean the filters once a month

Dirty filters are the most common reason for failures.

√ Keep leaves and debris away from the outside unit

Good air flow is essential to heat pump efficiency.

√ Listen periodically to the compressor

If it cycles on for less than a minute, there is something wrong. Call a technician and have it adjusted immediately.

√ Dust off the indoor coils of the heat exchanger at least once a year

√ Have the compressor tuned up

The technician will check its controls, filter, and refrigerant charge, and repair or help you identify and seal duct leaks. Have this service performed every year or two by a heating or cooling technician. (See the *Insulation* and *Cooling* chapters and page 78 of this chapter for additional discussion of sealing and insulating ductwork.)

Efficiency opportunities in air source heat pumps

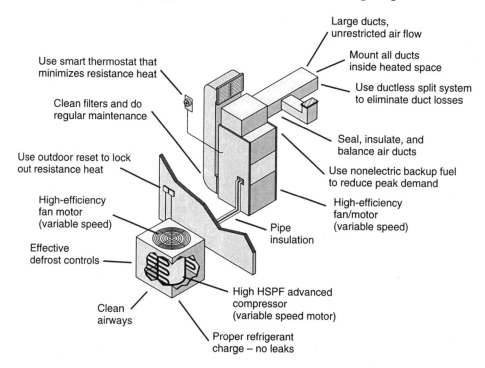

Some of the points in this illustration are best accomplished during new construction (sizing ducts, ensuring unrestricted air flow, and selecting efficient equipment, for example). A number are good retrofit measures: insulate piping, keep the outdoor unit free of leaves and debris, clean filter, and have it serviced regularly. Illustration courtesy of E SOURCE (1993), *Space Heating Technology Atlas*, p. 225, Boulder, CO.

Woodstoves

Wood heat is a mixed blessing. If harvested and used in a responsible manner, firewood can be a sustainable resource, though most wood-gathering is not done sustainably. There are 27 million wood-burning stoves and fireplaces in the U.S., and they contribute millions of tons of pollutants to the air we breathe. One woodstove emits 200 to 1,000 times as much particulates as a gas furnace. In Washington State, for example, wood heating contributes 90% of the particulates in two of the counties with the worst air-pollution problems.

√ Use a woodstove only if you're willing to make sure it burns cleanly

Woodstoves aren't like furnaces or refrigerators; you can't just turn them on and forget 'em. "Banking" a woodstove for an overnight burn doesn't make sense from an environmental perspective, as the wood usually just smolders and emits a lot of pollution. A well-insulated house will hold enough heat that you shouldn't need to keep the stove going overnight.

√ Burn well-seasoned wood

It should be split at least six months before you burn it. Never burn garbage, plastics, plywood, or other treated lumber.

√ Burn smaller but hotter fires

Make sure your stove gets plenty of air at all times.

√ If a woodstove is your main source of heat, be sure it is an EPA-approved model

New EPA regulations require woodstoves to emit less than one-tenth the pollution that older stoves spewed out.

√ Check your chimney regularly

Blue or gray smoke means your wood is not burning completely. If your fire is smoking, something is going wrong. Make sure you've done all the measures above.

Fireplaces

Fireplaces offer more of a light show than an effective source of heat. Fireplaces can even be a net heat loser because of the warm room air sucked up the chimney. A roaring fire can exhaust as much as 24,000 cubic feet of air per hour, and this air is replaced by cold air leaking into the house. Consequently, most fireplaces operate at a total efficiency of minus 10% to plus 10% (*i.e.*, some lose 10% more heat than they give). If you employ all the weatherization measures in Chapter 2 to seal your home, you may lack adequate fresh air for combustion. In extreme cases there is a danger of backdrafting the fireplace as the negative pressure draws air down the chimney.

√ If you never use your fireplace, put a plug in the flue of the chimney to reduce heat loss

Seal the plug to the chimney with good-quality caulk and be sure to tell anyone who may want to start a fire that the chimney is plugged. If you occasionally use the fireplace, you can make a tight-fitting plug for the fireplace opening with rigid board insulation, plywood with pipe insulation around the edge, or an inflatable DraftStopper™. Be sure you leave a sign on the fireplace, though, so someone doesn't inadvertently light a fire while the plug is in place (the DraftStopper™ comes with a warning strip).

Enviro-Energy, 6601 East Mill Plane Blvd., Vancouver, WA 98661, (800) 263-3674, sells the DraftStopper™.

√ Improve the seal of the flue damper

To test the damper seal, close the flue, light a small piece of paper and watch the smoke. If the smoke goes up the flue, there's an air leak. Seal around the damper assembly with refractory cement. (Don't seal the damper closed.) If the damper has warped from high heat over the years, get a sheet metal shop to make a new one.

Fireplace heat contribution versus heat loss

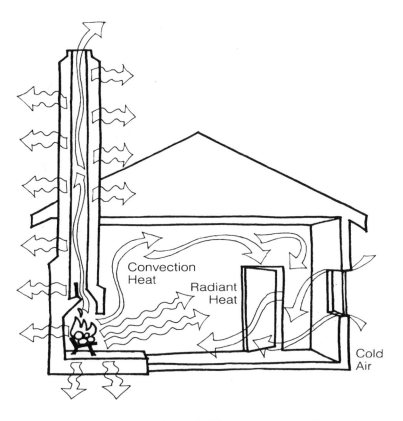

Fireplaces can be a net heat loss due to infiltration of cold air. Weatherization and insulation help, but the best measure, though often difficult and expensive, is to provide outside combustion air to the fireplace. Illustration courtesy Public Service of Colorado (1992), *Your Energy Guide to Heating, Cooling, and Home Appliances,* p. 26, Denver, CO.

√ **Install tight-fitting glass doors**

Controlling air flow improves combustion efficiency by 10 to
20% and also reduces air leakage up a poorly sealed chimney.

√ **Use tube grates made of C-shaped metal tubes**

Tube grates draw cooler room air into the fireplace to circulate
behind the fire, to warm up, and then to pass back to the room.
These grates can improve efficiency, but are expensive and can
deteriorate if placed too close to the heat of the fireplace.
Proper installation and periodic cleaning are essential.

√ **Caulk around the fireplace and hearth**

Do this where they meet the structure of the house, using a
butyl rubber caulk.

√ **Use cast-iron firebacks**

They are available in a variety of patterns and sizes, and improve fireplace efficiency by reflecting much of the fire's
radiant heat into the room.

√ **Locate the screen slightly away from the opening**

This allows the heated air to flow over the top of the screen.
While preventing sparks, firescreens can also prevent as much
as 30% of the heat from entering the room.

Buying a new heating system

If your old heating system is about to die, you're probably in
the market for a new one. Or, if you spend over $1,000 per
year on heating, it's likely that the $800 to $4,500 you would
spend on a more efficient heating system will reduce your bills
enough to pay for your investment in several years. Your sys-

tem will also be more reliable, as well as increase the value of your house. As you shop, it's worth keeping in mind a few things that will save you money and increase your comfort.

If you've weatherized and insulated your home, you can downsize the furnace or boiler without compromising the reliability of your heating system. An oversized heater will cost more to buy up front and more to run every year, and its frequent on-off cycles reduce system efficiency. Ask your heating contractor to explain any sizing calculations to verify that you don't get stuck with an oversized model.

Natural gas furnaces and boilers

It is always cost-effective to pay a little more up front to get a more efficient model. (It is not always cost-effective, however, to get the *most* efficient unit, since your reduced heating needs—now that you may have weatherized and added insulation—mean a longer payback for a super-efficient unit.) The differences between various models can be significant, and it is worth your while to examine efficiency ratings before making a decision. Consider getting a sealed combustion unit. A heating contractor or consulting engineer can help you decide whether to upgrade your system and what type of equipment and efficiency rating will best suit your needs and your pocketbook. Or you can use the section in Wilson's and Morrill's book listed at the end of this chapter to make the cost-effectiveness calculations yourself.

Fuel switching

It may be cost-effective to switch heating fuels from, say, heating oil to natural gas, but only if this does not also require expensive changes to your home's heat *distribution* system. For example, it probably wouldn't pay to replace the old steam boiler with a high-efficiency forced-air furnace or heat pump, since new forced-air ducts would need to be installed. Call a heating system engineer for information on systems that make sense for your situation, climate, and heating bills. You may not want to take our word for it, but we expect home heating oil, natural gas, and propane prices to remain low and stable for years (though prices are likely to continue to fluctuate with seasons and international tensions), while electricity prices are likely to rise only moderately and could even fall a bit in some areas.

Electric resistance heating

Electric baseboard heating is by far the most expensive way to warm one's home: it's cheap to buy and install, but it costs two to three times as much to heat with electricity as with gas, even accounting for the energy wasted in a typical gas-fired heating system. Including the higher installation cost of gas-fired furnaces and boilers, the life-cycle cost of electric resistance heating is, without exception, far higher, even in regions with very low electricity prices. If you do heat with electricity, it will be especially lucrative to weatherize, insulate, and install a programmable thermostat in your home. If you also use air conditioning and live in a mild winter climate, consider switching to a heat pump.

Heat pumps

Heat pumps are the most efficient form of electric heat. There are three types of heat pumps: air-to-air heat pumps, water-source heat pumps, and ground-source heat pumps. Heat pumps actually collect heat from the air, water, or the ground, concentrate the warmth and distribute it through the home. Heat pumps typically deliver three times more energy in heat than they consume in electric power. Heat pumps can also be used to cool homes by reversing the process—collecting indoor heat and transferring it outside the building. Some heat pumps are designed also to provide an inexpensive source of household hot water. See the *Hot Water* chapter for details.

Air-to-air heat pumps are the most popular and offer the lowest capital cost of the heat pump family. However, air-to-air units must rely on inefficient back-up heating mechanisms when the outside temperature drops below a certain point. That point varies from model to model, so be sure to buy one that's designed for your climate—some models can cope with much colder weather before resorting to back-up heat. A heat pump that's forced to run on back-up is, in effect, no better than standard electric resistance heating. Note that some newer pumps have more efficient gas-fired back-up mechanisms.

Ground-source heat pump

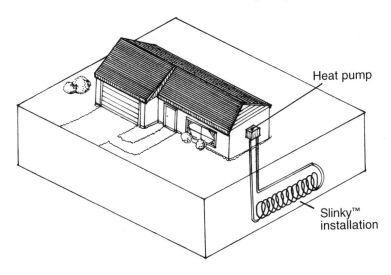

Ground-source heat pumps can be highly cost-effective in new construction over the life-cycle of heating and cooling equipment compared to more conventional options. Several designs are on the market; this illustration shows the Slinky™ design. Adapted from an illustration by E SOURCE (1993), *Space Heating Technology Atlas*, p. 227, Boulder, CO.

Not all heat pumps are created equal, but fortunately the Air Conditioning and Refrigeration Institute rates and tests all heat pumps on the market. If you're considering installing an air-to-air unit, look for the efficiency ratings and purchase a system designed for a colder climate. Also, contact your electric utility and State Energy Office for information on rebates and other incentives available to help finance the higher capital cost of these systems.

Ground- or water-source heat pumps require extensive outdoor plastic piping buried below the frost line in your back yard or installed into a well or pond. Ground-source systems can be expensive to install and are most cost-effective with new construction where pipes can be buried prior to landscaping.

Tens of thousands of ground-source heat pumps have been installed in Canada, New England, and other frostbelt areas. As indicated in the table at the end of this chapter, the life-cycle cost of ground-source heat pumps is very favorable compared to other heating and cooling systems.

People heaters

It often makes sense to buy a gas or electric radiant or convection heater to warm only certain areas of the home, or, as in the case of radiant heaters, keeping the *people* warm and comfortable. Radiant systems keep you and objects around you warm just like the sun warms your skin. This allows you to set the thermostat for the main heating system lower by 6–8F°.

Even if you heat with gas, electric convective or radiant spot heaters can save you money, depending on how the system is used. Radiant systems are designed and used more like task lights: turning them on only when and where heat is needed, rather than heating the whole house. Most central heating systems give you little control in this respect, since they are designed to heat the whole home.

As one old-timer, who was accustomed to sitting near a wood-stove, complained while pacing the floor at his son-in-law's house: "I don't know where to sit. Everything is the same temperature!"

Woodstoves and pellet stoves

Modern woodstoves have catalytic combustors and other features that boost their efficiencies into the 55–75% range while lowering emissions by two-thirds. Older woodstoves without

Advanced woodstove with catalytic combustor

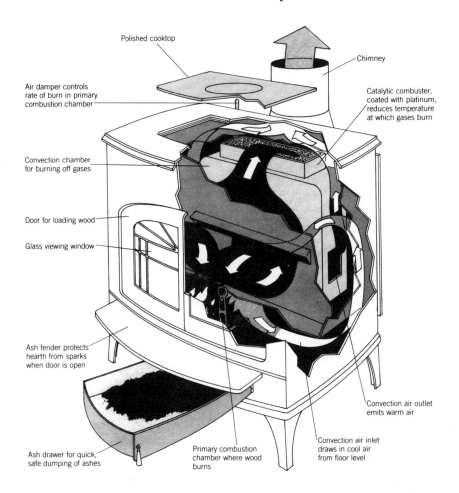

Polished cooktop

Chimney

Air damper controls
rate of burn in primary
combustion chamber

Catalytic combuster,
coated with platinum,
reduces temperature
at which gases burn

Convection chamber
for burning off gases

Door for loading wood

Glass viewing window

Ash fender protects
hearth from sparks
when door is open

Convection air outlet
emits warm air

Convection air inlet
draws in cool air
from floor level

Ash drawer for quick,
safe dumping of ashes

Primary combustion
chamber where wood
burns

New woodstoves are far more efficient and less polluting than older versions. Illustration courtesy of Reader's Digest (1991), *New Complete Do-it-yourself Manual*, p. 486, Pleasantville, NY.

air controls, such as Franklin stoves, have efficiencies of 20–30%. Wood burns at a higher temperature in a catalytic wood-stove, thereby minimizing pollution and creosote buildup.

If you're buying a new woodstove, make sure it's not too large for your heating needs. This will allow you to keep your stove stoked with the damper open, resulting in a cleaner and more efficient burn. Some stoves incorporate more cast iron or soap-stone as thermal mass to moderate temperature swings and prolong fire-life.

Pellet stoves have the advantage that the fuel—pellets of com-pressed sawdust, cardboard, or agricultural waste—is auto-matically fed into the stove by an electric auger. One hopper-full of fuel can last for a day or two.

Pellet stoves are cleaner burning than woodstoves, and the fuel is dryer than firewood, which improves combustion effi-ciency. But the pellets (which look like rabbit food) are more expensive than wood and not widely available around the country. Compared to woodstoves, pellet stoves have more mechanical parts that may require maintenance. Though they only use about 100 kWh of electricity a year (about $8 worth) to run the auger and fan, they will not operate during a power outage.

Fireplace inserts

A fireplace insert fits inside the opening of a fireplace, operates like a woodstove, and offers improved heat performance. An insert is difficult to install because it must be lifted into the fireplace opening and the space around it must be covered with sheet metal and sealed with a cement grout to reduce air leaks. Such inserts are 30 to 50% efficient, which is a good im-provement over a fireplace, but less efficient than a good free-standing woodstove. A better choice, though more expensive, is a certified woodstove insert.

A fireplace can be retrofitted with an airtight woodstove installed in front of the fireplace. This is the most efficient choice, since all six heat-emitting sides sit inside the living space, on the hearth. The stove's chimney is linked into the existing flue. Check the condition of your chimney with a chimney specialist first, as you may need a new chimney liner. Many woodstoves and inserts have glass doors, offering a view of the fire.

Some modern high-efficiency fireplaces combine furnace and woodstove features such as internal fans and thermostats and are EPA certified for acceptable levels of emissions.

Opel 2000, made by **RSF Energy** (PO Box 3637, Smithers, B.C., Canada, 604/847-4301) offers zoned heating capability and a catalytic combustor for reduced emissions. Available as a wood-burning fireplace or with a gas-conversion option. The company claims an extraordinary 80% overall efficiency rating. This unit may be used as a central heating system with ductwork extending from the fireplace.

Gas fireplaces

Gas fireplaces have combustion efficiencies up to 80%, whereas *gas logs* are only 20 to 30% efficient. However, many local codes require chimneys to be welded open, reducing their overall efficiency unless they have tight-fitting doors to cut exfiltration of heated room air.

Masonry stoves and fireplaces

Masonry stoves, also called Russian fireplaces, have long been popular in Europe. They are large free-standing masonry fireplaces with a closeable firebox in which the heat and smoke from the combustion process go through a twisting masonry chimney. The mass of the heater slowly warms up and re-radiates warmth into the room.

They are much more efficient than fireplaces, and because of their high mass, radiate an even amount of heat over a long period of time. They have relatively low emissions because of their high operating temperatures. As Mark Twain observed: "One firing is enough for the day ... the heat produced is the same all day, instead of too hot and too cold by turns."

Masonry stoves are expensive, but may be a good option for a new home. They are best suited to well-insulated homes with open floor plans that allow the heat to radiate freely.

Radiant fireplaces (also known as "Count Rumford" designs) have a broad, tall, and shallow opening to maximize radiative heating from the large masonry fireback exposed to the room.

Passive solar heat

Solar energy is the most environmentally friendly form of heating you can find. It can also be one of the cheapest. Passive solar heating uses no moving parts, just sunshine through insulating windows and thermal mass in the building structure to store the heat.

A carefully designed passive solar building can rely on the sun for half or more of its heating needs in virtually any climate in the U.S. Many successful designs cut conventional heating loads by 80% or better. Some buildings, such as Rocky Mountain Institute's own headquarters, have no need for a central heating system. In hot climates, shading and passive cooling strategies can eliminate a need for mechanical cooling.

Adding a greenhouse is one way to retrofit your home to take advantage of solar energy. If doable, you might also consider installing a new south-facing window to increase your home's solar gain; see the *Windows* chapter for more information on high-performance windows.

Contact the Passive Solar Industries Council (see the list at the end of the chapter) for information on passive solar design, and read the *Cooling* chapter of this book for ideas on how to cool your home passively.

We should point out, though, that using passive solar heating requires careful design of the home. It's best done in new construction or major remodels. Otherwise, put your money into weatherizing your home. See Chapter 10, *Doing it Right the First Time,* for additional discussion of passive solar design.

Sun path diagram

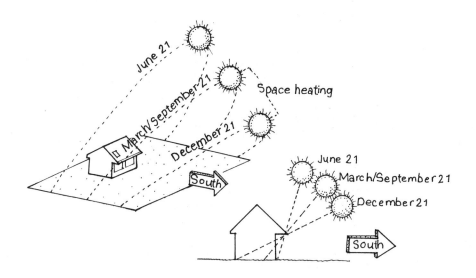

Passive solar heating is practicable in every climate. This simplified illustration shows the importance of a calculated roof overhang to allow solar heating in the winter but prevent unwanted solar heat gain in the summer. Adapted from an illustration by E SOURCE (1993), *Space Heating Technology Atlas,* p. 62, Boulder, CO.

Active solar heating

In many climates around the U.S., flat-plate collector systems can provide enough heat to make central heating systems unnecessary, but in most regions it would be prudent (and more cost-effective) to add a small back-up system for those cloudy periods. They are best incorporated into a passive solar design, and into new construction, although active solar systems can be added at any time to supplement space and water heating requirements. Solar thermal collectors are discussed in more detail in the *Hot Water* chapter.

Our favorite solar system for the Colorado climate is a radiant in-floor heating system supplementing passive solar gain and also heating the domestic hot water, backed up by a small medium-efficiency boiler that almost never has to be used. The system is quiet, comfortable, reliable, and cost-effective.

Cost

While operating costs will vary by climate and region, and fuel and electricity prices are different across the country, the following chart presents estimated installation and operating costs for selected heating and cooling systems in a typical single-family house. It assumes that heat pumps will provide air conditioning in summer as well as space heating in winter.

	Installation cost	Operating cost per year	Annualized cost
Annualized* cost of selected heating and cooling systems (in dollars; assumed life-expectancy is 20 years; estimated national average)			
Advanced gas furnace + high-eff A/C	7,200	746	1,455
Standard gas furnace + standard A/C	5,775	901	1,469
Gas-fired air-source heat pump	8,333	658	1,478
Advanced ground-source heat pump	9,250	682	1,592
Advanced air-source heat pump	8,940	822	1,702
Standard air-source heat pump	5,715	1,232	1,794
Advanced oil furnace + high-eff A/C	6,515	1,266	1,907
Electric resistance heat + standard A/C	5,515	1,769	2,312

Adapted from: Joan Gregerson *et al.* (1993), *Space Heating Technology Atlas*, E SOURCE, Boulder, CO, pp. 278–79, and Environmental Protection Agency (1993), *Space Conditioning: The Next Frontier*, Washington, DC.

* Annualized cost includes yearly operating cost plus the capital and installation cost recalculated as an annual payment (based on 20-year financing and a 10-percent discount rate to account for the time value of money).

Where to find

heating equipment and supplies

You can buy a setback, clock, or programmable thermostat at your hardware or heating supply store. You'll need to specify whether you are going to use it for electric baseboard heating, a furnace or boiler, or a heat pump. Your heating contractor can get components for upgrading your boiler or furnace. Most air-conditioner manufacturers also make heat pumps.

Carrier Corporation, Box 70, Indianapolis, IN 46206, (800) 227-7437, makes the "Weathermaker" sealed combustion gas-fired furnace.

Controlled Energy Corporation, Fiddler's Green, Waitsfield, VT 05673, (802) 496-4436 and (800) 642-3111 sells the "EcoTherm" direct vent room heater.

Dornback Furnace & Foundry, 9545 Granger Rd, Garfield Heights, OH 44125, (216) 662-1600, has a sealed combustion oil furnace.

Energy Federation, Inc. 14 Tech Circle, Natick, MA 01760, (800) 876-0660, has a selection of programmable thermostats, as well as foil-faced bubble wrap for radiator reflectors, high-temperature duct tape, and fiberglass pipe wrap.

Honeywell, 1985 Douglas Drive, Golden Valley, MN 55422, (800) 328-5111, is one of several makers of programmable thermostats.

Hunter Fan Company, 2500 Frisco Ave., Memphis, TN 38114, (901) 743-1360, makes programmable thermostats for heat pumps and conventional heating systems.

Lennox Industries, 2100 Lake Park Blvd, Richardson, TX 75080, (214) 497-5109, makes the "Pulse 21" sealed combustion pulse furnace.

Monitor Products, Inc., PO Box 3408, Princeton, NJ 08543, (908) 329-0900, makes a sealed combustion kerosene room heater.

Rinnai America Corp., 1662 Lukken Industrial Dr. West, La Grange, GA 30240, (800) 621-9419, sells a sealed combustion room heater.

Solar Works, Inc., 64 Main Street, Montpelier, VT 05602, (802) 223-7804, makes the "Solar Boiler."

SSHC, Inc., PO Box 769, Old Saybrook, CT 06475, (203) 388-3848, one of several electric radiant heater manufacturers, makes the "Ener-joy PeopleHeaters."

Teledyne Laars, 6000 Condor Drive, Moorepark, CA 93021, (805) 529-2000, makes the gas-fired "MiniCombo II" integrated space/water heater and the "MiniTherm" boiler series.

Trane Company, 6200 Troup Highway, Tyler, TX 75711, (903) 581-3200, makes a sealed combustion, gas-fired, condensing furnace (the XE-90), and the GS series of ground-source heat pumps.

Trianco-Heatmaker, Inc., 111 York Ave., Randolph, MA 02368, (617) 961-1660, makes the "HeatMaker" sealed combustion integrated hydronic space and water heating boiler.

information

State Energy Offices (see Appendix for phone numbers) often have free information on furnaces, heat pumps, maintenance tips, etc.

Consumer Guide to Home Energy Savings, by Alex Wilson and John Morrill. Loaded with the information you'll need—how heating systems work, when to upgrade, how to size of the system you'll need, and which models are most efficient. Check your local library for this year's edition. Available from ACEEE, 2140 Shattuck Avenue, Berkeley, CA 94704, (510) 549-9914.

The Energy Directory, Iris Communications, 258 East 10th Avenue, Suite E, Eugene, OR 97401-3284, (800) 346-0104, lists nearly 300 efficient furnaces, boilers, heat pumps, radiant heaters, and programmable thermostats.

Home Heating with Wood and Coal, Solar Ideas for Your Home or Apartment, and *Oil and Gas Heating Systems: Maintenance and Improvement* are available from the Massachusetts Audubon Society, 208 S. Great Road, Lincoln, MA 01773, (617) 259-9500.

Space Conditioning: The Next Frontier, EPA report 430-R-93-004. This EPA report is a detailed study of the efficiency and economics of a dozen different heating systems in six U.S. regions. Available from the National Technical Information Service, 5285 Port Royal Road, Springfield, VA 22161, (703) 487-4630.

Passive Solar Energy, by Bruce Anderson & Malcolm Wells, discusses how to add solar to existing homes and those being planned. Brick House Publishing Company, PO Box 256, Amherst, NH 03031, (800) 446-8642.

organizations

American Solar Energy Society, 2400 Central Avenue, Suite G-1, Boulder, CO 80301, (303) 443-3130.

Earth Energy Association, 777 North Capitol Street NE, Suite 805, Washington, DC 20002, (202) 289-0868.

Gas Appliance Manufacturers Association, 1901 N. Moore Street, Arlington, VA 22209, (703) 525-9565.

Hearth Products Association, 1101 Connecticut Avenue NW, Suite 700, Washington, DC 20036, (202) 857-1181.

International Ground-Source Heat Pump Association, PO Box 1688, Stillwater, OK 74076-1688, (800) 626-4747.

Masonry Heater Association of North America, 11490 Commerce Park Drive, Reston, VA 22091, (703) 620-3171.

Passive Solar Industries Council, 1511 K Street NW, Suite 600, Washington, DC 20003, (202) 628-7400.

Solar Energy Industries Association, 122 C Street NW, Fourth Floor, Washington, DC 20001, (202) 383-2600.

5

Home Cooling Systems: It's No Sweat to Stay Cool

The electricity used to air condition an average household causes about 3,500 pounds of carbon dioxide and 31 pounds of sulfur dioxide to be spewed from powerplant smoke stacks each year.

Most of us are familiar with only two ways for staying cool in the summertime: installing a monster air conditioner and cranking the beast up to max; or self-cooling by that time-honored physiological approach—sweating. These might work, but there are better, cheaper things you can do to increase your comfort and save money. Keeping your home cool and comfortable in the summer comes in four easy steps: reducing the cooling load, exploring alternative cooling methods, increasing the efficiency of your existing air conditioner, or buying new, efficient cooling equipment.

100

Reduce the cooling load

The best strategy for keeping a dwelling cool is to keep it from getting hot in the first place. This means preventing the outside heat from getting inside (reducing the *external* cooling load); and reducing the amount of unwanted heat generated inside by inefficient appliances and lights, unwrapped water heaters, and so on (reducing the *internal* cooling load).

A well-shaded house

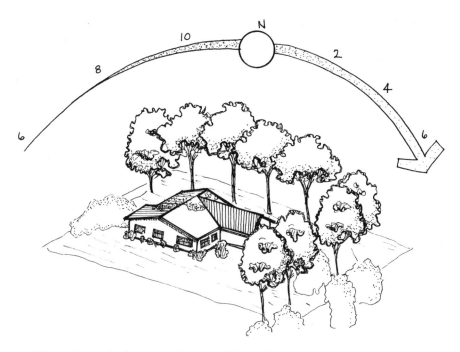

Mature trees shading your house will keep it much cooler by lowering roof and attic temperatures, blocking unwanted direct solar heat radiation from entering the windows, and providing a cooler microclimate outdoors. Adapted from an illustration by Saturn Resource Management, Helena, MT.

In a hot and humid climate, 25% of the total cooling load is the result of infiltration of moisture, 25% from the higher outdoor temperatures penetrating windows, walls, and the roof, 20%

from solar gain through windows, and the remaining 30% from heat and moisture generated within the home. It makes a lot of economic sense to cut these loads before getting that new air conditioner. You'll be able to get by with a smaller unit. Reducing your home's internal cooling load is essentially the subject of Part Three: *Hot Water, Appliances,* and *Lighting*.

Weatherizing and insulating, as well as doing some of the measures suggested in the Windows chapter, will reduce your cooling costs substantially. But there are still a few more tricks of the trade to keep the outside heat from getting inside.

Shading

Shading that blocks heat but not summer breezes is an effective way to keep your home cooler. Planting shade trees on the western, southern, and eastern sides of your house can greatly increase comfort and coolness. Awnings, porches, or trellises on those same sides of a building will reduce solar gain through the walls as well as through the windows. A home's inside temperature can rise as much as 20F° or more if the east and west windows and walls are not shaded. Trees will also absorb carbon dioxide as they grow, offsetting some of the CO_2 emitted by your electric powerplant.

Windows

Windows conduct warmth through the glass and the frame, permit warm, moist air to leak in around edges, and let in lots of unwanted heat in the form of solar radiation. See the *Weatherization* and *Windows* chapters for complete discussions of how to reduce this unwanted heat gain to your advantage.

Radiant barriers

Radiant barriers are thin plastic sheets coated with a shiny or metallized surface and are designed to reflect long-wave infrared heat radiation. Such barriers are typically stapled to the attic rafters or sloped trusses to lower high attic temperatures. (Laying the barrier on the attic floor is also an option, but some research indicates that the barrier's effectiveness is reduced by dust build-up.) Lowering high attic temperatures—which can easily reach 120°F on a hot sunny day—reduces heat penetration into the living space below and is frequently a cost-effective measure to lower air conditioning bills in many Sunbelt states. A study by the Florida Solar Energy Center found that properly installed radiant barriers reduced cooling loads by 7–21%. Radiant barriers reduce but don't eliminate high attic temperatures, and insulating to at least R-19 may be advisable to slow heat penetration into the living space.

Radiant barrier

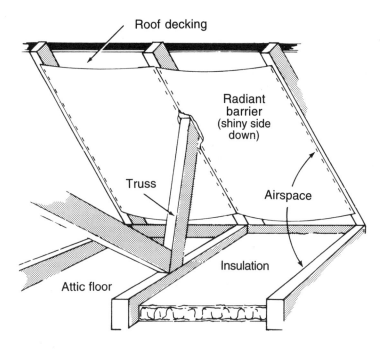

Stapling a radiant barrier to the attic's rafters will keep the attic and the rest of your home much cooler. Adding insulation may also be cost-effective. Illustration courtesy of Florida Solar Energy Center (1987), *Radiant Barriers: A Question and Answer Primer*, p. 1, Cape Canaveral, FL.

Insulation

Insulation slows heat transfer from outside to the inside of your home. If your attic, in particular, has little or no insulation, it may be cost-effective to increase it to R-19 or more. If you also need to heat your house in the winter, insulation is even more important (because of the much greater temperature differential between outside and inside), and you may want to add insulation to R-30 or even higher. In hot climates, if you already have some insulation, it may be more cost-effective to install a radiant barrier instead of adding more insulation. Contact local professionals or your State Energy Office (listed in the Appendix) for climate-specific recommendations.

Ventilation

Ventilating your attic is important, as roofs can reach temperatures of 180°F, more than hot enough to fry an egg, and poorly vented attics can exceed 120°F. To maximize the effectiveness of ventilation, both soffit and ridge vents should be installed. Dark roofs need better ventilation than light-colored roofs. In some cases, mechanical ventilation or fans may be recommended to reduce attic temperatures, but get a second opinion: a radiant barrier could be a far less costly option.

Capturing attic heat

Hot attic air can be used to your advantage. One Minnesota company is marketing a heat exchanger that soaks up the unwanted hot attic air and transfers the heat to your swimming pool or hot water heater. These units cost about $4,000 installed, and since pipes have to be installed from your pool's mechanical box to your attic, it may not be an easy or cost-effective measure for existing buildings. In new construction, such units may have a payback of three to eight years, depending on whether or not you heat your pool with natural gas or electricity, how many months you heat it, and so on.

Roof whitening

Roof whitening is another solution. If you are replacing a roof, using a white or reflective roofing surface can also reduce air conditioning loads. If you are not reroofing, coating the existing roof with white elastomeric paint is a cost-effective measure in some situations. Be sure to get a specialty paint specifically designed for roof whitening: normal exterior latex won't do. The Florida Solar Energy Center reports savings from white roofs of 25–43% on air conditioning bills in two poorly insulated test homes, and 10% savings in a Florida home with R-25 roof insulation already in place. Costs are relatively high—the coatings cost 30 to 70 cents per square foot of roof surface area—and adding insulation or a radiant barrier may be a more cost-effective measure. Light-colored asphalt or aluminum shingles are not nearly as effective as white paint in lowering roof and attic temperatures.

Weatherization

Weatherization, usually done in northern climates to keep heat in, can also effectively keep out heat and humidity in the hot, humid climates or seasons. Cutting air infiltration by half, which is easily done, can cut air conditioning bills by 15% and save $50–$100 per year in the average southern house. Since much of the work and comfort benefit of running an air conditioner is to remove moisture, reducing air infiltration is more important in humid climates than in dry ones.

Alternative cooling methods

Whole-house, ceiling, and portable fans

A whole-house fan is an effective means of cooling and is far less expensive to run than air conditioning. It can reduce indoor temperatures by 3 to 8F°, depending on the temperature

outside. Through prudent use of a whole-house fan, you can
cut air conditioner use by 15 to 55%. If it's cooler outside than
inside, a whole-house fan blows the hot air outside and draws
cooler air through the windows. It should be centrally located
so that it draws air from all around the house. Be sure your
attic has adequate soffit or ridge vents to get rid of the hot air.
To ensure safe and proper installation of a new whole-house
fan, have a professional do it, as codes will likely require automatic shut-off in case of fire.

A whole-house fan

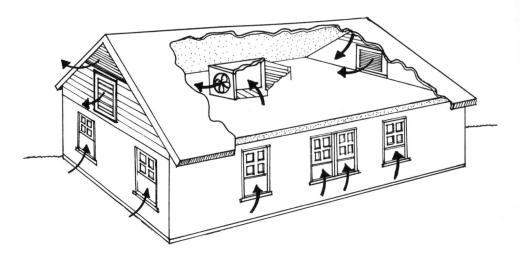

A whole-house fan can cool the house by bringing in cooler air—especially
at night—and lowering attic temperatures. Adapted from an illustration by
Illinois Department of Energy and Natural Resources (1987), *more for your
money ... Home Energy Savings*, p. 6-12, Springfield, IL.

Ceiling, paddle, or portable fans produce air motion across
your skin that increases evaporative cooling. A moderate
breeze of one to two miles an hour can extend your comfort
range by several degrees and will save energy by allowing you
to set your air conditioner's thermostat higher or eliminate the
need for air conditioning altogether. Less frequent use of air
conditioning at a higher setpoint will greatly cut cooling bills.

Passive night-time cooling

Opening windows at night to let cooler air inside is an effective cooling strategy in many states. This method is far more effective in hot dry areas than in humid regions, however, because dry air generally cools down more at night and because less moisture is drawn into the house, giving the air conditioner (A/C) a break on its most energy-intensive task: removing moisture.

The Florida Solar Energy Center found that when apartments in humid areas opened their windows at night to let the cooler air in, the air conditioners had to work much harder to remove the extra moisture that came along with that cool night air. In any case, storing "coolth" works better if your house has thermal mass such as concrete, brick, tile, or adobe that will cool down at night and help prevent overheating during the day.

Personal cooling

Buying a block of ice isn't cost-effective, but feeling cool is important. Cool drinks, small fans, less clothing, siestas, or sitting on a shady porch all work. Illustration courtesy of Saturn Resource Management, Helena, MT.

Improving air conditioner efficiency

Once you've reduced your external cooling load and taken advantage of alternative cooling methods, it makes sense to improve the efficiency of your air conditioner (A/C).

Air conditioner checklist

√ Have a technician check your central A/C's duct system for air leakage. Seal with duct tape or special mastic if necessary: most supply and return ducts are extremely leaky, and it's worthwhile to have them sealed. Your central A/C or heat pump should be on a regular maintenance schedule for a checklist of additional items: motor, compressor, air handler, ducts and leakage, oiling moving parts, dirt build-up, refrigerant charge, filter and coil cleaning, and so on. Proper maintenance will ensure maximum efficiency as well as the equipment's longevity.

√ Insulate cooling and return ducts that run through accessible areas in the attic (where temperatures can easily reach 120°F) and the basement or crawlspace with foil-faced fiberglass duct insulation. Fasten batts with ratcheting plastic ties, wire, metal tape, or glue-on pins. If you're not up for this kind of job, and your air conditioning technician can't do it for you, he or she may be able to recommend a qualified house doctor or insulation contractor.

√ Have the refrigerant charge checked. Under- or overcharging compromises performance: a 10% undercharge can reduce efficiency by as much as 20%. Make sure the technician won't vent the chlorofluorocarbon (CFC or HCFC) refrigerant to the air during servicing. Federal law now requires the capture and reuse of this environmentally hazardous chemical. See the *Insulation* chapter for a discussion of the environmental impacts of CFCs.

√ Set your A/C to the recirculation option—it takes a lot less energy than if the A/C is drawing hot and humid air from outside.

√ Set your A/C's thermostat at 78°F—or higher if you have ceiling fans. You'll save 3–5% on cooling costs for each degree you raise the thermostat.

√ Don't turn the A/C's thermostat lower than the desired setting—the house will not cool any faster and can get uncomfortably cold.

√ Turn off your A/C when you leave for more than an hour. It's worth it.

MYTH: It's more efficient to leave the A/C running than to shut it off and have to re-cool the house later.

FACT: You begin saving as soon as you shut off your A/C. If your house is tight and well-insulated, it may stay cool all day. This will only work, however, if you keep your house closed up all day. Opening windows not only heats up the house, but also allows the humidity back in that your A/C worked so hard to remove. The exception: on cool nights with low humidity, you're better off opening your windows and using ceiling or whole house fans.

√ Close off unused rooms (or close registers in those rooms, if you have central A/C).

√ Install a programmable thermostat for your central A/C system to regulate cooling automatically. Such a thermostat can be programmed to ensure that your home is cool only when you want it to be—when you come home from work, for example.

√ Trim bushes or shrubs around outdoor units so they have unimpeded air flow—a clear radius of two feet is adequate. Remove leaves and debris regularly.

√ Shade your room A/C or the outside condenser unit on a central A/C from direct sunlight if possible. This can increase the unit's efficiency by 5–10%.

√ Remove your window-mounted A/C each fall. Their flimsy mounting panels and drafty cabinets offer little protection from winter winds. If you don't remove it each fall, at least make sure that you close its vent after the cooling season.

√ Clean your A/C's filter every month or two during cooling seasons. Normal dust build-up can reduce air flow by 1% per week.

√ Clean the entire unit according to the manufacturer's instructions at least once a year. The coils and fins of outside condenser units of a central A/C should be inspected regularly for dirt and debris that can reduce air flow.

√ When the cooling season ends, turn off the power to the central A/C at the electrical panel. (Be sure to turn it back on at least a day before you need the air conditioning to prevent damage to the compressor.)

If you live in a humid climate

An important part of what a conventional air conditioner does is remove moisture from the air. This makes you feel a lot cooler. Unfortunately, some of the highest-efficiency models don't dehumidify as well as less efficient air conditioners. (Air conditioners that are too big for their cooling load have this same problem.) High humidity results in condensation problems and a sweaty mid-August New York City feeling. People tend to set their thermostats lower to compensate for the humidity, using even more energy. Here are better solutions:

√ Reduce your fan speed. This makes the coils run cooler and increases the amount of moisture that will condense in the A/C rather than on your books. (Don't worry, your air conditioner can handle it!)

√ Choose an A/C with a "sensible heat fraction" (SHF) less than 0.8. The lower the SHF, the better the dehumidification ability. The American Society of Heating, Refrigeration & Air Conditioning Engineers has information on SHFs.

√ Size your A/C carefully. Contractors should calculate dehumidification as well as cooling capacity. Most air conditioning systems are oversized—many by 50% or more. Ask any contractor you may be hiring to show you his or her sizing and SHF calculations to avoid being sold an oversized model or one that won't remove enough moisture.

√ Investigate the feasibility of using a Dinh heat pipe/pump. These devices use no energy to operate, cool the air before it runs through the air conditioner, and warm it again as it blows out of the air conditioner. They can help your existing air conditioner dehumidify severalfold more effectively; see the resource section at the end of this chapter.

√ Explore "desiccant dehumidifiers" which, coupled with an efficient A/C, may save you quite a bit of energy. Desiccant dehumidifiers essentially use a water-absorbing material to remove moisture from the air. This greatly reduces the amount of work the air conditioner has to do, thereby reducing your cooling bill.

√ Set your A/C to the recirculation option.

Buying a new air conditioner

Air conditioners have become much more efficient over the last 15 years. Top-rated models are 50 to 70% better than the current average. Federal appliance standards have eliminated the least-efficient models from the market (but builders and developers have little incentive to install a model that's more efficient than required by the standards, since they won't be paying the higher electric bills).

If you have an older, inefficient model, it may be cost-effective to replace it with a properly sized, efficient unit. The Office of Technology Assessment (a U.S. Congress research organization) estimates that buying the most efficient room air conditioner, costing $70 more than a standard unit, has a payback of six and a half years (or less, if one accounts for the additional features the better units include).

Air conditioner efficiency

When shopping, how can you tell which A/C units are the most efficient ones? *Room* air conditioners are rated by an Energy Efficiency Ratio (EER), which is their cooling capacity divided by their energy consumption. The higher the EER the better. Typical new room air conditioners have EERs of about 9, but the best ones are 12 or better.

Central air conditioners and heat pumps are rated on their Seasonal Energy Efficiency Ratio (SEER). Older central air conditioners have SEER ratings of 7 or 8. National appliance standards now require a minimum SEER of 10. The most efficient models have SEER values of 13 to 16, and the Florida Solar Energy Center currently recommends a SEER of at least 12 for cost-effectiveness.

Make sure the unit you purchase has a thermostat. If it doesn't, the machine may keep on cooling when it's not necessary.

Several studies have found that many, if not most, central air conditioning systems are oversized by 50% or more. To avoid being sold an oversized model or one that won't remove enough moisture, ask your contractor to show you the sizing calculations and dehumidification specifications. Many contractors may simply use the "one ton of cooling capacity per 400 square feet of living space" rule of thumb, which would be far larger than you need, especially if you have weatherized and done many of the other measures in this chapter to reduce heat gain and the need for cooling. (One ton of cooling capacity—essentially the cooling capacity of one ton of ice—is equivalent to 12,000 Btu per hour; room air conditioners range in size from $\frac{1}{2}$ ton to $1\frac{1}{2}$ ton, while typical central A/Cs range from two to four tons.)

Desuperheaters

As a special added bonus, it's possible to use the waste heat produced by your air conditioner! In hot climates where air conditioning is used more than five months per year, a desuperheater can use waste heat from the A/C to help heat household water. Some utilities give rebates to builders or homeowners who install such equipment.

Evaporative coolers

If you live in a dry climate, an evaporative or "swamp cooler" can save you 50% of the initial cost and up to 80% of the operating cost of an ordinary refrigerated A/C. An evaporative cooler cools the air by evaporating water, usually by drawing fresh outside air through wet and porous pads. As the dry air absorbs the water, it becomes cooler. "Indirect" or "two-stage" models that yield cool, *dry* air rather than cool, *moist* air are also available.

Heat pumps

If you live in a climate that requires heating in the winter and cooling in the summer, consider installing a heat pump in new construction or if you are replacing the existing cooling system. The air conditioning efficiency of a heat pump is equivalent to that of a typical air conditioner, but the heating mode will be much more efficient than the cooling mode.

Where to find

information

Air-Conditioning and Refrigeration Institute, 1501 Wilson Boulevard, Suite 600, Arlington, VA 22203, (703) 524-8800.

American Society of Heating, Refrigeration, & Air Conditioning Engineers, 1791 Tullie Circle NE, Atlanta, GA 30329, (404) 636-8400, has a technical inquiry service.

Association of Home Appliance Manufacturers, 20 North Wacker Drive, Chicago, IL 60606, (312) 984-5800, annually publishes the *Directory of Certified Room Air Conditioners*.

Energy Efficiency & Renewable Energy Clearinghouse, PO Box 3048, Merrifield, VA, 22116; (800) DOE EREC or (800) 523-2929, has several publications on air conditioning and space cooling that are worth checking out, including one on passive cooling.

Evaporative Cooling Institute, PO Box 3ECI, Las Cruces, NM, 88003, (505) 646-3948, has information on evaporative cooling strategies and equipment.

Florida Solar Energy Center, 300 State Road 401, Cape Canaveral, FL 32920, (407) 783-0300, has many publications on passive cooling, dealing with heat and humidity, shading techniques, radiant barriers, roof whitening, and other ways to reduce air conditioning bills in a hot climate.

Southface Energy Institute, PO Box 5506, Atlanta, GA 30307, (404) 525-7657 has information on duct sealing.

Consumer Guide to Home Energy Savings, by Alex Wilson and John Morrill, lists the most efficient room and central A/Cs. Ask for it at your local bookstore, or call the Publications Office of the American Council for an Energy-Efficient Economy, 2140 Shattuck Avenue, Berkeley, CA 94704, (510) 549-9914.

Your Home Cooling Energy Guide, by John T. Krigger, Saturn Resource Management, 324 Fuller Avenue, Suite S-8, Helena, MT 59601, (800) 735-0577, describes how to reduce unwanted heat gain, how to maintain mechanical cooling equipment, and how to size new swamp coolers and air conditioners. ($12.50 postpaid).

products and equipment

Carrier Corporation, PO Box 70, Indianapolis, IN 46206, (800) 227-7437, makes the high-SEER "Infinity," "Synergy," and "Tech" series of central air conditioners and air-source heat pumps.

Central Environmental Systems, PO Box 1592, York, PA 17405, (717) 771-7890, manufactures the York "HDS Series" central A/Cs with variable speed air handlers.

Heat Pipe Technology, Inc., PO Box 999, Alachna, FL 32615, (904) 462-3464, makes the "Dinh" heat pipe/pump.

Hunter Fan Company, 2500 Frisco Avenue, Memphis, TN 38114, (901) 743-1360, makes the "Air Stat" programmable thermostat for room air conditioners. This unit plugs into the wall socket and the A/C plugs into the thermostat.

Innovative Energy, Inc., 1119 West 145th Avenue, Crown Point, IN 46307, (800) 776-3645, makes "Astro-Foil" radiant barrier.

Key Solutions, Inc., 7529 East Woodshire Cove, Scottsdale, AZ 85258 (800) 776-9765, makes "KShield" radiant barrier and "Thermo-flex" reflective roof and wall coating.

Lennox Industries, 2100 Lake Park Boulevard, Richardson, TX 75080 (214) 497-5109, makes high-SEER central A/C equipment and air-source heat pumps.

SolarAttic, 15548 95th Circle NE, Elk River, MN 55330-7228, (612) 441-3440, manufactures an attic-cooling heat pump for heating the pool or household water.

Trane Company, 6200 Troup Highway, Tyler, TX 75711, (903) 581-3200, makes several high-SEER central air conditioning units.

6

Windows: Through the Looking Glass

Full frostbelt use of today's best windows would more than displace Alaska's entire oil output. —Amory Lovins

Windows are great for views, ventilation, and daylight, but they are also the weakest link in a building's insulating barrier. In winter, windows are responsible for 10–25% of a home's heat loss. This adds $50 to $125 to the average annual heating bill, and much more through inefficient windows in very cold climates. In warmer climates, ordinary windows admit too much solar radiation, often making a home unbearably hot. Unwanted solar heat gain through windows alone can account for 20–30% of your cooling bill, adding $50 to $80 to average cooling costs, though far more in poorly shaded homes. Reducing window heat gains and losses creates a tremendous national opportunity: if we cut residential window losses in half—readily achieved through measures described in this chapter—the nation would reduce its heating and cooling bills by $13 billion per year.

Nearly half of all residential windows in place are single-pane, which do little more than prevent the wind from blowing through homes. Whether you are building a new house or replacing windows (half of the 41 million residential windows sold in 1992 were replacement windows), this chapter gives you the information you need to choose windows that will make you more comfortable and reduce your heating and cooling bills substantially.

Replacing windows is a costly proposition. Certainly, you should upgrade to more efficient units if you are replacing windows anyway. Upgrading to better windows is most cost-effective if all of the following conditions are met: (1) you live in a cold and windy climate, (2) your home is already well-insulated and weatherized (otherwise it would be a better buy to add insulation and tighten up the house), and (3) you expect to replace your heating system in the near future. In this case, you can pay for part of the window upgrade by being able to downsize significantly (and pay less for) a smaller heating system. If you live in a hot or temperate climate, it is more likely that some of the simpler and less costly options discussed here will better suit your pocketbook.

Fortunately, there are both high- and low-tech ways to meet these challenges. In this chapter, we first look at cost-effective low-tech solutions for both cold and hot climates such as window films, shades, shutters, and insulation panels. Then, for those who are doing a major remodeling or who are building a new home, we discuss some relatively new window technologies: low-emissivity (low-e) windows and high-performance superwindows. These windows have superior insulating value and can block up to half of incoming solar radiation while letting in plenty of light. This means greatly enhanced comfort in your home, plus lower heating *and* cooling bills.

Cold weather window solutions

First, stop the wind from blowing in and around your windows and frames. Refer to the "Plug the Leaks" checklist in the *Weatherization* chapter. After you've cut infiltration around the windows, the main challenge is to increase the insulating value of the window while continuing to admit solar radiation. (If you're going to replace the entire window assembly, that'll do both jobs at once.) One average 3 x 4 ft. window loses about $20 worth of energy per heating season. Here are some suggestions for beefing up your existing windows in winter.

√ Install plastic barriers on the inside of windows

Such barriers work by creating an insulating dead-air space inside the window. After caulking, this is the least expensive temporary option to cut window heat loss. There are kits that allow you to do a tidy job using a heat-shrink clear plastic. Tape the plastic in place and run a hair dryer 3 to 6 inches away from the plastic to remove wrinkles. You'll scarcely notice there's something covering the window. Be sure not to cover windows that you'll need to open during the winter, especially those that might serve as a fire escape. Expect to pay about 20 to 40 cents per square foot—well worth it even for just one winter season, since such plastic barriers can cut the heat loss through single-pane windows by 25 to 40%.

√ Repair and weatherize exterior storm windows

If you already own storm windows, just replace any broken glass, re-putty loose panes, install them each fall, and seal around the loose edges with rope caulk.

√ Add new exterior or interior storm windows

Storm windows are more expensive than temporary options but have the advantage of permanence and better performance. It is also possible to have insulating low-e glass put into exterior or interior storm windows, providing even more comfort. For more information, see the section on low-e windows later in this chapter.

Storm windows cost about $7.50 to $12.50 per square foot of window area and can reduce heat loss by 25 to 50%, depending on how well the air seal performs. Exterior storm windows will increase the temperature of the inside window by as much as 30F° on a cold day. This decreases the window's heat loss, of course, and also keeps you more comfortable.

√ Install tight-fitting insulating shades

These shades incorporate layers of insulating material, a radiant barrier, and a moisture-resistant layer to help prevent condensation. Several designs are available. The whole unit rolls up during the day and to reduce air flow should be sealed against the window frame at night—either with magnetic tape or by rolling the shades down through a U-channel mounted on the window frame.

You can make insulating shades yourself with patterns available from fabric stores. Some sewing shops will make them for you. Be sure to use a fabric designed for insulation such as "Warm Window;" it has a built-in vapor barrier. The finished shade won't cost much more than using uninsulated fabrics, and you'll increase the insulating value several-fold.

There is one thing you should note when fitting insulating window shades: the actual window panes will get colder and therefore more moisture will be able to condense on the window. This could damage the sash and frame. This is why it's important to incorporate a moisture barrier and to seal the edges carefully to reduce air flow around the shade.

√ Construct insulated pop-in panels or shutters

Measure your windows and purchase rigid insulation from the building supply store. Cut the insulation so it fits snugly—

this will reduce condensation on the glass. Glue a lightweight decorative fabric, such as canvas, to the side of the insulation that will face the living space. Pop-in panels aren't ideal, as they require storage whenever you want to look out the window, but they are cheap and simple. They are especially good for windows you wouldn't mind covering for the duration of the winter. Just make sure the panel fits tightly so moisture doesn't enter the dead air space between the panel and the window and condense on the glass. The Energy Efficiency and Renewable Energy Clearinghouse (see the resource list at the end of the chapter) has a free publication on a simple do-it-yourself plan for making insulated movable shutters.

√ Build valances

While curtains are never as tight as shutters or insulating shades, you can use tightly fitting valances (wood or metal frames that go over the top of existing curtains). By securing the curtains on either side and at the bottom, you can keep the air from circulating behind the curtains and creating a chill. If this increases condensation on the colder glass, install the plastic films discussed above and seal well around the edges.

√ Close your curtains and shades at night

The extra layers increase R-value and you'll feel more comfortable not being exposed to the cold glass.

√ Open your curtains during the day

South-facing windows let in heat and light when the sun is shining. Removing outside screens for the winter on south windows can increase solar gain by 40%. Also remove pop-in insulation panels on south and west windows during the day.

√ Clean solar gain windows

You'll get better light and a lot more free heat. Keep windows dirty in the summer. (Just kidding!)

Warm weather window solutions

The main source of heat gain through windows is solar gain—that is, solar infrared radiation streaming in through single or double glazing. If you use air conditioning, a single 3 x 4 ft. window can cost as much as $24 per year in cooling costs. Here are some tips for saving that cash:

√ Install white window shades or mini-blinds

It's old-fashioned, but it works. (Since our grandparents didn't have air conditioners, they knew how to keep the heat out.) Miniblinds can reduce solar heat gain by 40–50%.

√ Close south- and west-facing curtains

Do this during the day, and keep the windows closed.

√ Build awnings

Another good, old-fashioned solution. Awnings work best on south-facing windows where there's no roof overhang to provide shade. Canvas awnings are more expensive than window shades, but they are certainly more pleasing to the eye, they work better, and they don't obstruct your view.

√ Hang tightly-woven insect screens or bamboo shades outside the window during the summer

They'll reduce your view but are inexpensive and stop 60–80% of the sun's heat from getting to the window.

√ Plant trees or build a trellis to block out radiation

Deciduous (leaf-bearing) trees planted to the south, east, and west of your building provide valuable shade. One mature tree can provide as much cooling as five air conditioners.

Deciduous trees block summer sun but drop their leaves to allow half or more of the winter sun's heat to warm you on those clear winter days. Evergreens planted to the north and east of your home will shield you from winter winds and lighten the load on your furnace.

√ Apply sun control or low-e retrofit window films

Do this to the inside of your east-, south- or west-facing windows and glass doors. Tinted films work in some situations, but may darken the interior too much. Low-e films are now available that block solar heat gain while transmitting most visible light. For more information, see "Retrofit films" below.

High-performance windows

Many people have never heard of low-emissivity (low-e) windows and superwindows, but they've been on the market for over a decade. In fact, over 30% of windows sold today are low-e. That share is growing fast because they dramatically outperform standard single and double glazings. Single-pane windows have an insulating value of R-0.9 and double-pane windows have R-1.75. Standard low-e windows insulate up to R-4.5; high-performance superwindows incorporating low-e coatings and gas-fills insulate up to R-12 (center of glass).

Low-e windows and superwindows allow in much more visible light than tinted or reflective glass, they block most ultraviolet rays (reducing fading somewhat, but not by as much as window manufacturers often claim, since visible light also causes fading), and are both more insulating than normal windows and more reflective of heat radiation. For hot climates, you can select low-e windows that reflect a high proportion of solar heat radiation, whereas in cold climates you'd specify high solar heat gain. They cost between 10% and 45% ($1.50–$2 per ft^2) more than standard double glazings. But if chosen and installed correctly, they will pay for themselves handsomely in energy savings and greater comfort.

Glazing types

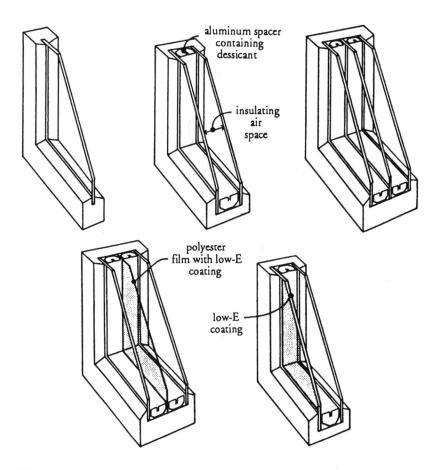

Which glazing type is best for you depends on your climate, finances, your home's shading and solar exposure, heating and air conditioning bills, level of insulation, rate of air infiltration, and so on. Low-e windows are cost-effective in most U.S. climate zones for new construction and replacements. Illustration courtesy of Montana Department of Natural Resources and Conservation (1990), *This New House: Crafting Houses for Comfort and Savings in Montana*, p. 15, Helena, MT.

If you've been shopping for new windows, you already know there is quite a selection on the market. To maximize your comfort and energy savings, it's important to choose the right type of window. Which window model is best for your home will depend on such factors as your energy bills, your climate, which direction your windows face, and to what extent your windows are shaded by awnings, trees, and other buildings.

Since conditions are so variable, we cannot tell you exactly which type of windows to get. Use the "Guide to Buying Windows" section later in this chapter, but seek additional advice from local window retailers, national window manufacturers, as well as local architects. (The resource section at the end of the chapter has lots of useful references, too.) The following section is designed to provide you with the background information you need to work with your supplier and get what's best for your home. (For descriptions of unfamiliar terms, please see "Window lingo" at the end of the chapter.)

How low-e windows work

Understanding how energy flows through windows—illustrated on the following page—makes it easier to figure out how low-e windows work.

The low-emissivity coatings allow visible light to pass through but selectively block infrared radiation (plastic films—tinted or low-e films—block ultraviolet radiation). Far infrared emitted by room-temperature objects is almost entirely reflected. This means that heat has a much harder time escaping on cold days and entering on hot ones. The R-value of the window is beefed up, making the window a much better insulator.

Near or solar infrared, on the other hand, is partially blocked, and different coatings transmit more, or less, solar radiation. When you buy a low-e window you have some choice in how much or how little solar infrared the window lets in. In hot

How heat moves through windows

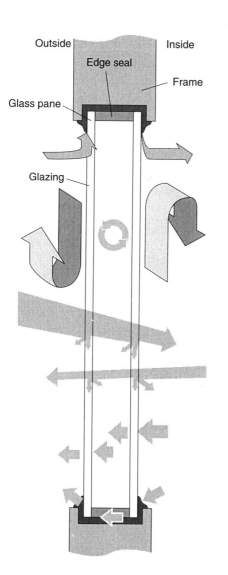

Infiltration

Air leaks around the frame, around the sash, and through gaps in movable window parts. Infiltration is foiled by careful design and installation (especially for operable windows), weather stripping, and caulking.

Convection

Convection takes place in gas. Pockets of high-temperature, low-density gas rise, setting up a circular movement pattern. Convection occurs within multiple-layer windows and on either side of the window. Optimally spacing gas-filled gaps minimizes combined conduction and convection.

Radiation

Radiation is energy that passes directly through air from a warmer surface to a cooler one. Radiation is controlled with low-emissivity films or coatings.

Conduction

Conduction occurs as adjacent molecules of gases or solids pass thermal energy between them. Conduction is minimized by adding layers to trap air spaces, and putting low-conductivity gases in those spaces. Frame conduction is reduced by using low-conductivity materials such as vinyl and fiberglass.

Windows lose heat (or gain unwanted heat) in four ways: infiltration, convection, radiation, and conduction. Illustration courtesy of E SOURCE (1993), *Space Heating Technology Atlas*, p. 104, Boulder, CO.

climates, reducing the amount of solar radiation entering through windows will increase your comfort and reduce your cooling bill. In cold climates, you can reduce your heating bill by allowing most solar infrared to pass into the home while significantly reducing heat loss.

Before you rush out to buy low-e windows, however, a word of caution is in order. Most salespeople won't be familiar with terms such as near or far infrared. Instead they will probably use window lingo—terms such as "visible transmittance" and "solar heat gain coefficient." And so a little translation is necessary. In hot climates, you want to get a window that lets in a lot of visible light but blocks heat from the sun (near infrared). In window lingo, this means a window with high visible transmittance and a low solar heat gain coefficient.

In cold climates, you want windows that insulate well—whole-window high R-value or low U-value. (For a definition of U- and R-values, see Part II, How Your Home Loses Heat.) If you want to heat your home passively in a cold climate, then you'll want to let in lots of heat from the sun. In window lingo, this means a high solar heat gain coefficient. And again, you'll probably want to allow in lots of daylight, which means high visible transmittance. Air tightness of window frames is also important, because significant air infiltration will add to your discomfort and your heating bills. See the "Guide to Buying Windows" at the end of the chapter for window selection tips.

Types of low-e windows

Low-e windows come in a variety of flavors. They vary in what kind of low-e coating they have, whether or not they are gas filled, what kind of edge seal they have, how well the frame insulates, and how resistant the window is to air infiltration. All of these will affect how well the window performs.

There are three kinds of *low-e coatings*: hard coat, soft coat, and Heat Mirror™ suspended films. Hard-coat low-e coatings, also called pyrolytic coatings, are quite durable and can be used on storm windows. Soft-coat low-e coatings are fairly fragile and need to be sealed within a double-glazed unit for protection. The coating is applied to one of the inner surfaces of glass in a double-glazed unit. Soft-coat low-e glazings generally insulate better than hard coatings. Worth noting is the Cardinal Glass Low-e^2 which insulates better than standard soft coats. Heat Mirror is described in the section on "Superwindows."

The insulating value of a low-e window can be improved with low-conductivity argon or krypton gas sealed inside the window instead of air. A number of manufacturers are now gas-filling many of their models. This can cut heat loss through the window by 15 to 20% at little or no extra cost. Don't worry: these are inert gases that occur naturally in the atmosphere, and are harmless even if the window breaks.

Also check a window's air tightness rating. Look for units with a rating no higher than 0.2 cfm/ft (cubic feet of air leakage per minute per foot of window edge under test conditions). The best windows are lower than 0.1 cfm/ft.

It is important to have a good *edge seal* on a double-glazed unit for two reasons. First, it is important to keep moisture out of the sealed window: if moisture gets in, it will condense on the glass inside. Second, if any low-conductivity gas escapes from the unit, the insulating value of the window will decrease. Look for durable double-seal systems. Find out what kind of warranty the manufacturer provides on the seal itself—the best have warranties of ten years or more.

The last feature to check when shopping for windows is the *frame*. Now that glazings have advanced so much, reducing heat flow through the frames of the window has become more important. Window *frames* and the metal *glazing spacers* can conduct a lot of heat if they do not incorporate a "thermal break" made of highly insulating material to reduce heat loss. Metal frames are especially good conductors and should have thermal breaks; it is worth shopping carefully if you are considering aluminum windows. Wood and vinyl frames are much less conductive, and usually do not have thermal breaks, but preferably incorporate a thermally broken glazing spacer. Some manufacturers are now making highly insulating fiberglass frames. Insulating frames and "warm edge" glazing spacers not only reduce heat loss, but also, therefore, prevent condensation from forming in all but the coldest weather. The "Where to find it" section lists several U.S. and Canadian manufacturers of wood, vinyl, metal, and fiberglass windows.

When choosing a new window, be sure to check whole-unit R-values or whole-unit U-values. This measurement tells you how well the whole window insulates—*including the frame.* If these numbers are not available for a given model of window, consider looking at other brands. (The National Fenestration Rating Council, listed at the end of this chapter, has recently published a *Certified Product Directory*, which lists whole-unit R and U-values for a wide range of windows.)

Superwindows

Residential windows are now widely available that offer superior performance in virtually any climate—Houston hot, Colorado cold, or Tennessee temperate. They go by many names: high-performance windows, superinsulating windows, spectrally selective windows, or just superwindows. Whereas standard low-e windows attain R-values of up to 4.5, superwindows insulate up to R-12 (center of glass).

Superwindows basically work the same way as regular low-e windows and incorporate the same advanced features, such as high visible transmittance, gas fill, good edge seals, insulated frames, and airtight construction. The big difference is that the low-e coating is applied not to the glass but to one or both sides of an invisible Heat Mirror™ plastic film. One or two sheets of this polyester film are suspended between the two panes of glass. The films reduce radiative and convective heat losses, since such windows have two or three air spaces, usually filled with low-conductivity gas such as argon or krypton. Several different window manufacturers (such as Craftline, Hurd, Milgard, Pella, Northwest, and Visionwall) use Heat Mirror to make superwindows.

Cross-section of a superwindow

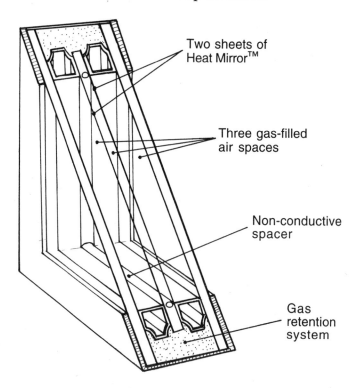

Two sheets of Heat Mirror™

Three gas-filled air spaces

Non-conductive spacer

Gas retention system

A superwindow incorporates one or two low-e coatings on polyester film or on the glass surface to reduce radiative loss, is filled with argon or krypton gas instead of air to slow conduction, has optimal spacing to minimize convection, and has an airtight and low-conductivity frame. Adapted from an illustration by Hurd Millwork, Medford, WI.

One particularly attractive feature of the Heat Mirror line of products is that you can select just how much solar infrared to allow through the glass. For example, Heat Mirror 66 or 44 is used for hot climates and blocks more near infrared than Heat Mirror 88, which is designed to maximize solar gain while reducing convective and radiative losses. Such windows are cost-effective in very cold climates, especially in new homes in which heating systems can be downsized, even eliminated altogether, as in Rocky Mountain Institute's own building. (Superwindows are not usually cost-effective in residential buildings in hot climates, where it is better to buy less expensive low-e or tinted windows and to provide good shading.)

Superwindows incorporating Heat Mirror 88 transmit less solar radiation than ordinary or low-e windows, and thus cut daytime solar gain. Remember, though, that in a wintertime climate, it's dark or cold for 16 to 24 hours every day, and the high insulating value of superwindows becomes a welcome feature. The net result is very much positive, even given the lower solar gain.

At least one company (Viking Industries) makes a high-performance window without suspended Heat Mirror films, instead using three panes of glass, two of which have low-e coatings. This window has a whole-unit U-value comparable to the best superwindows, but is priced competitively with regular low-e units. Other manufacturers include Craftline, Hurd, Pella, Pozzi, Visionwall, and Weather Shield.

Cost

Low-e windows in the U-0.5 to U-0.4 (whole-unit) range cost 10% to 15% more than standard double glazing; superwindows cost about 40% to 45% more than ordinary well-built windows. However, as mentioned above, Viking has introduced a gas-filled low-e window with superwindow perfor-mance at prices comparable to low-e windows. If you are planning to replace your windows, standard low-e windows will be a good bet in virtually any climate in the U.S. Super-windows usually make more sense in new construction (and cold climates), where you can save money by downsizing or eliminating heating and cooling equipment.

Cost vs U-value for different window types (All are retail prices for 3x5 foot casement window)			
	Whole unit U-value	*Retail price*	*Cost per square foot*
Single-pane, wood frame	0.90	$190	$13
Double-pane, wood frame	0.50	$205	$14
Double-pane low-e, wood frame	0.44	$240	$16
Double-pane low-e, gas fill, wood frame	0.38	$240	$16
Double-glass, plus suspended Heat Mirror	0.32	$270	$18
Triple-glass, 2 low-e coats, gas fill, vinyl frame*	0.22	$225	$15
Double-glass, plus 2 films, gas fill, wood frame	0.21	$360	$24

Source: J. Gregerson *et al* (1993), *Space Heating Technology Atlas*, E SOURCE, Boulder, CO, p. 115. Window prices vary greatly by manufacturer, frame type, and window type.
* New Viking Industries triple pane; only available in 13 western states as of March 1994.

Retrofit window films

Retrofit window films are coated plastic films installed directly onto an existing window to cut glare and block heat. Tinted and reflective retrofit films have been on the market for some time and used mainly in hot climates. Some films are suscepti-ble to peeling and radiating heat to the inside. Tinted window films will darken the interior substantially by blocking 40–60% of the visible light, and thus are less than ideal for residential windows. If you don't mind twilight all day long, tinted win-dows work well, and they are less expensive—and more cost-effective—than low-e retrofit films or new low-e windows. You may end up keeping the lights on more, however. Shade trees, awnings, trellises, and other shading techniques work well, too.

Southwall Corporation, listed below, has applied its Heat Mirror™ technology to produce Heat Mirror XIR. This retrofit window film blocks as much heat as other films but transmits much more visible light. These are for hot climates only; Heat Mirror XIR does not reflect far infrared and therefore does not increase a window's R-value.

3M Company manufactures light amber and medium amber retrofit window films that modestly improve R-value, but block more visible light than XIR film.

Most retrofit films need to be installed by a professional. Be sure to call around for prices and check the warranty of the product. While retrofit window films are quite expensive to install, ranging from $1 to $5 per ft^2 of window area, they can increase your comfort considerably, and they cost far less than new low-e windows.

Also consider the low-budget solutions discussed earlier in this chapter. See the "cold weather checklist" earlier in this chapter for information on air-gap films used, not for solar radiation control, but to create an insulating layer of air inside wintertime windows. Air-gap films are easy to install. While more expensive, low-e storm windows are another option.

Guide to buying windows

Many factors are important in deciding whether to replace your existing windows with better ones, or what type of windows to buy for a new home. Here are a few pointers:

Climate. Whether you live in a hot and humid or a cold and dry region makes a big difference in selecting windows. So does your own microclimate: your house might be well shaded, or on a sunny, south-facing slope, or facing north in a windy and unprotected area. You should choose a different window for each situation.

Your heating and/or air conditioning bills. You'll have more incentive to retrofit windows if your home is electrically heated and you pay 15 cents per kWh ($44 per million Btu) than if you heat with natural gas costing 40 cents per therm ($3.90 per million Btu). Since air conditioners always use electricity, and cooling bills are often very high, installing low-e solar heat gain control windows can be very cost-effective.

How long do you expect to live in your house? Windows are a big investment. Even though improving the comfort of your home may warrant the extra expense of superwindows, it may be hard to justify the added cost if you're only going to live in your house another year or two. Don't forget, though, that investments like these increase the value of your house, and high-performance windows can be a strong selling point. In new construction, the higher cost of high-performance windows will go into the mortgage, and the payback in energy savings and comfort is very favorable.

Do you expect to replace your heating or cooling equipment soon? If so, you can pay for a part of the window upgrade with money saved by downsizing such equipment.

Window direction may determine window type. In many climates it's best to vary window type by a combination of factors: direction, shade, direct sunshine by season, wind direction, etc. For example, in cold climates, high-performance superwindows are most cost-effective on the north side.

Other factors. Weatherization, insulation, shading, radiant barriers, and retrofit window films are all lower-cost measures you must also consider *before* you decide on a window retrofit.

Window selection chart

climate zone	side of house			
	north	south	east	west
Temperate (Pacific)	1* or 2	1 or 2	1 or 2	1, 2, or 3
Cold (Northern)	4	2 or 4	2 or 4	2, 3, or 4
Hot/Cold (Eastern, Central)	2	2 or 3	2 or 3	3
Hot (Southern)	2 or 3	3	3	3

*See key below for explanation of numbers.

Adapted with permission from Alex Wilson, "No Pane, No Gain," *Popular Science*, June 1993, p. 98. Substantial additions and changes by Rocky Mountain Institute.

Key to window selection chart

1. **Standard double-pane for temperate climates**
   Two (un-coated) panes of glass and a half inch airspace provides the basic insulating value (R-2); wood, vinyl, or metal frame (with thermal break).

2. **Low-e coating for cold to warm climates**
   Increases insulating value while allowing most solar radiation to pass through; emissivity of 0.1 to 0.2; half inch airspace with argon gas-fill boosts R-value; quality wood, vinyl, or metal frame (with thermal break). Look for high whole-unit R-value (or low U-value), high solar heat gain coefficient, low air tightness rating, and high visible light transmittance.

3. **Low-e coatings for hot climates**

   Reflects most solar radiation while transmitting most visible light, emissivity of ~0.04; half inch airspace with argon gas-fill (though gas-fills are less important in hot climates); wood, vinyl, or metal frame (with thermal break). Look for low solar heat gain coefficient, low air tightness rating, and high visible light transmittance. Combination of low-e and window tints is another option.

4. **Superwindows for cold climates**

   Maximum insulating values (generally double-pane with one or two suspended low-e coated plastic films (e.g., Hurd Insol-8, Pella InsulShield, or Weather Shield Super Smart; Viking 10000 Series is triple glass with low-e coats on two panes); argon and/or krypton gas-fill; improved edge seals; and wood or vinyl frame. Look for high whole-unit R-value (or low U-value in the 0.2 to 0.3 range), high solar heat gain coefficient, low air tightness rating, and high visible light transmittance.

Window lingo

Glazing.   The glass in a window unit.

Near infrared radiation.   Heat that is emitted from very hot objects, such as the sun.

Far infrared radiation.   Heat radiation that is emitted from room temperature objects, such as people, furniture, or walls.

Low-emissivity coatings.   Low-e coatings (thin and invisible coats of metal) are applied to glass or polyester film. They block far infrared and partially block near infrared while allowing most of the visible light to pass through. Clear glass has an emissivity of 0.84, whereas the best low-e coatings have values as low as 0.03. Emissivity refers to the ability of a surface to radiate infrared energy, and range from zero for a non-emitter to one for a perfect emitter. Generally, the lower the emissivity the lower the solar heat gain.

Tinted windows or retrofit films. Glass with color added in the manufacturing process, or tinted polyester film. The tints reduce solar heat gain and visible light transmittance.

Solar heat gain coefficient (SHGC). Fraction of total solar energy transmitted (including ultraviolet, visible light, and infrared) through the window. The higher the solar heat gain coefficient, the *more* solar energy is allowed to pass through. (The related term "shading coefficient," which is relative to the solar energy transmitted by a sheet of clear glass, is being phased out in favor of "solar heat gain coefficient.")

Visible transmittance. The fraction of visible light transmitted through the window, ranging from zero to one. For most homeowners, the higher the better.

Center of glass R-value. Resistance to heat flow measured at the center of the glass, not including heat flow through the frame. The *higher* the R-value the better. Equal to the reciprocal of center of glass U-value. That is, center of glass R-2 is the same as center of glass U-0.50, R-4 is the same as U-0.25, and so on.

Center of glass U-value. Center of glass U-value measures the heat conductivity at the center of glass, not including the frame, and is defined as the reciprocal of R-value ($U = 1/R$). The *lower* the U-value the better.

Whole-unit R-value/U-value. Calculated or measured R-value or U-value that takes into account heat flow through the whole window, including the frame. Whole unit R-value can be as low as one-half the center of glass R-value.

Gas fill. A low-conductivity gas such as argon or krypton sealed between two panes of glass to increase the R-value of the window.

Thermal break. An insulating material built into a window frame or glazing spacer (in double- or triple-pane windows) to reduce heat loss.

Superwindow. A superinsulating window with low-conductivity gas fill and low-e Heat Mirror™ film suspended between the panes of glass. Several window manufacturers achieve superwindow performance at lower cost with two low-e coats on triple-pane windows instead of using Heat Mirror.

Air tightness rating. New windows are rated in terms of how much air penetrates around the window under 25 mph wind conditions in units of cubic feet of air per linear foot of window edge. Values range from 0.01 for the tightest windows to over 0.5 for loose windows. Casement and awning windows are typically tighter than double-hung and sliders, but there are great differences between brands.

Frame losses. This generally refers to conductive heat losses (or gains in cooling climates) through the wood, vinyl, or aluminum window frame. Edge losses refers to heat loss through the glazing spacer separating (and sealing) the two panes of glass in double- or triple-pane windows.

Where to find

cold weather window solutions

Look in the Yellow Pages under "Window Treatments." You might also find information at a fabric store. Many hardware and building supply stores carry heat shrink air gap window films.

Appropriate Technology Corporation, Box 975, Brattleboro, VT 05302 (800) 257-4501, manufactures an insulated track-mounted window shade called "Window Quilt."

Energy Efficiency & Renewable Energy Clearinghouse, PO Box 3048, Merrifield, VA, 22116, (800) DOE-EREC and (800) 523-2929, EREC has a pamphlet called *Movable Insulation*.

Warm Products, 16110 Woodenville-Redmond Road, #4, Woodenville, WA 98072, (800) 234-9276, manufactures a quilted material for constructing roman shades.

Thermal Shutters and Shades, by William Shurcliff, Brick House Publishing, PO Box 256, Amherst, MA 03031, (800) 446-8642. Good ideas for do-it-yourselfers. Out of print; check the library.

warm weather window solutions

Look in the Yellow Pages under "Windows," "Window Treatments" and "Awnings." For information on low-e or tinted retrofit window films, see LOF, Southwall, Courtalds, and 3M on following pages.

Global Releaf, American Forestry Association, PO Box 2000, Washington, DC 20013, (202) 667-3300, has information on landscaping options that reduce energy costs.

Phifer Wire Products, PO Box 1700, Tuscaloosa, AL 35403, (800) 633-5955, makes plastic and metal window screens.

United Textile and Supply, 5175 Commerce Drive, Baldwin Park, CA 91706, (800) 456-6282, has retractable awnings.

window manufacturers

Look in your Yellow Pages under "Windows." Most window representatives and salespeople know what type of window works best in your climate. You will want to order them locally because they are heavy and fragile and don't ship well. Manufacturer, associations, and window specifiers (consultants) are listed in the next sections.

Alenco, 615 Carson Street, PO Box 3309, Bryan, TX 77805, (409) 779-7770, makes aluminum windows with thermal breaks.

Anderson Windows, PO Box 3900, Peoria, IL 61614, (800) 426-4261, makes wood low-e windows for hot and cold climates.

Better-Bilt Aluminum Products, PO Box 277, Smyrna, TN 37167, (615) 459-4161, makes aluminum windows with thermal breaks.

Blomberg Window Systems, 1453 Blair Avenue, Sacramento, CA 95822, (916) 428-8060, makes "pultruded" fiberglass windows.

Craftline, 1125 Ford Street, Maumee, OH 43537, (800) 283-3311, makes wood and aluminum clad high-performance windows.

H Window, 1324 East Oakwood Drive, PO Box 206, Monticello, MN 55362, (800) 242-4946, imports this superwindow from Norway.

Hurd Millwork, 575 South Whelen Avenue, Medford, WI 54451, (800) 433-4873, makes wood and vinyl-clad windows and doors.

Kolbe & Kolbe Millwork, 1323 South 11th Avenue, Wausau, WI 54401, (800) 477-8656.

Marvin Windows, PO Box 100, Warroad, MN 56763, (800) 328-0268, offers "Southern" and "Northern" low-e windows.

Milgard, 1320 Industrial Place, Dixon, CA 95260, (916) 678-8406, uses Heat Mirror in its high-performance windows.

Northwest Windows, 1514 East Broadway, Spokane, WA 99212, (800) 541-6200, makes aluminum and vinyl windows and doors.

Peachtree Windows & Doors, 4150 Blue Ridge Industrial Parkway, Norcross, GA 30071, (404) 497-2000.

Pella Corporation, 102 Main Street, Pella, IA 50219, (800) 348-3344, makes triple-pane, "smart sash," and other low-e windows.

Pozzi Window Company, 62845 Boyd Acres, PO Box 5249, Bend, OR 97701, (503) 385-1498, makes triple-pane and low-e windows.

Viking Industries, PO Box 20518, Portland, OR 97220, (503) 667-6030, or (800) 722-6030, makes triple-pane low-e windows.

Visionwall, 14904 123rd Avenue, Suite 110, Edmonton, Alberta, Canada, T5V 1B4, (403) 451-4000.

Weather Shield Manufacturing, 531 North 8th Street, PO Box 309, Medford, WI 54451, (715) 748-2100 or (800) 477-6808 x201, makes wood and vinyl triple-pane low-e windows and doors.

Winter Seal, 1300 Dussel, Maumee, OH 43637, (419) 897-9500, makes "pultruded" fiberglass windows.

glazing manufacturers

These three glass manufacturers make about 80% of the glass used by the window manufacturers above. All of them have consumer information packets.

Cardinal Insulated Glass, 12301 Whitewater Drive, Minnetonka, MN 55343, (612) 935-1722.

Libby Owens Ford (LOF), 811 Madison Avenue, Toledo, OH 43695, (419) 247-4884, makes low-e glass for windows and storms.

PPG Industries, 1 PPG Place, Pittsburgh, PA 15272, (412) 434-2858.

window specifiers and engineering consultants

Enermodal Engineering, Inc., 1554 Emerson Street, Denver, CO 80218, (303) 861-2070. Canada office: 368 Phillip Street, Unit 2, Waterloo, Ontario N2L 5J1, (519) 884-6421.

Tech-Line, Inc., 5249 Quail Hollow Court, Boulder, CO 80301, (303) 530-1388, specializes in window specification.

Westlab, 907 West Dean Avenue, Monona, WI 53716, (608) 221-9510. California office: 1851 Heritage Lane, Suite 187, Sacramento, CA 95815-4922, (916) 568-2487.

retrofit solar gain control films

Courtaulds Performance Films, PO Box 5068, Martinsville, VA 24115, (800) 345-6088, makes retrofit window films.

3M, Woodbury, MN, (800) 364-3577 (general) or (800) 480-1704 (construction products), makes tinted and air-gap window films.

Southwall Corporation, 1029 Corporation Way, Palo Alto, CA 94303, (800) 365-8794. Southwall licenses Heat Mirror™ film technology to window manufacturers and also produces Heat Mirror XIR retrofit window film for hot climates.

associations, books, and videos

American Architectural Manufacturers Assoc., 1540 E. Dundee Rd., Palatine, IL 60067, (708) 202-1350. AAMA has two publications, *Window Selection Guide* and *Windows: A Consumer Guide.*

California Association of Window Manufacturers, 2080-A North Tustin Avenue, Santa Ana, CA 92701-2418, (714) 835-2296.

National Fenestration Rating Council, 1300 Spring Street, Suite 126, Silver Spring, MD 20910, (301) 589-6372. NFRC has recently published a *Certified Product Directory* (available for $10) and has a video for architects and builders.

National Wood Window and Door Association, 1400 East Touhy Avenue, Des Plaines, IL 60018, (708) 299-5200. NWWDA has printed *A Guide to Energy-Saving Windows.*

Vinyl Window and Door Industry Association, 355 Lexington Avenue, New York, NY 10017, (212) 351-5400.

Window Design Decisions, a 20 minute video appropriate for owner-builders, architects, and home buyers, from Iris Communications, 258 East 10th Avenue, Suite E, Eugene, OR 97401-3284, (800) 346-0104, $20.

Low-E Glazing Design Guide, by Timothy Johnson, describes window technology, passive solar heating, and passive cooling. Butterworth Architecture, 80 Montvale Avenue, Stoneham, MA 02180.

Part Three

Bright Lights, Hot Showers, and Cold Beer

It's not easy being green.   —Kermit the Frog

Part Two discussed keeping the inside of our home warm in the winter and cool in the summer. Part Three looks at ways to save energy, water, and money on hot water, appliances, and lighting. The focus of chapter 7 is on saving hot water, but also gives tips on saving cold water inside and outside your home. Chapter 8 covers efficient use of kitchen, laundry, and other electricity-using appliances, and gives tips on what to look for when shopping for new appliances. Chapter 9 suggests many ways to cut lighting bills while improving lighting quality.

On average, these three categories make up nearly sixty percent of a family home's energy use, or a hefty $860 per year. No doubt you could find more interesting ways to spend this money. Read on, and explore this library of suggestions for using less money and energy to get the same hot showers, cold beers, and well-lit rooms.

Annual water heating, appliance, and lighting expenditures

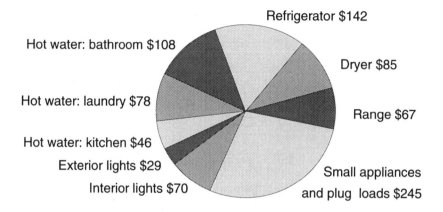

Estimated average energy expenditure for equipment within the home, based on households of three to five persons. Water heating expenditure for clothes washers and dishwashers are allocated to those appliances. Mixed gas and electric appliances such as dryers and water heaters are averaged. Adapted from Energy Information Administration (1993), *Household Energy Consumption and Expenditures, 1990*, pp. 10, 114, and 123, Washington, DC.

7

Hot Water:
A Terrible Thing to Waste

Installing efficient showerheads and faucet aerators will save an average family $60 to $120, cut water use by 17,000 gallons, and prevent more than a ton of carbon dioxide from entering the atmosphere—every year.

You can take off those overalls now. Saving energy by cutting hot water use is clean, fast, and perhaps the most lucrative way to save energy in most homes. Water heating is probably your second largest energy expense after heating or cooling your home. It costs a typical family $160 to $200 a year to heat water with gas or $260 to $390 a year with electricity.

This chapter takes a three-step approach: first, reducing the amount of water we need by installing efficient showerheads and faucets; second, improving the efficiency of the hot water supply by turning down the thermostat and insulating your water heater; third, seeking out the most efficient and properly sized type with the lowest life-cycle cost when you buy a new water heater. Measures to reduce total water consumption—including outdoor watering—are also discussed.

The cold facts about saving hot water

Americans spent over $15 billion to heat residential water in 1990. Rocky Mountain Institute estimates that two-thirds or more of this energy and expense can be saved if all households implemented the simple and cost-effective improvements described below. We could also retire twenty large powerplants in the process, and avoid their pollution.

Retrofitting a household's showerheads and faucets will

• Save about 17,000 gallons of water each year.

• Save (if you heat water with electricity) approximately 1,080 kWh of electricity each year and avoid the annual emission of about 2,010 pounds of carbon dioxide (CO_2), six pounds of nitrogen oxides (NO_x), and 13 pounds of sulfur dioxide (SO_2) from the average powerplant.

• Save (if you heat with natural gas) about 4,800 cubic feet of natural gas per year, displacing the annual emission of 580 pounds of carbon dioxide.

• Cut energy bills by $36 (gas) to $86 (electric) and reduce average water bills by $33 per year.

Calculations by Rocky Mountain Institute.

Saving one "typical" U.S. kWh prevents the emission of 1.86 lbs. of CO_2.

Water (and money) saving tips

√ Start here

• Don't leave the hot water running when washing or rinsing dishes, or brushing your teeth or shaving. A simple wrist action can save you hot water and cold cash.

• If you have a combination bathtub-shower and the tub filler spout continues to flow after you switch to shower, you're wasting hot water down the drain. Chip away any caulking and unscrew (counter-clockwise) the whole spout. If soaking it in warm vinegar (to remove the scale) doesn't help, get a new spout at a hardware or plumbing supply store.

• It's also a good idea to fix leaky faucets. A leaky faucet won't just keep you up at night—a drip per second will cost you up to a quarter a day in wasted hot water. Buy new washers at the hardware store. You'll be able to get all the pieces back together, we promise. Just remember to shut off the water valve under the sink before you start taking the faucet apart.

Where does the hot water go?

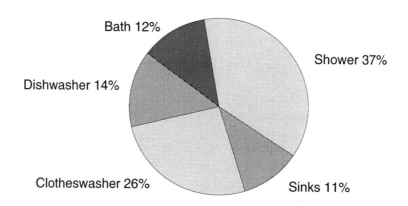

Typical hot water consumption by place of use. Adapted from E source (1991), *State of the Art: Water Heating*, p. xvi, Boulder, CO.

- Wash clothes in cold or warm water. Always rinse in cold water. Wash full loads.

- If you're thoughtful about water usage, washing dishes in the sink will use less hot water than the 7–14 gallons of hot water your dishwasher uses. If you do use a dishwasher, wait for a full load. (See the *Appliance* chapter for more tips.)

- Don't turn on the hot water spigot when all you need is a little cold water. Many of us habitually turn on the hot water tap when all we need is a little water. The hot water leaves the tank, but doesn't reach the tap.

√   Install efficient showerheads

For $10–$20, you can cut conventional showerhead water use by one-third to one-half—*without sacrificing the quality of your shower.* (Savings will be lower if your water pressure is low or you don't turn the shower on full.) Even if they are free, don't settle for "flow restrictors," which are little washers fitted between the showerhead and arm. These deliver something more like a drizzle than a downpour. You're not going to save money or the environment if your shower loses its charm and you switch to baths; a bath uses more hot water than an ordinary inefficient shower. Of course, if you're like some of us and you get in the shower and sing 'til the water turns cold, well, a water-efficient showerhead won't save you a nickel. It will make the hot water last longer, though, and perhaps get you through all of *Old Man River.*

To check the flow rate of your existing showerhead, turn the shower on all the way and see how long it takes to fill a one-gallon plastic milk jug. (You may have to cut a piece of the neck off the jug so it will fit over the showerhead.) If the jug takes more than 24 seconds to fill, you already have an efficient showerhead that uses fewer than 2.5 gallons per minute. If it takes 15 seconds or less, you have a not-so-efficient show-

erhead that should be replaced. Standard showerheads have
flow rates of 3.5 to 6 gallons per minute. A five-minute shower
uses about 25 gallons and costs 33 cents for electrically heated
water.

Efficient showerhead

A Spa 2001 showerhead. Adapted from a drawing by Energy Technology
Laboratories, Modesto, CA.

There are dozens of models of efficient showerheads. Your local hardware store or home center should carry some of them.
But remember: not all water-saving showerheads are as efficient as what we've described. Be sure the one you get delivers
no more than 2.5 gallons per minute rated at 80 pounds per
square inch (psi); 1.2 to 2.0 gallons per minute is even better.
The "feel" of the shower—misty, pounding, etc.—varies widely with brand and model. To save even more money, get a
model with a fingertip flow control valve that makes it easy to
shut the water off while you're shampooing.

Water-efficient showerheads are a snap to install. Unscrew your old showerhead, smear some pipe goop on the shower-arm threads (or apply a half-dozen turns of Teflon tape—both are available from your local hardware or plumbing-supply store), and screw the new showerhead into place. That's it!

You may need to use a wrench to loosen the showerhead and a pair of pliers to keep the shower arm from twisting out of its fitting, which can make a real mess. (Turn off the cold water supply at the valve in the basement or mechanical room to avoid flooding the bathroom in case a fitting comes loose.)

If your shower arm ends in a ball rather than in threads and you can't unscrew the ball from the arm, you'll need to install an adapter, which should be available at your local hardware or plumbing-supply store. An alternative is to replace the shower arm in the wall with a threaded arm—a $3 to $5 item. Now, that's not so bad, is it?

Where to get an efficient showerhead

Water-saving showerheads are available from most of the mail-order outlets listed in the Appendix. For $1, Rocky Mountain Institute will send you a pamphlet entitled *Water Efficiency for Your Home: Products and Advice Which Save Water, Energy, and Money.*

√ Install efficient faucet heads

Faucet aerators, faucet widgets, faucet heads. Call them what you will, but the little metal devices that fit on the end of most faucets are inexpensive, easy to replace, and can save a heck of a lot of hot water. The tradeoff is that it takes a little longer to fill the sink or for the water to turn hot. If you have a habit of letting the water run, a fingertip shutoff lever on the faucet head is a handy way to slow the flow to a trickle without losing the hot/cold mix.

High-efficiency faucet heads save 4 to 7 percent of your total home water consumption. That may not sound like much, but the aerator will repay its initial cost within a few months in water savings alone. If you include hot water savings, you'll recoup the $4 to $10 investment for two aerators in a matter of weeks. Some of you might already have an aerator—but beware, as it might not be water-efficient. Unscrew it and look inside: if the only thing you see is a screen, then it's definitely a loser. It's not saving you money or energy; read on and get your hands on the real stuff.

There are a couple of different types of efficient faucet heads. Faucet *aerators* mix air with the water, making the water flow seem bigger than it is. *Laminar* faucets line up the water molecules for a sculptured, clear stream that rinses like magic.

Efficient faucet head

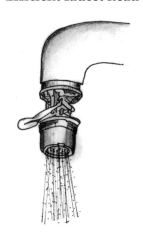

Adapted from a drawing by Energy Technology Laboratories, Modesto, CA.

A bathroom faucet head that delivers a half gallon per minute instead of two to four gallons per minute will work fine for brushing your teeth, washing or shaving. If for some reason you regularly fill the sink, you'll want one that delivers about one to one and a half gallons per minute. Since you'll be filling pots and pans in your kitchen sink, you'll want a flow of two to two and a half gallons per minute there. The flow rate is usually listed on the package or stamped on the barrel of the aerator.

Installing faucet aerators is easy. Once you get your tools together, it should be a ten-minute operation—definitely worth the effort.

1. Unscrew your old faucet aerator and screw on a new one. If the old one is corroded, a pair of pliers will help.

2. If the threads are on the inside of the faucet aerator, it has female threads. If the threads are on the outside, they're male.

3. If a nickel fits into it easily, it's a "kitchen" (regular) faucet aerator.

4. If a nickel doesn't fit but a dime does, it's a "bathroom" (small) faucet aerator.

Where to get high-efficiency faucet aerators

It's best to check hardware and plumbing supply stores, rather than trying to buy one through the mail. But if you can't find what you want locally, most of the mail-order outlets listed in the Appendix carry them. Your electric utility or water authority may have a giveaway or rebate program for water-efficient showerheads and faucet aerators.

√   Insulate your hot-water tank

This gives you savings of 4% to 10% on your water heating bill. Standby losses in a poorly insulated electric water heater tank can cost you $50 or more per year. Easy to install and inexpensive, tank-insulating blankets are available at hardware stores for $10 to $20. Your investment will pay back in lower bills in three months to a year (depending on your type of water heater). To insulate your tank, use at least an R-7 wrap (R-11 if you can find it). You might double up with R-5 jackets since R-11s are less common. Don't use duct tape—it'll fall off in a few years. Acrylic tape lasts much longer.

Wrapping the water heater

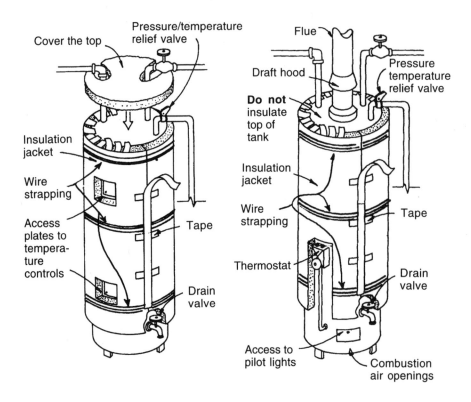

Basic steps for wrapping an electric (left) and a gas (right) water heater. Be sure not to cover the combustion air inlets of a gas water heater. Illustrations courtesy of New Mexico State University Cooperative Extension Service, *Saving Energy in Your Mobile Home*, p. 20 and 21, Las Cruces, NM.

Leave the thermostat(s) uncovered. On gas water heaters, keep the blanket away from the burner and controls and above the drain at the bottom and away from the flue collar at the top. (Note of caution: if the jackets are not taped securely they can slip down and interfere with the air flow to the burner, thereby reducing the heater's efficiency.) Additional insulation is not just for old clunkers; it's worth it for new models, too.

√ Set your water heater thermostat to 120°F

In addition to saving energy, a lower setting will keep your kids from scalding themselves. Your water heater will build up less efficiency-robbing scale inside the tank, and it may last longer. For each 10F° reduction, you'll save 3–5% on your water-heating bill (since most water heaters are set at 145°F or so, you'll save $26 to $57 per year with this easy measure).

It's simple to do. For an electric water heater, turn off the electricity at the fuse box and remove the side panels on the water heater with a screwdriver. Then set the thermostat to 120°F. (If yours doesn't list temperatures, 120°F is just below midway between "low" and "medium." If you find two thermostats, set them both to 120°F. If in doubt, use a meat or candy thermometer to check the water temperature from a nearby tap.

The only time lowering water-heater temperature is a problem is if you use an older-model dishwasher that does not have a booster heater. To find out if your dishwasher has one, check the product literature or call the manufacturer. Without a booster heater, you may need to turn the hot water heater back up to 130°F or even 140°F ("medium"). The better your pipes are insulated, too, the less the temperature will drop between the heater and the tap.

√ Turn down the water heater thermostat when you go on vacation

This saves energy when you are going to be gone longer than two days. Many gas water heaters have a "vacation" setting on the dial at the bottom of the tank, or you can turn it down to the lowest setting. In vacation homes that are unoccupied for weeks or months at a time, turn *off* the water heater. The pilot alone will use about $3 of gas each month. Only turn it off, however, if *you* know how to re-light the pilot (it's easy), otherwise you *lose* money by having to pay someone to turn it back on. Electric water heaters can be turned off at the circuit breaker panel. They take about an hour to reheat the water once you flip the circuit breaker back on. (Gas or oil heaters take less time to reheat.)

√ Insulate both cold- and hot-water pipes

Do this within three feet of the hot water tank. Ten feet of insulation will cost less than $5. Cover the cold-water inlet and the pressure relief pipes, too, for a few feet starting right where they enter the tank. *Keep foam insulation at least six inches from the flue of a gas water heater.* If you use split foam-rubber pipe insulation, use the right size so the slit closes. Put the slit on the underside and tape the insulation in place.

√ Do preventive maintenance

You, or your plumber, should check your water heater every year or two for certain life-shortening problems. Sediment on the inside bottom of gas water heaters reduces heating efficiency, and should be flushed out. Check the heater's "sacrificial" anode (which inhibits rust); replacing the anode as needed—preferably with a magnesium rod—will easily double the water heater's life. Also check the vent, drain valve, and pressure relief valve. Clean and adjust the burner on gas units. If your heater doesn't provide enough hot water, check the dip tube (which, if broken, mixes cold water with the hot at the top of the tank). The *Water Heater Workbook* listed in the "Where to find" section discusses the how-to's of maintenance.

√ Install water heater timers

You can save an additional 5% to 12% of water heating energy by turning water heaters off for certain periods, such as midday or overnight (when little or no hot water is used) or during a utility's peak demand times. You can control your own water heater with a timer that automatically turns the heater off for pre-set periods. The $60–$80 investment is paid back in lower bills in 6 to 14 months. Some utilities use radio signals or separate meters to cut electricity to the water heaters of participating customers during periods of high electric demand, rewarding those customers with lower rates. The shut-off periods are brief enough that you'll never get cold water in the shower—yikes!—because of participating in such a program.

Wrapping water pipes

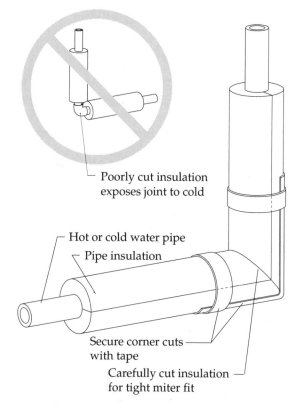

Poorly cut insulation
exposes joint to cold

Hot or cold water pipe
Pipe insulation

Secure corner cuts
with tape
Carefully cut insulation
for tight miter fit

Wrap both the cold and hot water pipes for the first three to five feet from the water heater (but not closer than six inches to the flue of a gas heater). Illustration courtesy of Bonneville Power Administration (1992), *Builder's Field Guide to Energy Efficient Construction*, p. 176, Portland, OR.

Buying a new water heater

When choosing a new water heater, it may be tempting to select a model that is inexpensive to buy, ignoring how much it will add to your energy bill each month. Such a strategy will cost you dearly in the long run. That "cheap" $425 electric tank heater can cost you $5,500 (13 times its purchase price) in energy costs over its typical 13-year life.

Also, if you've installed efficient showerheads and faucets, rinse clothes in cold water, and otherwise conserve, you can buy a smaller, less expensive unit. Your current water heater may have been sized using a rule of thumb such as 120 gallons of hot water per day per family of four, or 70 gallons of hot water needed in the morning. Now you might only need half as much hot water during the period of greatest demand for those same uses. Check the first-hour rating of new water heaters. (These are listed for efficient water heaters in Wilson's and Morrill's *Consumer Guide to Home Energy Savings* referenced at the end of this chapter.)

Federal appliance efficiency standards and labeling requirements have greatly improved water heater efficiencies. Newer ones are better insulated, certain models have anti-convection valves built in, and some systems drain hot water back into the tank. Even so, it pays to shop carefully, read the EnergyGuide labels, and consider the life-cycle cost of each option. Shop for models that have easily accessible anode rods; preferably two (magnesium) rods. The chart on the next page offers comparisons of life-cycle costs for several types of water heaters.

If you are in the market for a new water heater, call your local electric and gas utilities and inquire if they offer a rebate for buying the most efficient model. Many utilities have water heater retrofit programs, and may come to your house to install a water heater wrap and an efficient showerhead.

Life-cycle costs of several water heating options*

Water heater type	Purchase price**	Annual energy cost	Total cost over 13 years
Indirect with efficient gas or oil	$700	$150	**$2,275**
High-efficiency gas	500	145	**2,385**
Tankless gas	650	160	**2,503**
Conventional gas	425	163	**2,544**
Electric heat pump	1,200	160	**3,280**
Solar with electric back-up	3,000	140	**3,770**
Oil-fired free standing	1,100	228	**4,487**
High-efficiency electric	500	374	**5,337**
Conventional electric	425	390	**5,495**
Tankless electric (2 units)	600	400	**5,590**

* Based on hot water needs for typical family of four and energy costs of $0.082/kWh for electricity, $0.60/therm for gas, $1.00/gallon for oil.

** Approximate; includes estimated installation costs. Purchase price is amortized over the expected equipment lifetime, an estimated 13 years for most types listed above, but varies from 8 years for oil-fired water heaters to 30 years for indirect units.

Adapted from and reprinted with permission from Alex Wilson and John Morrill, *Consumer Guide to Home Energy Savings*, 3rd ed., 1993, p. 147, American Council for an Energy-Efficient Economy, Washington, DC.

√ Install anti-convection valves and bottom boards

When you're installing a new water heater, ask your plumber to install anti-convection valves to reduce the heat lost by convection of hot water through the cold and hot water pipes. They cost only a few dollars ($5–$7 a pair plus labor) and can save you $9 to $27 per year. You can have them added to your tank in less than half an hour. If you have hard water, anti-convection loops (a complete 360° bend in both pipes above the tank) are a better idea; they're as effective and can't clog.

When installing a new electric water heater, have the plumber add a "bottom board" of rigid insulation under the tank so the heat doesn't leak into the floor. Bottom boards should be avail-

able from your local plumbing- or building-supply store. Or
make your own with a two-foot square piece of two-inch rigid
extruded polystyrene insulation, cut it into a rounded shape
with a bread knife, and slip it under the tank *before* you or the
plumber solder in the new water heater.

Anti-convection valves

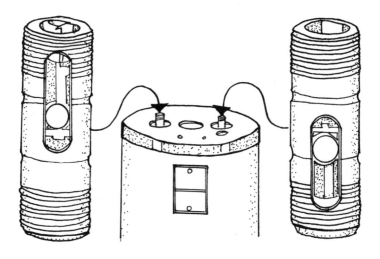

When there is no demand for hot water, the spheres in the valves are
"seated" to prevent convection of hot water through the hot and cold water
pipes. When a hot water tap is turned on, the flow lifts the sphere from its
seat; the opposite happens in the cold-water inlet. Adapted from an illustration by Perfection Corporation, Madison, OH reproduced in E SOURCE (1991),
The State of the Art: Water Heating, p. 156, Boulder, CO.

Conventional electric resistance water heaters

If you already own an electric water heater, your most cost-
effective options—reducing hot water use and improving the
heater's efficiency—are discussed above. You may be doing
your pocketbook a favor by considering the life-cycle cost of
switching to solar and/or gas water heating. If you are building a new home and gas service is available, don't even think
about installing a conventional electric heater: it won't pay.

Electric heat pump water heaters

If you're stuck with electricity, look into a *heat pump water heater*. For an initial cost of around $800 to $1,200, heat pumps can cool and dehumidify your house *and* heat your water using less than half the electricity of an ordinary electric water heater. Heat pump water heaters are most appropriate for moderate and warm climates where more heat is available year-round to transfer to the water, but they're routinely used in new superinsulated Swedish houses, where heat recovered from ventilated exhaust air is ample to meet all water-heating needs.

Therm-Stor Products of Madison, Wisconsin (800-533-7533) manufactures a ventilating heat pump (VHP). Therma-Stor's *Therma-Vent* is basically a heat pump water heater with a powerful exhaust fan, and *Envirovent* is a VHP unit that offers some space heating and cooling as well as water heating. *Envirovents* are recommended for milder climates, or as a match for homes with electric resistance heat. *Envirovents* are not cheap, costing about $1900 plus $300–400 for ducts and accessories. In some areas the utility company offers substantial rebates to support the purchase of VHPs.

Ground-source heat pumps absorb heat from the soil several feet underground where temperatures remain around 50–55°F throughout the year, and thus work well in cold climates. Thousands of such units have been installed in New England and Canada.

In hot climates where air conditioning is used at least five months of the year, consider a *desuperheater* that uses the waste heat from a central air conditioner to help heat household water. Some units capture waste heat from heat pumps and heat water whether the pump is cooling or heating your home. Some utilities offer rebates to encourage the installation of desuperheaters and other efficient heat pumps. See the *Heating* and *Cooling* chapters for additional discussion of heat pumps.

Gas water heaters

If at all possible, buy a *natural gas or propane water heater* rather than an electric model. It'll be cheaper to operate and easier on the environment. In conventional storage tanks, heating with gas costs half as much as heating with electricity; the relative cost-effectiveness of gas is somewhat smaller if compared to heat pump water heaters. Shop carefully; even though gas water heaters have become much more efficient on average, it'll pay to buy a more expensive model that is designed to capture more of the energy of the burning gas and is better insulated to keep the hot water hot. Look for sealed combustion and condensing units for the highest efficiencies.

Tankless water heaters

Tankless water heaters, also called demand water heaters, heat water instantly when a faucet is turned on. When the faucet is turned off, the burners or electric elements shut off automatically. Heating water only when you need it eliminates the nearly 15% standby heat losses common in conventional electric storage tank water heaters (thus saving about $65 worth of electricity per year). The net savings is smaller in gas units with a standing pilot light.

Tankless heaters are more durable than storage tanks, reportedly have less of a scaling problem, and will provide endless hot water but only up to a maximum flow-rate. Sizing is very important when choosing a tankless, and the capabilities of the water heater should be carefully matched to your hot water requirements.

RMI uses an *AquaStar* tankless water heater in combination with its solar system. The incoming cold water is first pre-heated in tubing imbedded in the wall of the greenhouse, then heated in four solar collectors before being stored in a 1,500 gallon insulated tank. When hot water is being drawn, it passes through the demand heater, where an aquastat senses whether additional heating is necessary.

Tankless heaters are thus best for families whose need for hot water at any one time is moderate. You will not be able to run a high-flow shower while running the clotheswasher. Water flow from demand water heaters is limited to about 3.0 to 3.5 gpm (2 to 3 gpm for electric units), so they work best when combined with efficient showerheads and faucets, or if separate units service the bathroom and the kitchen. Larger flow rates can be achieved by integrating a tankless heater with a solar hot water system. Electric models may require new wiring since they need 5 to 7 kilowatts to run.

Solar water heating

You can add a solar water heater at any time. Although this requires a hefty initial investment, it may be worthwhile for you, especially if you have an electric water heater. Which type of solar system is best for you depends on the amount of sunshine and other climatic factors, your water heating bills, the temperature of the incoming cold water, and so on. The cost of solar systems adequate for families of two to five people range from $2,000 to $5,000. In general, there are three types of solar systems: batch, flat plate, and geyser-pump:

- **Batch water heaters** are the simplest and cheapest, and consist of a water tank enclosed in a glazed, insulated box exposed to the sun. Sunlight strikes the batch tank and preheats the water before it flows to the conventional hot water tank. Batch heaters can be home-built for as little as $300, but they do not provide as much hot water as other types of systems.

- **Flat plate collectors** are the most common type of collection system. These systems heat a fluid circulating through tubes connected to a dark-colored absorber plate housed in an insulated metal box. This heated fluid—usually antifreeze— then heats the water in the hot water tank through a heat exchanger. Thermo-siphoning flat plate systems circulate

the heated water or antifreeze by natural convection into
the storage tank, which must be located at least a foot higher than the panels.

- **Geyser-pump systems** (also called phase-change systems)
  work like a coffee percolator. Rather than using an electric
  pump to circulate the solar-heated fluid, such systems use
  the energy generated when a water-alcohol mixture boils
  into a vapor to circulate the heat from your roof panels
  down to the heat exchanger. In such systems, the heat
  exchanger and hot water tank can be located up to 20 feet
  below the panels without using a pump.

Solar water heating system

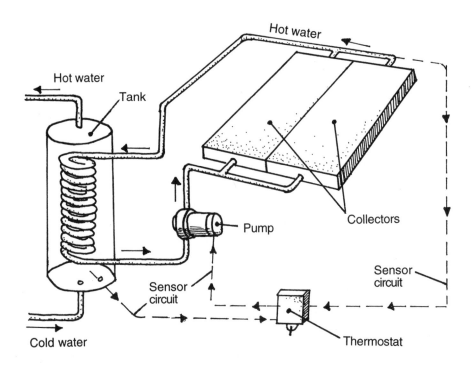

Flat plate solar panels, circulating pump, sensor circuit, and hot water
storage tank with a heat exchange loop. Illustration adapted from Reader's
Digest (1982), *Home Improvements Manual*, p. 369, Pleasantville, NY.

Most solar systems use a conventional water heater as the storage and backup heat source. During sunny periods, your solar heater can provide 100% of your water heating needs. When it is cloudy, the conventional heater will take over. A demand water heater can also be used as a backup to boost the water temperature.

Solar panels are used in thousands of homes to heat swimming pools. The **Florida Solar Energy Center** has useful information on such systems and other ways to cut your pool heating expenses. You can get information on state and regional solar energy associations from the **American Solar Energy Society**. The **Solar Rating and Certification Corporation** tests and certifies solar hot water collectors and systems.

Solar water heating can also be integrated with space heating systems by running the heated water though hydronic baseboards or radiant floor heating coils. In colder climates a gas-fired backup system is installed for use during cloudy periods. Such integrated systems provide heat and hot water very efficiently, and little back-up fossil energy is needed.

Integrated or combination water heaters

If you're contemplating replacing your furnace or boiler too, a new integrated water- and space-heating system may be the best way to go. By combining space- and water-heating, manufacturers have been able to include efficiency measures that are not cost-effective in a stand-alone water heater. Some of these units are built to make good use of solar preheated water. Integrated systems heat water in a storage tank by circulating the water through the furnace or boiler as it is being used for space heating. Other units are basically large water heaters that also circulate hot water through a heat-exchanging coil in the air-handler of a warm-air furnace. While such systems can be very efficient during the heating season, their efficiency may drop the rest of the year, depending on the type of system. Combined with an active solar system, however, it can be the most efficient way to heat both water and your home. Several manufacturers are listed in the "Where to find" list.

Combination water and space heating system

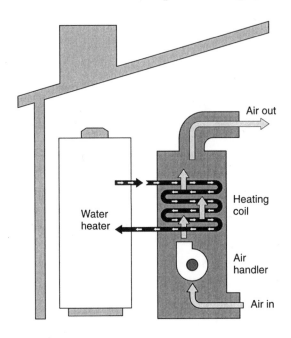

This combination system heats water in a large tank and transfers heat through a heat-exchange loop in the air handler of the space-heating system. Other integrated units work in reverse by heating water in a boiler for storage in a tank. Illustration courtesy of E SOURCE (1993), *Space Heating Technology Atlas*, p. 263, Boulder, CO.

Saving cold water

Cold water is worth saving too. Providing clean water to American households costs the environment plenty. The average family uses between 68,000 and 112,000 gallons per year for indoor water consumption alone. Although the annual bill is only around $200, it takes a lot of money and energy to treat, pump, and deliver water, to build the facilities, dams, and pipelines, and to clean up the water before it's returned to the river. As taxpayers, we help invest several billion dollars per year in such infrastructure. Like energy, water is too cheap, and we end up using far more water than we really need. We can readily save 17,000 gallons annually through hot water efficiency alone, but there is much more we can do.

Water-efficient toilets

Conventional toilets are one of the biggest water-wasters in the home, using 3.5 to 7 gpf (gallons per flush) and a total of 32,000 gallons per four-person family per year. Water-efficient

Efficient toilet

The 1.6-gallon Ifö Cascade toilet. Adapted from an illustration by Mansfield Kilgore Norris Plumbing Products (the U.S. distributor), Perrysville, OH.

toilets, by comparison, use 1.0 to 1.6 gpf while providing the same quality of performance as water-wasters. Installing such toilets can save 23,000 gallons annually and, based on the average cost of water ($1.76 per 1,000 gallons), can reduce your water bill by $40 per year. If you live in a cold climate, installing water-efficient toilets will also save you $15 to $25 worth of space-heating energy, since you'd flush less heated water down the drain.

Water-efficient toilets cost no more than conventional ones, and are available in designer colors and styles. Most plumbers and plumbing supply stores either carry them in stock or can order them. Some municipalities and water utilities around the country offer rebates on efficient models; it's worth inquiring.

Even if you decide not to replace your conventional toilet, do repair leaking toilets, since they can waste as much as 5% (or about $10 worth in a year) of your household's water. Inserting a toilet dam or gravel-filled plastic gallon jug into the tank of your existing toilet certainly reduces the volume of water used per flush, but conventional toilets are designed to use the full amount of water, and doing this *may* degrade its performance. It's worth a try. (Putting a brick in the toilet is not recommended, as it can eventually crumble and gunk up the works.) Also fix dripping faucets—especially, of course, if it's a hot water faucet that's leaking.

Outdoor watering

As any suburbanite knows, lawns and other exterior vegetation soak up a lot of water. An hour of watering can easily use 300 gallons, and by summer's end a small lawn may have cost you $50 to $200 to keep green. Lawns are usually over-watered (and under-fertilized). There are many ways to cut down on outdoor watering:

• Set sprinklers on timers. You can buy battery-powered timers for hose bibs, too. Use a gypsum block or electronic moisture sensor to avoid watering when there is already enough moisture in the soil. Some "smart" gypsum blocks can be used to control an automated or timed sprinkler system.

- Water more deeply, but less often, to wet the roots. Observe how long it takes for runoff to occur, and set timers accordingly. Except in spring and fall, do your watering in the evening: on sunny days in a dry climate, half the water from a sprinkler can evaporate before it ever hits the ground. Avoid watering driveways and sidewalks.

- Consider storing the water runoff from your roof in a cistern or garden pond. Water can be gravity fed or pumped with a submersible pump.

- Landscape with low-water-use plants. Plant drought-resistant, native, or less thirsty grasses, shrubs, flowering plants, and trees. Add moisture-retentive mulches, limit turf areas, and landscape with rocks, gravels, bark, etc.

- Install drip irrigation or subsurface trickle irrigation for non-grassy areas.

- Since requirements vary so much, asking lawn and garden experts who know your climate is the best way to find out what will work best for you—and your pocketbook.

Where to find

information on getting into hot water

Consumer Guide to Home Energy Savings lists the ratings of the most efficient water heater models, including heat pumps and makers of solar panels. Available at bookstores or from ACEEE: 2140 Shattuck Avenue, Suite 202, Berkeley, CA 94704, (510) 549-9914.

The New Solar Home Book, by Bruce Anderson, Brick House Publishing Company, PO Box 256, Amherst, NH 03031, (800) 446-8642, discusses how solar water heating works.

The Water Heater Workbook, by Larry and Suzanne Weingarten, Elemental Enterprises, PO Box 928, Monterey, CA 93942, (408) 394-7077, discusses why water heaters fail, how to maintain them for efficiency and long life, and what to look for when shopping for a new water heater.

American Solar Energy Society, 2400 Central Avenue, Suite G-1, Boulder, CO 80301, (303) 443-3130.

Earth Energy Association, 777 N. Capitol Street NE, Suite 805, Washington, DC 20002, (202) 289-0868. Information on ground- and water-source heat pumps.

Energy Efficiency and Renewable Energy Clearinghouse, PO Box 3048, Merrifield, VA, 22116, (800) DOE EREC and (800) 523-2929 has information on water- and energy-saving technologies.

Florida Solar Energy Center, 300 State Road 401, Cape Canaveral, FL 32920, (407) 783-0300 has information on solar water heaters and solar pool heating.

International Ground Source Heat Pump Association, PO Box 1688, Stillwater, OK 74076-1688, (800) 626-4747 and (405) 744-5175. Information on ground- and water-source heat pumps.

Solar Rating and Certification Corporation, 777 North Capitol Street NE, Suite 805, Washington, DC 20002, (202) 408-0603, tests and certifies solar hot water collectors and systems.

water heating and water saving equipment

The following is a partial list of hundreds of manufacturers of water heating equipment and water and energy saving widgets. See the "Where to find" section in chapter 4: *Fine-Tuning Your Heating System* for additional listings and the Appendix for mail-order companies selling water heater tank wraps, showerheads, solar systems, etc.

American Water Heater Group, PO Box 4056, Johnson City, TN 37602, (800) 937-1037, makes the "Polaris" water heater that can be combined with a heat exchanger to provide space heating.

Controlled Energy Corporation, Fiddler's Green, Waitsfield, VT 05673, (802) 496-4436 or (800) 642-3111, imports the "AquaStar" gas- or propane-fired tankless water heater used at RMI.

Crispaire Corporation, 3570 American Drive, Atlanta, GA 30341, (404) 458-6643, makes the "E-Tech D-SuperHeater" that extracts heat from central air conditioners, heat pumps, or other mechanical chillers, and pumps hot water to a separate storage tank.

DEC International, PO Box 8050, Madison, WI 53708, (800) 533-7533, offers the "Therma-Stor" line of heat pump water heaters.

Energy Technology Laboratories, 2351 Tenaya, Modesto, CA 95354, (800) 344-3242, makes the "Spa 2001," "Spradius," and other models of efficient showerheads and faucet aerators.

Kohler Corporation, 44 Highland Drive, Kohler, WI 53044, (414) 457-4441, makes water-efficient toilets, faucets, and showerheads.

Nordyne, 1801 Park 270 Drive, St. Louis, MO 63146, (314) 878-6200, makes the "Powermiser" heat pump water heater that also heats and cools the home.

Paloma Industries, 1440 Howard Street, Elk Grove Village, IL 60007, (312) 806-1010, manufactures tankless water heaters.

Perfection Corporation, 222 Lake Street, Madison, OH 44057, (216) 428-1171, manufactures anti-convection valves.

Sage Advance Corporation, PO Box 23136, Eugene, OR 97402, (503) 485-1947, manufactures the geyser-pump "Copper Cricket" solar thermal system used at RMI.

SolarAttic, 15548 95th Circle NE, Elk River, MN 55330-7228, (612) 441-3440, manufactures an attic-cooling heat pump for heating the pool or household water.

SUN Utility Network, 5741 Engineer Drive, Huntington Beach, CA 92649, (714) 898-2084, makes a passive solar water heater.

Temptec Energy Efficient Products, 421 Nugget Avenue, #3, Scarborough, Ontario M1S 4L8, (905) 472-1224, makes a simple anti-convection heat trap.

Water Heater Innovations, 3107 Sibley Memorial Hwy, Eagan, MN 55121, (612) 688-8827, makes the "Marathon" efficient gas-fired water heater; sold as the "Survivor" by Sears, Roebuck & Co.

cold water savings

First call your water utility and ask about publications on reducing outdoor watering needs. Many water utilities also offer rebates on water-efficient toilets. While Federal water-efficiency standards have banned the manufacture of toilets using more than 1.6 gallons per flush (and showerheads and faucets using more than 2.5 gallons per minute), many states still allow the sale of water-wasting equipment manufactured prior to January 1994. All U.S. plumbing manufacturers can provide you with high-performance water-saving equipment.

American Society of Landscape Architects, 4401 Connecticut Avenue NW, 5th Floor, Washington, DC 20008, (202) 686-2752.

American Water Works Association, 6666 West Quincy Avenue, Denver, CO 80235, (303) 794-7711, operates the Water Efficiency Clearinghouse, (800) 559-9855.

National Xeriscape Council, PO Box 767936, Roswell, GA 30076-7936, (404) 998-5899, has information drought-resistant plants.

U.S. Bureau of Reclamation has regional Water Conservation Centers. The Washington, D.C. Center number is (202) 208-7587.

U.S. Environmental Protection Agency operates the Drinking Water Hotline, (800) 426-4791, and the National Small Flows Clearinghouse, (800) 624-8301.

8

Appliances: Keeping Up With the Lovinses

All the televisions in the United States, when turned to the "off" position, use the equivalent in output of one Chernobyl-sized power-plant.

Refrigerators with thin insulation and inefficient compressors, stoves with pilot lights, TVs that still draw power even when switched "off"—all of these consume far more energy than needed to provide the services we want. All told, we spend $43 billion annually to run our appliances, an average of $560 per year per family. If every household in the U.S. replaced old appliances with efficient models already on the market, we would save at least $15 billion per year and enough electricity to retire 36 large powerplants. This would prevent the emission of 175 million tons of carbon dioxide annually.

We aren't asking, of course, that everyone rush to the show-room to buy expensive new appliances. There are many simple and cost-effective things we can do to make our appliances use less energy and run more efficiently. But for those of you about to take the big dive on a major new appliance, we have some suggestions for making a smart choice.

Refrigerators and freezers

The refrigerator is likely to be the largest single power-user in your home aside from space conditioning and water heating. Keeping milk cold and food fresh nationally consumes the output of 37 large powerplants. Right now, it may not be worth scrapping your 15-year-old clunker to buy a new energy-efficient model. But by all means, when it does quit, buy the most efficient model available. In the meantime, there are several things you can do to improve the performance of the refrigerator you now own.

√ Cover liquids and wrap foods stored in the refrigerator. Uncovered foods release moisture and make the compressor work harder.

√ Clean the door gasket and where it seals on the refrigerator. Replace the gasket if it is damaged. You can check to see if you are getting a good seal by closing the refrigerator door on a dollar bill. If you can pull it out without resistance, replace the gasket. On newer refrigerators with magnetic seals, you may instead need to put a flashlight inside some evening, turn off the room lights, and check for light leaking through the seal.

√ Unplug the extra fridge (or freezer) in the garage. The electricity the fridge is using costs you far more (typically $130 a year) than the six-pack you've stashed there. *Take the door off so kids don't accidentally get stuck inside.*

√ Move your refrigerator out from the wall and vacuum its condenser coils; they should be cleaned once a year. (The coils may be under the refrigerator.) Your refrigerator will cycle on for shorter periods with clean coils. Leave enough room (at least a couple of inches) behind it for air to circulate and carry off waste heat.

Cleaning a refrigerator's coils

Simply vacuuming the refrigerator's heat-dissipation condenser coils once or twice a year will improve the refrigerator's efficiency. Illustration courtesy of Public Service of Colorado (1992), *Your Energy Guide to Heating, Cooling, and Appliances,* p. 3, Denver, CO.

√ Install an electricity-saving GreenPlug (but only if your fridge is a few years old, as it won't save much if you have a new fridge). The circuitry inside this device reduces the voltage of the electricity feeding into the refrigerator, which makes it run more efficiently. The GreenPlug will reduce your refrigerator's electricity consumption by 3% to 20%, depending on your line voltage and the efficiency of your fridge. Savings are greatest if your line voltage is above 120V (you can get a voltage meter at Radio Shack) and if you have an older, less efficient fridge. At a cost of $35–$40, the payback ranges from a year and a half to never (if your line voltage is below 110V), but reportedly averages four to seven years. GreenPlugs are available at home centers and hardware stores. Follow the installation instructions, as some simple adjustments are required.

The GreenPlug

Adapted from an illustration by Green Technologies, Boulder, CO. Green Technologies also makes a GreenPlug for washing machines and dryers.

√ Check to see if you have a power-saving switch or a summer-winter switch. Many refrigerators have a small heater (yes, a heater) inside the walls to prevent condensation build-up on the refrigerator walls. If yours does, switch it to the power-saving mode.

√ Defrost your fridge if significant frost has built up.

√ Turn off your automatic ice maker. It's more efficient to make ice in ice trays.

√ If you can, move the refrigerator away from the stove or dishwasher and out of direct sunlight.

√ Set your refrigerator's temperature to between 38°F and 42°F and your freezer to between 10°F and 15°F. You'll need a thermometer for this because temperature dials don't tell you the real temperature.

√ Keep cold air in. Remember to open the door as infrequently and briefly as possible. Know what you're looking for. Labeling frozen leftovers could save a little head-scratching time while the door is open. If you're not into stuffing the fridge with food, put in a few empty or water-filled milk jugs so less cold air will spill out. Don't pack it too tight or block the fan or the cold air can't circulate.

You can get a "**Chillshield**"—a system of vinyl flaps that help keep the cold air inside when you open the door—from **The Conserve Group**, PO Box 1560, Bethlehem, PA 18016-1560, (610) 691-8024.

Super-efficient refrigerators

Federal appliance efficiency standards have greatly reduced the electricity consumption of modern refrigerators. Compared to models made in the early seventies, which use an average of over 1,700 kWh per year, refrigerators of the same size meeting Federal standards now use fewer than 700 kWh annually. The U.S. Environmental Protection Agency, in collaboration with 25 utilities, promoted the adoption of advanced technology through a design competition in 1993. The winning entry, a 22 ft^3 side-by-side by Whirlpool—marketed under the KitchenAid, Kenmore, and Whirlpool brands—is available within the service territories of the 25 participating utilities, and will be available nationwide by early 1995. The SERP model and other Whirlpool models do not use CFCs as refrigerant or in the foam insulation. Inquire with your utility or local appliance dealer; Whirlpool and the Super-Efficient Refrigerator Program (SERP) are listed at the end of the chapter.

The race for efficiency continues, and manufacturers' innovations, such as vacuum insulation panels, dual compressors, efficient motors and fans, and non-CFC refrigerants, will yield another 10 to 30 percent savings by 1998.

Average refrigerator electricity consumption 1972–95	
Model or year	*kWh per year*
1972 Refrigerator/freezer (average sold, 18-ft^3)	1,726
1987 Refrigerator/freezer (average sold, 20-ft^3)	974
1990 Refrigerator/freezer (Federal standard, 21-ft^3)	965
1990 Refrigerator/freezer (average in use)	1,300
1993 Refrigerator/freezer (Federal standard, 21-ft^3)	691
1993 Best available model (Sun Frost, 18-ft^3)	240
1995 Whirlpool (SERP model, 22-ft^3 side-by-side)	670
1998 Consumption target (1994 industry agreement, 22-ft^3)	490

Sources: Shepard, Lovins, Neymark, Houghton, and Heede, *The State of the Art: Appliances*, 1990, E SOURCE, Boulder, CO, p. 37; Energy Information Administration (1993), *Household Energy Consumption and Expenditures, 1990*, Washington, DC, p. 10; Whirlpool Corporation, Benton Harbor, MI; and Natural Resources Defense Council, San Francisco, CA.

Meanwhile, Sun Frost has made super-efficient refrigerators for years. Thicker insulation, dual top-mounted compressors, better gaskets, and manual defrost result in measured savings of 14 to 40+% compared to the best mass-produced models.

Sun Frosts are popular with homeowners on "off-grid" or independent electric systems where the high cost of photovoltaic (solar) panels or wind turbines justifies the higher cost of super-efficient refrigerators. Vestfrost, a Danish manufacturer, also markets an efficient, CFC-free 10.6-ft^3 fridge in the U.S.

Design improvements of Whirlpool's SERP refrigerator

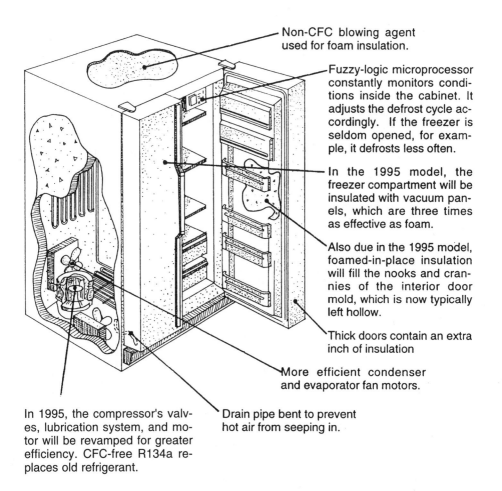

Non-CFC blowing agent used for foam insulation.

Fuzzy-logic microprocessor constantly monitors conditions inside the cabinet. It adjusts the defrost cycle accordingly. If the freezer is seldom opened, for example, it defrosts less often.

In the 1995 model, the freezer compartment will be insulated with vacuum panels, which are three times as effective as foam.

Also due in the 1995 model, foamed-in-place insulation will fill the nooks and crannies of the interior door mold, which is now typically left hollow.

Thick doors contain an extra inch of insulation

More efficient condenser and evaporator fan motors.

In 1995, the compressor's valves, lubrication system, and motor will be revamped for greater efficiency. CFC-free R134a replaces old refrigerant.

Drain pipe bent to prevent hot air from seeping in.

Whirlpool's winning entry into the Super-Efficient Refrigerator Program included the improvements depicted above. Adapted from an illustration in *Popular Science*, "The $30 Million Refrigerator," January 1994, p. 66.

Buying a new refrigerator

A new, more efficient refrigerator can typically save you $70–$80 a year, and will pay for itself in about nine years (longer if you buy a fancy model). If you use your air conditioner a lot, replacing an inefficient refrigerator will also reduce your air conditioning bills. Since all of the electricity used by your refrigerator is converted into waste heat vented out the back of the fridge, saving 1,000 kWh per year by buying a new fridge will also cut your cooling bills by about $30 per year. This will reduce your payback from nine years to about seven years.

As an additional incentive to buy a new refrigerator, your electric utility may be willing to help you buy one. It's often cheaper for the utility to give customers a financial incentive (usually around $100) to buy a more efficient fridge than it is for them to build and operate the generating capacity needed to run an inefficient model.

Typical energy cost for the best new refrigerators (1994)

Style	Volume (cubic feet)	Energy use (kWh/yr)	Energy cost ($/yr)
Top freezer	14.4	496	41
Top freezer	18.2	591	49
Top freezer	21.6	650	54
Top freezer *	22.3	726	60
Side-by-side *	21.7	759	62
Side-by-side **	22.0	760	62
Side-by-side *	23.6	799	66
Side-by-side *	26.6	898	74

All of the above have automatic defrost.

* Denotes through-the-door ice.

** Whirlpool's SERP model; see text for explanation.

Adapted from Alex Wilson and John Morrill (1993), *Consumer Guide to Home Energy Savings,* American Council for an Energy-Efficient Economy, Washington, DC, pp. 157–160.

If you buy a new refrigerator, it's important to shop wisely, carefully read the EnergyGuide label found on each appliance, and buy a refrigerator that is no larger than you need. It is much more efficient, however, to have one large refrigerator than two smaller ones. Refrigerators come in lots of styles and features, and the least efficient models are no longer on the market, thanks to Federal appliance standards. The above chart on typical energy cost lists the energy consumption and annual operating cost of the most efficient mass-produced models, and will give you some guidance when comparing models, sizes, and features.

EnergyGuide labels

MODEL A	MODEL B
Cost: $545.00	Cost: $485.00

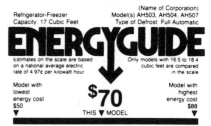

These labels compare two 17-ft³ automatic-defrost refrigerator-freezers. Note that the simple payback on the more efficient model (A) is 3.2 years (purchase differential divided by operating differential: $60/$19 = 3.2 years). You can make similar calculations when shopping for any new appliance. Illustration courtesy of New Mexico State University Cooperative Extension Service, *New Mexico Home Energy Guide*, p. 28, Las Cruces, NM.

Refrigerator shopping checklist

- Automatic defrost on older fridges is an energy consumer, but some new fridges use "smart" controls and a smaller heater that only operates when frost accumulates. The result is that auto defrost models perform almost as efficiently as manual defrost models. Look for this feature.

- Models with top- or bottom-mounted freezers generally use about 12% less energy than side-by-side designs.

- Features like through-the-door ice and ice-water dispensers increase the purchase price by about $250 and generally increase energy consumption and maintenance costs. You'll recoup *some* of this higher energy cost *if* you'll open the freezer door a lot less with through-the-door ice.

Disposing of the old fridge

Make sure the refrigerant (CFCs) is recovered when you dispose of your old fridge. First call your electric utility to see if they will pick up the refrigerator or freezer and properly dispose of it and its CFC refrigerant charge. Ask them if they will also shred the refrigerator's foam insulation and recover its CFC content.

If the utility can't help you, call a local recycling organization, solid-waste company, the municipal dump, or appliance repair folks to see if they can recover the CFCs. Your State Energy Office or the U.S. Environmental Protection Agency (see Appendix) may also be able to find out who can responsibly recycle your refrigerator.

Unfortunately, appliance recycling programs often don't recover either the CFC refrigerant or the CFCs in the foam insulation. (Of the 2.5 lbs of CFCs in a typical fridge, 2 lbs is in the foam insulation.) The global warming caused by releasing the

CFCs will far outweigh any decrease in CO_2 emissions from the powerplant as a result of buying a more efficient fridge.

Encourage your utility or local government to start a comprehensive appliance recycling program; in the meantime, hold on to used appliances until such a program exists in your area.

Again, when you store or dispose of a refrigerator, be sure to remove the door from its hinges so playful kids won't entomb themselves.

Stoves and ranges

Cooking uses about 6.5% of the average home's consumption of electricity. Households with an electric range typically use 750 kWh per year for cooking. Whether your main cooking fuel is gas (42% of households) or electricity (58%), most of the following tips can reduce the amount of energy you use for preparing meals.

√ Make sure that your range has adequate ventilation to remove smoke and fumes. If you are remodeling your kitchen, install a vent hood with a quiet fan (sone rating less than 1.5) so you're more likely to use it.

√ Use pressure cookers. These use 50 to 75% less energy than ordinary cookware.

√ Use toaster ovens instead of conventional electric ovens when possible. Because they are smaller, they use a third to a half the power of an electric oven.

√ Microwave ovens use one-fifth to one-half as much electricity as a conventional electric range/oven—particularly when reheating small portions. Using pre-packaged microwavable foods, however, often uses more energy than cooking from scratch—if you add in the energy used in processing, pre-cooking, packaging, and transporting such items.

√ Ever wonder whether you should stick a casserole in the oven or the microwave? Below is an estimate of the cost of different options for cooking just such a dish.

Energy costs* of various cooking methods	
Electric oven	16 cents
Convection oven (electric)	11 cents
Toaster oven	8 cents
Gas oven	7 cents
Frying pan	7 cents
Crock pot	6 cents
Microwave oven	3 cents

*8 cents per kWh for electricity and 60 cents per therm for natural gas.

Adapted from Wilson and Morrill, *Consumer Guide to Home Energy Savings*, American Council for an Energy-Efficient Economy, Washington, DC, p. 174.

√ Cover pots (except pasta, of course).

√ If your stove is electric, don't put a small pot on a large burner: this can waste 40% of the energy. If you cook with gas, don't turn the flame on really high unless you're using a large pot.

√ The metal grease plates under the burners will be more effective at reflecting heat if they are kept clean.

√ Cook several dishes at the same time in the oven, or cook larger portions and re-heat for another meal. Re-heating takes less energy than cooking, and you'll have fewer dishes to wash.

√ Lower oven temperature (by about 25F°) if you use ceramic or glass pans. Covering oven racks with foil reduces heat flow and increases cooking time. Use thermometers or timers to avoid overcooking.

√ If you have a self-cleaning oven, plan to clean it right after you've finished baking something; that way it doesn't have to start from cold.

√ If you are in the market for a new range, consider buying a gas unit. Always get the best-insulated model. A model with a solid door or small glass window will be better insulated than one with a large glass window. Also, a self-cleaning oven is better insulated than ones with the never-clean feature. Culinary preferences aside, gas cooktops and ovens use much less energy than their electric counterparts, because three or four units of fuel must be burned at the powerplant to make one unit of electricity.

√ Magnetic induction and halogen cooktops are more efficient than conventional electric ranges, but they are quite expensive, and induction cooktops require that you use only iron or steel pots and pans.

√ If you are looking for a free lunch, you may want to cook your casserole in a solar oven. These ovens are simply insulated boxes with a glass lid and reflective surfaces that concentrate the sun's energy. Placed outdoors facing the sun, they can collect enough solar heat energy to provide oven temperatures as high as 450°F.

√ If you have air conditioning, remember that the less energy is wasted in heating food, the less your air conditioner will have to work to keep your home cool. Conversely, some of the heat given off in the kitchen offsets space heating requirements, but such savings are smaller than the extra cost imposed on your cooling system.

Clothes washers and dryers

Heating water accounts for some 86% of the energy consumed by a clothes washer, and minimizing the use of hot water for washing is a simple energy conservation measure. Use the warm or cold wash cycle, rinse in cold water, and wash full loads (or use the low water-level setting).

Just switching your washer's setting from hot to warm water can cut a load's energy use in half. Full-sized conventional machines use about 15 to 20 gallons of water on the small-capacity setting and twice that for an extra-large load.

√ Wash clothes in cold water using enzymatic cold-water detergents. Greasy stains may require hot water, however. Always rinse in cold water.

√ Wash and dry full loads. If you are washing a small load, be sure to use the appropriate water-level setting.

√ Dry clothes outdoors on a clothesline to make clothes smell fresher, look better, and last longer. If your house has an excessive moisture problem, you may not want to hang-dry clothes inside in the winter.

Clothes line

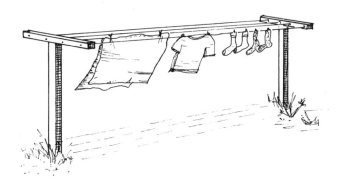

Adapted from an illustration by Saturn Resource Management, Helena, MT.

√ Dry towels and other heavy cottons in a separate load from lighter clothes. Dry two or more loads in a row, so you can make use of the heat already in the dryer.

√ Don't overdry your clothes. If your machine has a moisture sensor, use it. Taking clothes out while still a little damp reduces wrinkling, which saves on your time and the energy cost of ironing.

√ Clean the lint filter in the dryer after every load to improve air circulation (and while the dryer is running if you're doing a linty load).

√ Use the cool-down cycle to allow the clothes to finish drying with the residual heat in the dryer.

√ Check the outside dryer vent. If it doesn't close tightly, replace it with one that does; you'll reduce air infiltration and heating bills.

Cost of washing a load of laundry (average cost per load, in cents)				
Wash/rinse setting	Electric water heater		Gas water heater	
	140°F	120°F	140°F	120°F
Hot/hot	66	52	20	15
Hot/warm	50	39	15	10
Hot/cold	34	27	10	7
Warm/warm	34	27	10	7
Warm/cold	18	15	5	4
Cold/cold	3	3	3	3

Adapted from Alex Wilson and John Morrill, *Consumer Guide to Home Energy Savings*, 1991, p. 186. Assumes typical equipment and 8 cents per kWh and 60 cents per therm.

Drying laundry in a electric dryer costs 30 to 40 cents per load *vs* 15 to 25 cents in a gas dryer.

Buying a new washer or dryer

If you're in the market for a new washer, look into a horizontal axis (H-axis) machine. These use about half to a third the energy of vertical-axis top-loaders because they need less water

to get the same load of wash just as clean (and since these machines use less water, you'll also save ~$9 in water plus ~$36 a
year in detergent). While these washers cost $200–$500 more
than conventional machines (even higher for the European
models), the energy, water, and detergent savings will pay
back the higher up-front cost in three to nine years (based on
electric water heating; with a gas-fired water heater you'll save
a little less money per year, and the payback will be longer).

Conventional clothes washer and two horizontal-axis models

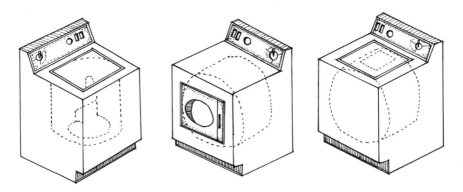

Horizontal-axis machines use a lot less hot water. Next to the conventional
vertical-axis machine (left) are figures of front-loading (center) and top-load-
ing (right) H-axis clothes washers. Adapted from Alex Wilson and John
Morrill (1993), *Consumer Guide to Home Energy Savings*, p. 186, American
Council for an Energy-Efficient Economy, Berkeley, CA.

Horizontal axis machines cost a total of about $45 per year to
run, *vs* $110 for conventional machines (only about one-third
of this cost is for energy, the rest is for water and detergent).
Since they wring more water out of the wash during the spin
cycle (they spin faster than vertical axis machines), you save
on drying energy, too. Staber introduced its System 2000 H-
axis model in 1994. Frigidaire's existing model (sold under the
Gibson and White-Westinghouse labels) will be redesigned for
1995. Maytag plans to introduce an H-axis model in late 1995,
and Whirlpool has announced plans for a 1996 model. Several
European machines are already available in the U.S.

When buying a new dryer, see that it has a moisture sensor, which can save 15% of a load's energy needs. It will save you about $13 per year while being gentler with your clothes by avoiding overdrying. Gas clothes dryers are cheaper to operate and easier on the environment than electric ones. The cost of drying a load of laundry is about 31 to 40 cents in an electric dryer compared to 15 to 25 cents in a gas dryer.

If you have a choice, don't install dryers in a cold or damp basement as it will make the dryer work harder to get your clothes dry.

Dishwashers

A typical dishwasher will use between seven and fourteen gallons of hot water for a full cycle. Washing dishes by hand can use less hot water than using a dishwasher, but only if you use conservative washing habits.

√ Leaving the water running when washing or rinsing will cost you four cents per minute. Installing a low-flow faucet head with a finger-tip on-off valve makes it easy to shut the flow to a trickle between uses.

√ A modern dishwasher will save energy and water, but only if you don't rinse the dishes, or rinse them with cold rather than hot water.

√ Wash only full loads. Using the "light wash" or "energy-saving" cycles (which use less hot water) also cuts down on electricity use.

√ Dishwashers with a switch to allow air-drying of dishes use considerably less electricity than those using electric heating elements for drying. These switches are mandated on all new models.

√ Buy a model with a water booster heater; most new dish-washers have them. These will boost the water tempera-ture up to the 140°F level needed to prevent the spotting of glassware, but will save your water heater from having to keep a whole tank at that higher temperature. Only 20–40% of the hot water used by a dishwasher needs to be at 140°F. Booster heaters heat only the amount of water that actually needs to be at that peak temperature. See the *Hot Water* chapter for additional discussion.

Waterbeds and electric blankets

The 17 million waterbeds in this country consume the electri-cal output of five large powerplants. One waterbed will typi-cally use nearly as much electricity as a refrigerator, and will cost about $70–$120 per year to heat. While a waterbed will help heat your room, too, it isn't an efficient use of electricity, and makes your air conditioning bills higher in the summer.

If you use an electric blanket, consider this: electric current generates an electromagnetic field (EMF), and sleeping under an electric blanket that is on *may* be hazardous to your health (research remains inconclusive). Don't take the risk; better to warm up the bed before you retire, and turn the blanket off for the night. Or use old-fashioned hot water bottles.

Here are some tips to reduce your waterbed's energy costs:

√ Make the bed and cover it completely with a thick quilt. A quilted cover can halve your waterbed's heating bill.

√ Insulate. Use one-inch foam (or Foil-Ray™ or Reflectix™) beneath (make sure the reflector is rated for your water heater temperature) and around the sides of your mattress to reduce heat loss. Buy an "egg-carton" foam pad and put it under your bed's mattress pad to insulate the top. If you

make your bed and insulate it as suggested you should be able to set your waterbed temperature lower. The insulation will cost about $40, but you'll save $25 to $80 per year.

√ Plug the heater into a timer and set it to turn off from 6 a.m. to 6 p.m. Adjust the timer's setting as necessary.

√ Look for an insulated, soft-sided model when shopping for a waterbed. They use half the electricity of the older styles. Fiber-filled waterbeds—designed to suppress waves—reduce heating demand by about 12%.

Televisions

You may think that when you turn off the tube it's truly "off." Actually, the beast is not dead but only sleeping; your TV when turned off may still draw 1.5 to 8 watts. The nation's 200 million TV sets consume the output of 21 large powerplants. It takes the output of one such powerplant to run all American TVs *when they are "off."* This constant power draw is for electronic tuning, remote control, and instant-on capability—so that you don't have to wait for the tube to warm up.

To see if your TV has the instant-on feature, compare how long it takes to bring up a picture normally and then immediately after plugging it into the wall. If the latter takes longer, then it has the instant-on feature. Most color TVs do, although new solid-state sets take less time to warm up, and don't need the instant-on feature (but still draw a little power for tuning and remote control).

Until a couple of years ago it was recommended that you unplug your older color TV (or plug it into a switchable outlet), but this would shorten its life and only save about $3 per year, so it isn't worth it. The best way to reduce a TV's power consumption is to read a book.

Home office equipment

One-third of American homes now have computers, and many have fax machines, printers, and copiers. It's both possible and profitable to get consumer electronic products that are state-of-the-art in terms of performance *and* energy efficiency. Many computer manufacturers are collaborating with the U.S. Environmental Protection Agency to make and market energy-efficient computers, components, software, printers, and peripherals. Models meeting certain standards—especially those allowing "sleep" options during periods of inactivity—are now sold bearing EPA's EnergyStar label.

The computational power of personal computers has grown phenomenally over the past ten years while power consumption has dropped manyfold. This progress has been likened to a Rolls Royce Silver Ghost costing $2.50 and getting a million miles per gallon.

Battery-powered portable computers use >99% less electricity than desktop models and are immune to power failures and lightning strikes (unless the charger is plugged in). Mono-chrome computer monitors use half the power of color moni-tors. Inkjet and dot-matrix printers are far easier on energy bills than laser printers. They use, respectively, 13 to 46 watts when printing, or 85 to 96 percent less electricity than a laser printer. Inkjet printers produce pages about as clear and crisp as laser printers; they're just a bit slower. The same goes for inkjet fax machines like the Panafax UF-300. Cold-fuser copiers such as Canon's line of personal copiers cost far less to buy and operate, as they use one tenth as much electricity, and they make copies perfectly acceptable for home-office use (although you wouldn't want to copy your résumé on one).

The best way to save electricity is to turn computers, printers, and copiers off when not being used for an hour or more. Modern hard drives are designed to handle some 40,000–

250,000 on-off cycles before failure, and you're not likely to approach this number over the average computer's five to seven year life. (Computers often last longer, but most people upgrade their machines after a few years.) You may think that using your computer's screen-saver feature also cuts the monitor's power consumption, but it doesn't. It saves the screen's phosphors from imprinting "ghosts" of any text that is left on the monitor for a long time. To save *electricity*, turn the monitor off: that doesn't affect the operation of the computer, only whether you can read the screen.

When on vacation

Have you ever exclaimed after a long vacation, "Hey, we were gone for a month—what's with this power bill?" Here are a few tips for reducing post-vacation shock:

√ Unplug television sets, cable TV converters, and all other appliances that aren't too difficult to reprogram. Also unplug the little transformers and chargers for cordless vacuums and phones: they use 1–8 watts each, all the time.

√ Set water heaters to the vacation setting or "off" if you'll be gone for more than a few days.

√ Turn the pool or spa heater off if you'll be gone for more than a couple of days. Spas cost about $20–$40 per month to heat and keep the pumps running. Even though pool pumps use about 160 kWh per month ($13 worth), it is best to keep them running; covering the pool allows you to reduce the amount of time the circulation pump is on.

√ A heat pump can draw 30 watts continuously; turning it off at the circuit breaker panel will save you $1.60 per month. Be sure to switch the breaker on a couple of hours before you turn the heat pump itself back on.

√ Set your heating or cooling system's thermostat for temperatures appropriate for vacation time. Better yet, *prepro-*
gram your programmable thermostat (you should have
one by now!) for a vacation setting when you are not in a
rush to leave, and check it to make sure it is properly programmed. Pull window shades to reduce solar heat gain.

While the people are away, the appliances will play

Illustration courtesy of *Home Energy* magazine, July/August 1993, p. 32.

√ Put both interior and exterior lights on timers or photo-
sensors. A couple of incandescent porch lights on for a
month will cost you $3.50. Install compact fluorescents.

√ If you will be gone for a long time, it may be worth empty-
ing your refrigerator and turning it down to the lowest
possible setting, but not off. The refrigerator will use 40%
less electricity, saving you up to $12 per month.

Small and "phantom" loads

Hidden energy loads, like the clock on a coffee maker, VCRs on perpetual standby, transformers and chargers for "dustbusters" and telephone answering machines, television "instant-on" features, the furnace fan, even an innocent-looking aquarium can surprise homeowners with high energy bills. Richard Perez wrote in *Home Power* magazine that such hidden or "phantom loads" in the U.S. equal the electricity use of Greece, Peru, and Vietnam combined. It is hard to reduce such loads—estimated to consume nearly 700 kWh per year in one typical California home—but you can at least unplug chargers, transformers, and coffee makers when not in use. Other tips:

Plug your car's engine block heater into a timer set to start preheating the engine an hour or so before you plan to leave in the morning: you'll save about 50 cents per night, and heating the engine on cold mornings will prolong its life and save fuel.

One thing you should not do is use batteries instead of line power in electronic equipment that offers the choice, such as cassette players and radios. While they are convenient, batteries are extremely expensive: you'll end up paying between $130 and $1,980 per kWh (for D cell and 9-volt batteries, respectively).

Instead of keeping coffee hot on the unit's heating pad, pour freshly brewed coffee into a thermos. The coffee will retain its flavor better, and you'll save about 10 cents worth of electricity per day.

The table on the next two pages shows many surprising loads (and expenses) for appliances and gadgets thought to use no, or very little, electricity. The list includes annual electricity consumption, cost, and carbon dioxide emissions for many ordinary appliances.

Approximate electricity use of home appliances and widgets

Product	Average kWh used per year	Average cost per year, in $	CO_2 emissions per year, in lbs
Air conditioner (room)	1,070	86	1,990
Air conditioner (central)	3,230	258	6,008
Aquarium, terrarium	600	48	1,116
Car engine block-heater	500	40	930
Coffee maker	100	8	186
Clock	25	2	47
Clothes dryer	1,060	85	1,972
Clothes washer (including hot water)	1,080	86	2,009
Clothes washer (excluding hot water)	99	8	184
Dehumidifier	400	32	744
Demand water heater (electric)	350	28	651
Dishwasher (including hot water)	935	75	1,739
Dishwasher (excluding hot water)	330	26	614
Electric blanket	120	10	223
Exhaust fan	15	1	28
Fan (whole-house)	80	6	149
Fan (ceiling)	50	4	93
Fan (room)	20	2	37
Furnace fan	600	48	1,116
Hair dryer	50	4	93
Home computer	130	10	242
Humidifier	100	8	186
Iron	50	4	93
Lighting (average home consumption)	844	68	1,570
Lighting (two outside lights)	730	58	1,358
Microwave oven	220	18	409
Pipe and gutter heater	100	8	186
Pool pump	1,500	120	2,790
Range	840	67	1,562

Product	Average kWh used per year	Average cost per year, in $	CO_2 emissions per year, in lbs
Refrigerator (average in use)	1,300	104	2,420
Refrigerator (21-ft^3 1993 model)	650	52	1,209
Safety outlets (5 GFIs)	48	4	89
Spas, hot tub	2,300	184	4,280
Stereo and radio	75	6	140
Space heater	500	40	930
Sump pump	40	3	74
Telephone (cordless)	36	3	67
Telephone answering machine	36	3	67
Television, black & white	50	4	93
Television (cable TV box)	144	12	268
Television, color (average use)	197	16	855
Television, color (when turned off)	33	3	61
Toaster oven	50	4	93
Vacuum	25	2	47
Vacuum (cordless)	36	3	67
VCR	40	3	74
Waterbed	960	77	1,786
Water heater	5,300	424	9,858
Water heater (standby losses only)	788	63	1,466
Water heater (distribution losses only)	795	64	1,479
Well pump	360	29	670

Sources: Washington State Energy Office, Seattle, WA; Shepard, Lovins, Neymark, Houghton, and Heede (1990), *The State of the Art: Appliances*, E SOURCE, Boulder, CO, p. 10; Energy Information Administration (1993), *Household Energy Consumption and Expenditures, 1990*, p. 10; and Alan Meier, "What Stays on When You Go Out?" *Home Energy*, July/August, 1993, p. 34.

Average costs are based on an electric rate of 8 cents per kWh.

Carbon dioxide emissions are based on an RMI estimate that the consumption of a "typical" U.S. kWh emits 1.86 lbs of CO_2.

Where to find

information

Contact your electric utility to find out if it offers a rebate program to help you replace inefficient appliances, air conditioners, or water heaters—many do. If your utility has a test meter available, borrow it and check out the amount of electricity your appliances use.

Consumer Guide to Home Energy Savings will help you get the most out of your existing appliances. They also list the most energy-efficient refrigerators, water heaters, clothes washers, dryers, dishwashers, and heat pumps. It is available at bookstores or from ACEEE: 2140 Shattuck Avenue, Suite 202, Berkeley, CA 94704, (510) 549-9914.

Directory of the Most Energy-Efficient Refrigerators and Freezers for 1993, Florida Solar Energy Center, 300 State Road 401, Cape Canaveral, FL 32960, (407) 783-0300.

The Smart Kitchen: How to Design a Comfortable, Safe, Energy-Efficient, and Environment-Friendly Workspace, by David Goldbeck, is an innovative guide for those interested in both cooking and saving energy. Ceres Press, PO Box 87, Woodstock, NY 12498. ($17.95).

"Refrigerators for a Wiser World," *Consumer Reports*, February 1994, pp. 74–85.

Association of Home Appliance Manufacturers, 20 North Wacker Drive, Chicago, IL 60606, (312) 984-5800, has a directory of air conditioners, humidifiers, dehumidifiers, refrigerators, and freezers, listing models by size and energy use.

Gas Appliance Manufacturers Association, 1901 North Moore Street, Arlington, VA 22209, (703) 525-9565.

Super-Efficient Refrigerator Program, 2856 Arden Way, Suite 200, Sacramento, CA 95825, (916) 974-3999.

appliance manufacturers

AEG/Andico Appliances, 64 Campus Plaza, Edison, NJ 08837, (800) 344-0043, is the distributor of this German H-axis clothes washer.

Appliances International, 2807 Antigua Drive, Burbank, CA 91504, (800) 672-8297, imports an integrated H-axis washer/dryer.

Asko, 903 North Bowser, Richardson, TX (214) 238-0794, (214) 644-8593, is the distributor of this Swedish H-axis clothes washer.

Conserve Group, PO Box 1560, Bethlehem, PA 18016-1560, (610) 691-8024, makes the "Chillshield" for refrigerators, and plans on marketing an insulating waterbed cover in 1995.

Frigidaire, PO Box 7181, Dublin, OH 43017, (800) 451-7007, markets Gibson and White-Westinghouse H-axis clothes washers.

Green Technologies, 5490 Spine Road, Boulder, CO 80301, (800) 600-1100, makes "GreenPlugs" for refrigerators, washers, and dryers.

Maytag, Inc., 1 Dependability Square, Newton, IA 50208, (800) 688-9900, is developing an H-axis washing machine.

Miele Appliances, 22D World's Fair Drive, Somerset, NJ 08873, (800) 289-6435, is the distributor of this German H-axis clothes washer.

Photocomm, Inc., 7681 E Gray Road, Scottsdale, AZ 85260, (800) 223-7973, imports the Vestfrost refrigerator from Denmark.

Solar Cookers International, 1724 11th Street, Sacramento, CA 95814, has solar oven construction plans, or buy one from **Burns-Milwaukee,** 4010 West Douglas Avenue, Milwaukee, WI 53209.

Staber Industries, 4411 Marketing Place, Groveport, OH, 43125, (800) 848-6200, is test-marketing a water-efficient H-axis washer.

Sun Frost, PO Box 1101, Arcata, CA 95591, (707) 822-9095 makes several models of efficient refrigerators and freezers.

Watt Stopper, 400 Chisholm Place, Plano, TX 75075, (800) 879-8585, makes a smart powerstrip/sensor for computer workstations.

Whirlpool Corporation, Consumer Services, 2303 Pipestone Road, Benton Harbor, MI 49022, (800) 253-1301, makes the efficient SERP refrigerator, and will market an H-axis washer in 1996.

9

Super-Efficient Lighting

Mullah Nasruddin was once asked which is more valuable, the moon or the sun. "Why, the moon!" he replied—"because it shines at night, when we need the light more." —Amory Lovins
Sermon at St. John the Divine, 17 January 1993

Residential, commercial, industrial, and municipal lighting uses about 22% of all the electricity generated in the U.S. and accounts for 39 million tons of our carbon dioxide emissions. Rocky Mountain Institute estimates that the technology already exists to cost-effectively save 50–90% of the power now consumed by lights in the U.S. That would save $30 billion a year, enough electricity to retire 70 to 120 large powerplants, and reduce CO_2 emissions by 20 to 35 million tons per year.

We hope you'll take advantage of the relatively simple measures listed below. Keep in mind that lighting accounts for only 12% of a typical home's electric bill—$38 per year for a small home with low electric rates to $244 a year for a large home with high rates. While saving lighting energy is easy and cost-effective, the "bang-per-buck" is better with other measures. Your greatest opportunities to cut energy use are still with weatherization, insulation, hot water savings, and heating system improvements. Don't overlook the water heater just to install a light bulb!

An incandescent light bulb will only set you back 75 cents or less at the store, but it will typically cost six to ten times that for electricity over its relatively short (750 hour) life. This is because incandescent lights put out more heat than light. In fact, 90% of the electricity that runs an incandescent is lost to heat, while only 10% is emitted as light (5–15 lumens per watt—a measure of light output/watt, its *efficacy*—or lm/W). In total, only 3% of the energy contained in powerplant fuel ends up as light—better than the conversion efficiency of a candle (~0.5 lm/W), but far less than the most efficient lamps (150+ lm/W).

New compact fluorescent bulbs (25–75 lm/W) developed in the 1980s are four times more efficient than incandescents and last 9 to 13 times as long. Coupled with sensible use of daylighting and lighting controls, the use of efficient bulbs can greatly reduce the amount of electricity consumed by the nation's 2.8 billion conventional incandescent light sockets.

General tips

As you ponder your lighting needs, remember that we light our homes not only to see but to create a pleasing and comfortable atmosphere and to be safe and secure. A lot of fancy lighting design work can be done elegantly using less electricity. Use dimmers, lamps with lower light output, uplights, tasklights, low-wattage colored lights, creative daylighting, low-voltage lighting, and different lamp types, for example.

Varying light levels to improve light quality can also save energy. If the light on your work surface is three to four times brighter than the amount of background light, the contrast will be just right. Much more, though, will cause tiring eyestrain.

Since changing lighting systems in your home can be expensive, your first step should be to stop buying light bulbs on the basis of wattage; instead, think about the amount of light you need and where it's needed.

Daylighting

As much as possible, use natural daylight. In addition to being free, natural light is the healthiest light available. To bounce the sun's light deeper into the room where you're reading your paper, use light-colored furnishings, light-colored wall and ceiling surfaces, and reflective louvers or blinds.

But didn't we just say in the *Home Cooling* chapter that you should keep your blinds closed to keep the heat out? We did indeed. For hot climates, it might make the most sense to close west-facing blinds. But there's more you can do. Using the low-emissivity coatings described in the *Windows* chapter, you can get natural daylight while cutting solar heat gain. And for cold climates you can use superinsulating windows to get all the daylight and solar gain you want without losing precious heat through the glass.

Task lighting

Task lighting is one of the simplest and most effective ways to save energy while enhancing lighting quality. Instead of brightly lighting every room, it may be more attractive and practical to focus the light where you need it—on your desk, by the night table, and so on. When determining your lighting needs, figure out what you really need the light for—then design your lighting scheme. Provide reading lamps where you need to see detail. Lower your background lighting levels with lower-wattage bulbs to save energy and create more contrast in a room. Mounting height also makes a big difference when it comes to lighting level, as the amount of light falls by three-quarters if you double the distance from the lamp to where you need the light.

Clean and dim your light fixtures

Accumulated dirt can significantly reduce a bulb's light output. (Don't wipe bulbs with a wet rag while they're hot, though—they can crack or explode.) Some fixtures—with lenses or plastic covers, even lamp shades—can reduce a bulb's light output by half, particularly if dirty. Poorly designed fixtures, or mismatched recessed cans and bulbs, for example, absorb and squander a high fraction of a bulb's light output.

Use dimmers for incandescents

Dimming incandescents in hallways, bathrooms, guest rooms, and anywhere you need low lighting levels is an effective way to reduce electricity use. Do not install compact fluorescent bulbs on circuits controlled by a dimmer. For incandescents, dimmers save energy and extend the life of bulbs as follows:

Incandescent lighting	Electricity saved	Extends lamp life
10% dimmed	5%	2 times
25% dimmed	15%	4 times
50% dimmed	30%	20 times
75% dimmed	50%	over 20 times

Use bulbs appropriate for the fixture

Selecting the appropriate lamp and reflector design for a given fixture and application is critical. In general, installing the largest diameter reflector the fixture can accommodate results in the greatest light output and efficiency.

In fixture applications where you want to aim the light, such as in recessed down-light cans or track-mounted cans, a reflector lamp of half the wattage delivers the same amount of light on the task compared to an ordinary bulb.

Use airtight recessed fixtures

Replace, if possible, *recessed ceiling fixtures* with units that reduce both air leakage and are rated for insulation contact. Some manufacturers now make recessed "cans" that are airtight to prevent air leakage and can be insulated to reduce heat loss; each one can save you $5 to $10 per year.

Airtight fixtures help avoid moisture condensation in the attic's insulation. Air leakage through a conventional recessed fixture has been measured at 2–10 ft^3 of air per minute, dumping about one-third of a gallon of moisture per day into a cold (32°F) attic or nine gallons per month. Moisture condensation destroys the insulating value of insulation and promotes rot and mildew.

Don't believe everything you see

Watt Miser, Energy Choice, Supersaver, and *Econo-Watt* incandescents are simply lower-wattage bulbs (typically by 10%), and they are no more efficient per watt than regular full-wattage bulbs. In fact, they are somewhat less efficient, since lower wattage bulbs have lower light output per watt consumed. This also means that you shouldn't substitute two lower-wattage bulbs for one with twice the wattage, as this will decrease efficiency—unless you leave one bulb off a lot.

Long-life incandescents are less efficient than standard incandescent bulbs. The manufacturers make these bulbs last longer by using different filaments that burn cooler. While such bulbs last 2,000 to 5,000 hours, they use as much electricity, emit less light, and cost about twice as much as regular incandescents.

A better buy in the realm of extended-life incandescents is the 130-volt bulb. Putting one on a normal 120-volt circuit dims the bulb a little but extends service life to 2,000 hours, compared to 750 hours for ordinary incandescents, and costs only a little more. There are also long-life 130 volt bulbs available. If you want to get both long life *and* high efficiency, use compact fluorescent bulbs.

Warning! Many "energy-saving buttons," often available next to the checkout counter at hardware stores and in mail-order catalogs, may actually waste energy. They are placed inside the incandescent socket before you screw in the bulb. These reduce the wattage of a particular bulb, but they generally reduce light output even more. You'd get the same benefit by simply using a lower wattage bulb. The diode and thermistor kinds of buttons do not save energy or extend bulb life. The exceptions are integrated circuit (IC) units. They have two advantages: they come programmed to turn lights off automatically after a certain period of time, and they "soft-start" the bulb for longer life. These IC buttons are available at many home centers and hardware stores, or from Beacon Lighting (referenced in the resource box) for about $10.

An *"auto-off" incandescent* was introduced by Philips Lighting in 1994. This bulb has a built-in timer that automatically turns off the light after 30 minutes; the off-command can be overridden by switching the light on again after it blinks a minute before it turns off. Even though the bulb will retail for about $5, it might be cost-effective to use it in places such as pantries, garages, or closets if you are forgetful about turning lights off.

Another option is to install integrated circuit socket buttons that screw into the socket under regular incandescents and also automatically turn the bulb off after a certain amount of time. These buttons are not compatible with compact fluorescents, however. For most situations, a better solution is to install dial timers or occupancy sensors.

Tungsten-halogen bulbs

A new generation of incandescents, tungsten-halogen lamps, is the bulb of choice where color quality is critical and the lights may need to be dimmed. They are more expensive than regular incandescents (about $5–$6 apiece) but are 10% more efficient and last up to three times as long. Among the latest developments in halogens is the Halogen-IR™ lamp, which is up to 50% more efficient than conventional incandescents and costs about $11–$13 each. A Halogen-IR bulb achieves greater efficiency because the inside of the lamp base is coated with an infrared-reflective surface that redirects the infrared energy back onto the filament. The bulb uses less electricity to heat the filament to operating temperature. Halogen lamps are now available in a wide variety of floodlight, spotlight, and general-service models, all of which screw into standard sockets.

Compact fluorescent lamps (CFLs)

Not only do CFLs give you a warm-colored light, comparable to incandescents, they are also generally four times as efficient and last 9–13 times as long. But at $8 to $25 a pop for the initial purchase, CFLs aren't cheap, though they *are* cost-effective, with payback periods of three to four years (assuming four hours of use per day). Once a light fixture has been adapted to modular CFLs, plug-in replacement lamps are $3 to $8.

In order to achieve energy savings with a reasonable payback, install CFLs where they'll be used a lot. They're not a wise investment in, say, closets, because those lights are off most of the time. How quickly CFLs pay for themselves will also depend on your electric rate. A person living in Seattle paying five cents/kWh may not want to bother with infrequently used fixtures, but a person in New York paying 16 cents/kWh would find it cost-effective to replace more incandescents.

Regardless of your rate, CFLs are ideal in kitchens, living rooms, next to your favorite reading chair, or in frequently used exterior lights. Temperatures above 95°F may shorten the life of some CFLs. When installing them in enclosed fixtures indoors, select a CFL that is rated to operate up to 140°F.

> **Do not** install CFLs on any circuits controlled with a dimmer, as they will overheat and become a fire hazard.

At present, dimmable, screw-in CFLs are not available; they are expected to enter the market in 1995.

Compact fluorescent bulbs

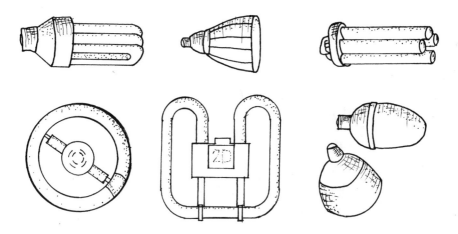

Compact fluorescent bulbs are available in dozens of sizes and shapes, and can replace ordinary incandescents in nearly every application. Install CFLs only in your frequently-used sockets. Illustration by Rocky Mountain Institute, Snowmass, CO.

Because some people may be sensitive to standard magnetically ballasted fluorescents (the light switches on and off at 60 cycles per second), we recommend electronically ballasted fluorescents, which oscillate faster than 20,000 cycles per second, far beyond the range our eyes can detect. They are about 20% more efficient and start instantly. (Magnetically ballasted bulbs may start with a slight delay or momentary flicker.)

Although they're getting more compact every year, many CFLs are larger than their incandescent counterparts and may not fit the same fixture. Measure the maximum width and length that a fixture can accommodate before choosing a replacement. There are lots of different sizes and shapes available—from round globes and cylindrical shapes to floodlights and "halos." You should be able to find one that works for your fixture. If not, a harp extender is a simple, inexpensive way to fit larger CFL bulbs into table and floor lamps (the harp is the rigid piece that supports the lampshade).

CFLs are substantially heavier than standard incandescents. Make sure a CFL won't make your table or floor lamps too top-heavy. This shouldn't be a problem with most electronically ballasted CFLs, which are relatively lightweight.

Retrofit guide to compact fluorescent bulbs

Fixture applications   **Replacement CFLs**

 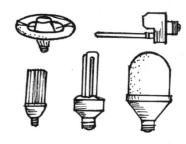

Table and desk lamps are among the easiest fixtures in which to install CFLs. You may need to remove harps, get a harp extender, or use other accessories to accommodate the CFL. Be sure the lamp base is stable and wide enough to support the heavier bulbs. Thirty-watt circlines provide good reading light. CFLs will work with three-way switches—at full light output—in the second and third switch positions, although a few labels forbid such use.

Fixture applications   Replacement CFLs

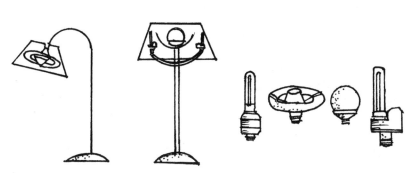

Floor lamps are also easy fixtures to retrofit. Circlines work well in most single-socket floor lamps. Many floor lamps have multiple sockets and can achieve a high light output by using two or more CFLs.

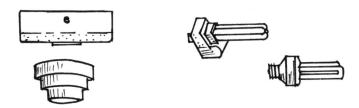

Wall fixtures are among the most difficult to retrofit, because generally there is little room in the fixture. Compact triple lamps and very low-wattage CFLs are good options for wall fixtures where space is tight.

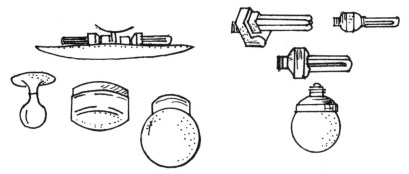

Capsules should be used in bare-bulb applications for aesthetic and safety reasons. Offset ballasts, with ratcheting bases, work well with flat lens ceiling fixtures, which usually have two horizontal sockets: 9- and 13-W quad lamps work well, as higher-wattage units are too heavy. Do not use CFLs in totally enclosed fixtures with little room around the lamp, or heat build-up will cause the product to fail prematurely.

Fixture applications   **Replacement CFLs**

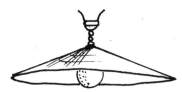

The 15-W globe capsule looks fabulous in a pendant, and provides a soft warm light for dining (where these fixtures are often found). You can install virtually any product in these fixtures, but the globe remains the most appropriate.

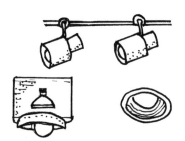   

Track lights generally have little room for CFLs, but where possible, the lightweight electronic units are recommended. For recessed fixtures, either use a reflector product or adapt a 15- or 18-W capsule by adding a reflector collar. Be certain not to install CFLs in any fixtures controlled by a dimmer switch, as many recessed fixtures are.

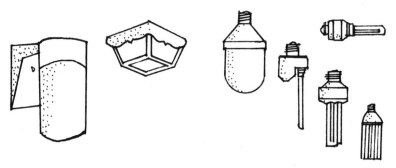

In outdoor fixtures, electronic CFL units start well in temperatures as low as 0°F. Magnetic-ballast CFLs are not recommended for use below 32°F. But if magnetic twin CFLs are protected from the elements, they will light in temperatures down to 10°F, although they will take some time to get to full brightness. All CFLs used outdoors should be protected from rain and moisture. CFLs may not work with some types of timers and photocells.

Outdoor and cold weather applications

CFLs are great as porch lights or security lights that might be on 6 to 12 hours every night. Whereas two 100-watt incandescents will use 700 kWh and cost you around $60 per year, two 27-watt CFLs will consume 200 kWh and cost less than $17 annually, reducing your electric bill enough to pay back the cost of the CFLs in a little over a year. (This calculation does not count the ten incandescent replacement bulbs you'd have to buy; avoiding that further improves the payback.)

If you need a CFL for your porch, garage, or another cold location, confirm that the lamp will work in your climate. Temperatures below freezing inhibit some CFLs in starting and attaining full brightness. While electronically ballasted bulbs start easily in the cold, get smaller wattages (5-, 7-, or 9-watt) if you're buying magnetically ballasted CFLs. Most packaging will identify operating temperatures. Installing the CFL in an enclosed outdoor fixture will temper its environment a little, allowing it to operate below its lowest rated temperature.

Integral versus modular

CFLs can be purchased either as one integral unit or in modular form. Integral units combine a ballast, a screw-in adapter, and a fluorescent tube in one sealed package which must be replaced as a complete unit when the tube "burns out." (Actually, it's the special chemical compounds inside that get exhausted.) In contrast, modular CFLs use a screw-in adapter/ballast and a removable fluorescent tube (usually two to four inches long). Tubes themselves are rated at a 10,000-hour average life, after which they can be replaced.

Since the ballasts used with the fluorescent tube are generally engineered to last for 40,000 to 70,000 hours, a modular compact fluorescent usually represents a better investment than an integral assembly. Both integral and modular CFLs are available with bare bulbs, decorative globes or chimneys, or other accessories to dress them up or distribute the light better.

CFLs are expensive ... or are they?

The price of CFLs has come down dramatically, in part due to utility rebates to both retail customers and manufacturers. Also, improved manufacturing technology and increased demand have driven prices lower. It is now common to be able to buy CFLs for $4 to $12 each with rebates. Check with your utility to see if rebates are available. More discount stores are now carrying CFLs at reasonable prices. If you can't find them locally, several of the mail-order businesses listed in the Appendix sell them.

A tale of two light bulbs— life-cycle costs of two lighting options		
	Incandescent	*Compact fluorescent*
Watts consumed	75 W	18 W
Rated lamp life	750 h	10,000 h
No. lamps used over 10,000 hours	13	1
kWh used over 10,000 hours	750 kWh	180 kWh
Cost per kWh (average)	$0.083	$0.083
Electricity cost per 10,000 hours	$62.25	$14.94
Cost per bulb	$0.75	$20.00
Bulb cost per 10,000 hours	$9.75	$20.00
Total life-cycle cost	$72.00	$34.94
Total savings from this one compact fluorescent = $37.06		

Sound like a good investment? It is, but don't expect the payback to be really fast. Because the lamps last such a long time, you'd have to use one lamp four hours daily for over two years before you'd earn your investment back in lower bills.

In the meantime, however, it will do one of the following:

- Spare the earth more than 1,500 lbs of carbon dioxide and about 20 pounds of sulfur dioxide spewing from the stack of a coal-fired power plant.

- Avoid the production in a nuclear plant of half a curie of high-level radioactive waste (which is a lot) and two-fifths of a ton TNT-equivalent of plutonium.

- Keep an oil-fired power plant from burning 1.25 barrels of oil—enough to run a family car for a thousand miles or to run today's best super-efficient prototype car across the United States from Los Angeles to New York and on to Miami before it needed gas.

One light bulb does all this—and you can screw it in yourself!

A word of caution

Like all fluorescents, CFLs contain very small amounts of mercury vapor, which is integral to the light-generating process. Free mercury will evaporate rapidly into the air if a fluorescent lamp is broken. Such a minuscule amount of mercury is not a health hazard, but if you do break a bulb in a small unventilated area, you may want to take the precaution of leaving the room until it has had time to ventilate, since mercury is an inhalable, cumulative poison.

Magnetically ballasted CFLs also contain a very small amount of krypton-85 or promethium-147, radioactive isotopes that help start the bulb. The amount of radiation that you'll encounter from working in close proximity to such bulbs is less than one millionth of one percent of typical background radiation. Even at a lamp-manufacturing plant, a worker who is handling these bulbs all day long will, over the course of a year, receive less radiation than the cosmic bombardment an airline passenger receives on a flight from Chicago to New

York. We don't consider these levels of radioactivity a concern, but if you do, get electronically ballasted integral CFLs, which contain no radioactive elements. They're also more efficient.

Tube fluorescents

Standard fluorescent tube lighting has come a long way from the ghostly, flickering, humming light often associated with it. Now, high-frequency electronic ballasts eliminate flicker while reducing power consumption 25–40% compared to electro-magnetic ballasts. High-performance electronic ballasts, which cost a little more, also eliminate hum. Special tri-chromatic, rare-earth phosphors produce a high-quality light that shows colors accurately. These lamps are available in various color temperatures, and you can select warmer or cooler tones. Skinny T-8 tubes, one inch in diameter, are more efficient than older tubes, and lamps with electronic ballasts use less elec-tricity than magnetic ones.

Specialty manufacturers make the most of efficient bulbs by combining electronic ballasts, better reflectors, diffusers, and lenses to create state-of-the-art systems. Since a great variety of well-designed fixtures is available, you can now install tube fluorescents in more places than just the basement.

Full-spectrum

Many lighting manufacturers make full-spectrum fluorescent tubes to emulate natural sunlight. Some users think these lights are more pleasing and render colors more accurately. Costs are around $4 or $5 per bulb. People suffering from Sea-sonal Affective Disorder may indeed benefit from using full-spectrum lighting, but be cautious about accepting wild-sounding claims for the health benefits of full-spectrum light-ing: one company has been ordered to cease making unsub-stantiated claims about its lamps.

Sensors, photocells, & photovoltaics

Want to automate your lighting system? Here are a few convenient control devices to light your way. Occupancy sensors,
which cost about $25 to $50, detect the presence of people in
an area, indoors or out, and turn lights on and off as people
come and go. They'll greet you with light as you enter driveways, walkways and entryways. They are also handy for areas
like workshops and laundry rooms, where you often have
your hands full and it's a drag to fumble in the dark for the
switch.

An occupancy sensor

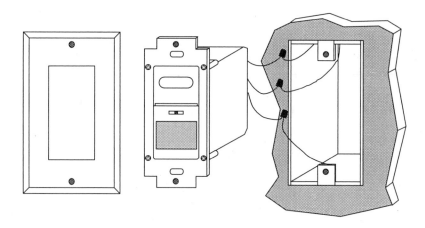

Occupancy sensors, which are usually mounted in ordinary lightswitch
boxes, turn lights off after they detect no motion or heat from occupants for a
pre-set period of time. Illustration courtesy of WattStopper, Inc., Plano, TX.

Some occupancy sensors directly replace existing wall switches, and others can be built into new fixtures or come as self-
contained units. Some new room sensors are designed to be
turned on manually and off automatically if there's no motion
in the room for a specified period of time.

Occupancy sensors have infrared and/or ultrasonic sensors. Use the infrared units where the sensor can "see" the entire area you want covered; use the ultrasonic option where the sensor must "hear" changes in the ultrasonic "signature" of the room. Infrared sensors detect heat radiation emitted by warm bodies, whereas ultrasonic units emit an ultrasonic pulse and detect changes in the reflected signal.

Photocell controls sense daylight and switch your lights on at dusk and off at dawn. Timers provide a convenient way to turn your lights on and off at preset times. Photocell controls cost $10 to $25 and timers $10 to $75. To provide the ultimate in convenience and efficiency, you can use any combination of these controls in tandem. Just make sure the controls are electrically compatible with each other as well as the light source.

It often makes sense to install photovoltaic (PV) lights in places where running electric wiring is expensive, such as a garden, walkway, or driveway. Electricity generated during sunlight hours by small integrated panels is stored in batteries; this electricity is then used at night to light the way. Motion sensors are sometimes built in to turn the lights on only when needed.

Where to find

CFLs, occupancy sensors, photocells, and timers

Most lighting showrooms, home centers, and hardware stores should be able to get them, or you should be able to pick them up yourself from a good electrical supply house. Several of the mail-order houses listed in the Appendix also sell efficient lighting equipment.

Beacon Lighting, 723 West Taylor Avenue, Meridian, ID 83682, (208) 888-5905, sells the Bulb Boss™ integrated circuit socket buttons.

Energy Federation, Inc., 14 Tech Circle, Natick, MA 01760, (800) 876-0660, sells occupancy sensors and timers no more difficult to install than a light switch. Also sells several brands of CFLs.

General Electric, (800) 626-2000, makes compact fluorescents, halogens, the new "Genura" induction lamp, and other lamps.

Intersource Technologies, 130 Kifer Court, Sunnyvale, CA 94086, (818) 248-2116, makes the radio frequency E-Lamp (which is expected on the market in 1995).

Juno Lighting, 2001 Mt. Prospect, Des Plaines, IL 60018, (800) 323-5068, makes airtight recessed fixtures.

Lights of America, 611 Reyes Dr., Walnut, CA 91789, (800) 321-8100, makes circline and other compact fluorescent lamps.

Osram Sylvania, Customer Service, 18725 North Union, Westfield, IN 46074, (800) 842-7010, makes compact fluorescent lamps..

Panasonic, One Panasonic Way, Mail Code 4A-4, Secaucus, NJ 07094, (800) 545-2672, makes compact fluorescents and other lamps.

Philips Lighting, 200 Franklin Square Drive, Somerset, NJ 08875-6800, (908) 563-3000, makes compact fluorescent lamps.

Real Goods Trading Corporation, 966 Mazzoni Street, Ukiah, CA 95482, (800) 762-7323, sells a wide selection of compact fluorescents, photovoltaic (PV) battery chargers, and PV yard lights. Also publishes the useful guide to lighting products *Book of Light*.

Watt Stopper, 400 Chisholm Place, Suite 314, Plano, TX 75075, (800) 879-8585, makes a variety of occupancy sensors.

lighting technology and design

"Energy-Efficient Lighting for the Home," by Jeanne Byrne, *Home Energy* magazine, November/December 1994, pp. 53–60.

Guide to Energy-Efficient Building Products: Lighting Products, Florida Solar Energy Center, 300 State Road 401, Cape Canaveral, FL 32920, (407) 783-0300. $5.

Lighting Options for Homes, is a 21 minute video available from Iris Communications, 258 East 10th Avenue, Suite E, Eugene, OR 97401-3284, (800) 346-0104. $20.

Lighting Options for Homes is also the title of a book published by Bonneville Power Administration, Public Information Center, PO Box 3621, Portland OR 97208, (503) 230-3478.

The Lighting Pattern Book for Homes, Russell Leslie, Kathryn Conway, Lighting Research Center, Rensselaer Polytechnic Institute, Troy, NY 12180-3590, (518) 276-8716. $50.

Rising Sun Enterprises, 40 Sunset Drive, Suite 1, Basalt, CO 81621, (303) 927-8051, does complete turn-key residential and commercial efficient lighting design and installation.

organizations

American Lighting Association, 435 North Michigan Avenue, Suite 1717, Chicago, IL 60611, (312) 644-0828.

Green Lights, U.S. Environmental Protection Agency, 401 M Street SW, Washington, DC 20460, (202) 775-6650.

Lighting Design Laboratory, Seattle City Light, 400 East Pine, Seattle, WA 98101, (800) 354-3864.

Lighting Research Center, Rensselaer Polytechnic Institute, Troy, NY 12180-3590, (518) 276-8716.

National Lighting Bureau, 2101 L Street NW, Suite 300, Washington, DC 20037, (202) 457-8437.

10

New Home Construction: Doing It Right the First Time

If you cannot afford to do it right the first time, how come you can afford to do it twice? —Ivar Eidsmo, master builder

Building a new home? Remodeling an existing one? You've got a once-in-a-lifetime opportunity to do it right. While it may cost a little extra to build a resource-efficient home, the additional cost will be rapidly repaid by big savings on your energy bills. The investment will also make your home more attractive, comfortable, and valuable, and the cost is tax-deductible with your mortgage, whereas energy bills are not.

In very cold climates, the key to energy efficiency in new construction is passive solar design coupled with superinsulation. The extra insulation may even pay for itself immediately by making it possible for you to install smaller, less expensive heating and cooling systems—or none at all.

Please note that this chapter is not a comprehensive guide to building a resource-efficient home. Instead, it simply lists the areas new home builders should consider and offers a framework in which to think about the challenge. By building correctly for your climate, you can reduce energy bills and live more comfortably and lightly on the planet.

While building a state-of-the-art low-energy home is environmentally responsible and will benefit your pocketbook, it is not enough. We must also reduce the amount of energy "embodied" in and the environmental impact caused by harvesting and manufacturing the materials that go into the home. As Alex Wilson of *Environmental Building News* points out, the energy necessary to build an energy-efficient home may be greater than it will consume over its fifty-year life. Architects and builders must improve planning and construction methods to reduce materials waste, and environmentally responsible materials should be selected. (For further information, see RMI's *A Primer on Sustainable Building,* and other resources listed at the end of the chapter.)

Renewable energy

Thousands of homes across the country rely exclusively on the sun, wind, wood, or flowing water for energy to power or heat their home. Electric "off-grid" homes are usually located a half a mile or more from utility power lines. Other homes rely on photovoltaic panels or other renewable technology to generate most of the electricity needed, but are also hooked up to the utility grid. Superefficient design is imperative, with particular attention paid to electric efficiency to reduce the expense of the photovoltaic, wind, or microhydro electricity generating equipment. See the Appendix for books and organizations that can help you get the most appropriate, reliable, and cost-effective renewable electric system for your home.

Photovoltaic and wind system on a home

Solar, wind, and small hydro systems can generate electricity for independent homes in town or in the back woods. Such systems are far more cost-effective if the home incorporates the electricity-saving technologies described in this book. Adapted from an illustration by Real Goods Trading Corporation (1990), *Alternative Energy Sourcebook*, p. 9, Ukiah, CA.

Passive solar design

In new home construction throughout America, solar design principles can be incorporated to save anywhere from 10 to 95+% of a building's heating requirements. Solar design can be as simple as orienting the house to face south, with windows collecting enough solar heat to reduce heating bills by 10 to 20%. A more comprehensive solar design carefully calculates solar gain through windows or a greenhouse, rate of heat loss, and heat absorption and storage in walls and floors made of brick, stone, concrete, adobe, rammed earth, or tile.

Solar homes can look just like conventional houses. The essential components of a well-designed passive solar house are siting, orientation, climate-based design, high-performance windows (which allow solar gain but control overheating and reduce heat loss), proper shading techniques (especially calculated overhangs), superinsulation, and walls or floors that store the heat gained during the day. Windows can easily provide more net heat gain per square foot than solar collectors. Other ways to store heat energy—rock beds, Trombe walls, and water systems—have proven effective, but often involve greater expense, complexity, or loss of views. See the end of the chapter and Appendix for in-depth passive solar resources.

Basic components of a typical passive solar house

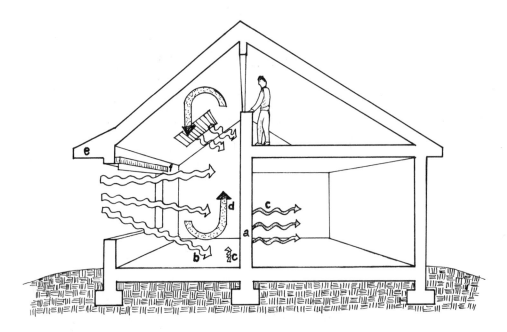

An effective passive solar home balances four key design elements: *collection* through south-facing windows; *storage* in (a) thermal mass wall and (b) tile floor; *distribution:* radiant heat from (c) wall and floor and (d) natural convection; and *control* by (e) overhang to block summer sun and (f) sun-control blinds or climate-specific high-performance windows. Illustration courtesy E SOURCE (1993), *Space Heating Technology Atlas*, p. 62, Boulder, CO.

Typical additional construction costs range from $1,000 to $5,000. It is possible to build a passive solar home that costs no more than (or less than) conventional construction if the extra insulation and high-performance windows allow heating and cooling equipment to be downsized or eliminated. It often makes sense to incorporate active solar space and water heating systems; see the *Home Heating* and *Hot Water* chapters.

Before you build

√ Planning

This is one of your best investments and easiest ways to avoid mistakes you might regret for decades. Here is where you'll make nearly all of the decisions that will determine the long-term cost and performance of your home, not to mention its comfort, beauty, and environmental impact.

√ Choosing the site

Before you design your house (or even as you look for land to buy), consider the local environment: where does the sun rise, travel, and set over the four seasons? Ask a solar professional to do a solar survey for you. Which trees or buildings shade the sun during the day? Which views do you most want to preserve (or block) from your home? Where do prevailing winds come from? Ask your future neighbors for advice. Spend some time on the land to familiarize yourself with the environment. Consider living near where you work, shop, play, or your kids go to school to reduce driving and facilitate walking, bicycling, or using mass transit.

√ Hiring the architect

Select an architect familiar with passive solar design, optimal insulation levels for your climate, efficient appliances, high-performance windows, and good energy and building design principles. Ask for references, visit the architect's completed homes, and, if possible, talk to the owners. Ask prospective architects (and builders) to sign energy performance contracts.

√ House shape

A building's shape will influence where chilling winds enter the house, where snow piles up outside, how cooling breezes flow through, and how much solar gain you can count on. Simplifying a building's layout and footprint makes it easier and less expensive to build, tends to improve its insulating value and air tightness, and requires fewer construction materials. A lot of time and resources can be saved if designs are based on typical lumber sizes and framing patterns.

√ Use shading

Think carefully about structural and exterior shading for solar gain control: roof overhangs, covered patios, canvas covering, and awnings. Shading options will be different for each side of the house and for every climate. (See the *Cooling* and *Heating* chapters for more information.)

√ Preserve trees

Preserve as many of the trees on the site as you can, particularly in hot climates where shade trees can help keep a lid on your air conditioning bills. Vegetation reduces ambient outdoor temperatures, blocks and channels wind, and provides habitat for birds and other backyard wildlife.

√ Hiring the builder

Pick a builder familiar with energy-efficient construction, insulation, and air leakage control techniques. Resource-efficient building techniques are evolving quickly, and many builders simply don't keep up with new materials and techniques.

√ Active solar heating

If you are interested in cost-effective and appropriate use of solar space and water heating for your climate, call a local solar contractor. Modern solar equipment is more reliable and efficient than it used to be, but system selection and installation quality varies: get references from contractors, visit the sites of completed installations, and talk to the owners. Call your regional solar or sustainable energy society for referrals. (The American Solar Energy Society—listed in the Appendix—can refer you to the nearest association.)

√ Construction materials

Consider using alternative construction materials such as rammed earth and genuine adobe in dry climates, straw bales, and recycled plastic siding and roof shingles, or request lumber that is certified as sustainably grown and harvested. These types of materials are not widely available, but more consumer requests will help bring such materials to market.

The rising cost of lumber—wrongly blamed on efforts to protect ancient forests and wildlife—has increased interest in alternative building materials. Many systems use recycled or waste materials, frequently cost less and perform better, and are often less destructive to the environment than conventional materials. (The Appendix lists many books, magazines, and organizations you can consult for further information.)

Design homes with available lumber sizes in mind to minimize cutting waste. Plan for waste minimization and materials recycling at the job site. Use natural materials and low-VOC adhesives and wood preservatives.

√ Insulation

Remember—it is almost always cost-effective to exceed building energy and insulation codes. While there are diminishing returns with additional amounts of insulation, the optimal level for your climate is often more than called for by local building codes, architects, and builders. Be sure to specify foundation or stemwall insulation. If you're planning on pouring a slab on grade in a cold climate, it is best to insulate under the slab; in hot climates, it's usually better to keep the slab coupled to the cooler earth below by *not* insulating under it. (Please see the *Insulation* chapter for details.)

√ Radon

Test your site for the presence of radon in the soil. If radon is a potential problem, design and install a system to avoid its infiltration into the house. It is far cheaper to do it right as you build than to correct a radon problem after the house is done.

√ Window selection

Provide good daylighting with windows or clerestories. Only specify skylights if you plan on buying ones suitable for your climate; skylights can be tremendous sources of unwanted heat gain or heat loss. Proper window selection is critical in every climate. (See the *Windows* chapter for details.)

√ Recycling

Design spaces in your kitchen and garage for easy handling of recyclables and compostables. Plan pantries and storage places to facilitate the use of bulk foods to reduce packaging waste.

√ Water recovery

Plan on capturing and storing the water (or melting snow) from your roof in a cistern, small pond, or on the roof itself. If this is done right—and if you revegetate with native plants, grasses, shrubs, and trees—most of your outdoor watering can be so supplied. After all, nobody watered *before* you built.

√ Pollution

Make sure you design and build a safe, healthy house. The best way to avoid household pollution problems is to avoid toxic materials in the first place. Read up on energy-efficient housing design and insist that the architect and builder use healthy, nontoxic materials for you and the planet. (See the Indoor Air Quality section in the *Weatherization* chapter)

Bigelow Homes

Perry Bigelow has built energy-efficient custom and townhomes in the Chicago area for years. Realizing that customers may not value the special features of efficient construction, he offered a guarantee to new homebuyers that their heating bills will not exceed $200 per year (many residents spend less than $100 annually) or Bigelow will pay the difference. The company's emphasis on well-insulated walls, attics, and basements, good air-sealing techniques, low-e gas-filled windows, an integrated water- and space-heating system, and efficient lighting pays off for the homeowners. Bigelow has succeeded in adding value and competitiveness to his homes while only adding an estimated $500 to $700 to their cost, compared to conventional design and construction.

Source: *Home Energy*, February 1994, pp. 13-18. Bigelow Homes is based in Palatine, IL

As you build

√ Air leaks

Seal potential air leaks while building. Use sill seals under framing walls and on top of foundation walls. Fill plumbing and electrical penetrations with fiberglass to prevent air leakage—especially those holes between the living space and the basement, crawlspace, and attic. Seal and flash around the chimney and other penetrations. Pay particular attention to sealing potential leaks in the attic and around the foundation.

Use caulk, expanding foam, gaskets, insulation, and other air-sealing materials. Don't forget to seal and insulate ductwork. In areas with radon, seal cracks in slabs on grade after curing.

√ Weatherstripping

Weatherstrip all windows and doors, including doors to an unheated basement, garage, and the attic door or hatch.

√ Moisture

Be sure to address potential moisture problems. Local conditions and recommendations vary, particularly in humid climates, so check with local builders who keep well-informed. (See the moisture section in the *Weatherization* chapter.)

√ Ventilation

Locate operable windows or vents both high and low so that excessive warm air can escape naturally. In hot climates, consider installing a whole-house fan. You may need to provide mechanical ventilation to handle moisture and air quality problems. In cold climates it is usually cost-effective to install heat recovery ventilators. Install a whole house air-to-air heat exchanger with intakes in the bathrooms and above the kitchen stove to provide fresh air.

√ Framing

In colder climates, use 2x6 construction at 24 inches on center and consider wrapping the exterior with rigid foam insulation boards. Window and door headers should be well insulated. Some builders, unfamiliar with good framing technique, will over-frame and leave only 70% as insulatable voids. This wastes lumber and reduces overall wall insulation, since framing conducts three times more heat than insulation. Block off or seal against air conduits in walls, between floors, into the attic or roof structure, and from the basement.

Advanced framing technique

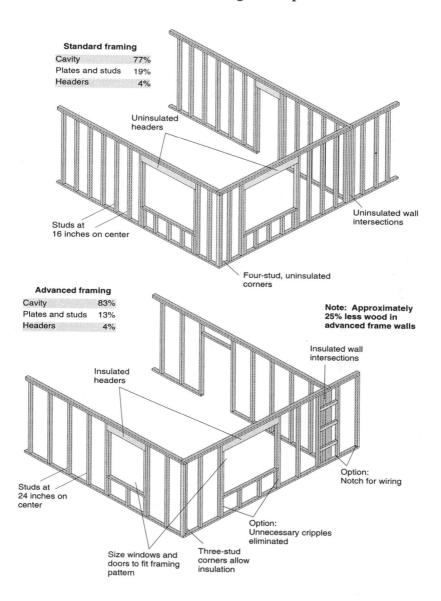

Standard framing

Cavity	77%
Plates and studs	19%
Headers	4%

Uninsulated headers

Studs at 16 inches on center

Uninsulated wall intersections

Four-stud, uninsulated corners

Advanced framing

Cavity	83%
Plates and studs	13%
Headers	4%

Note: Approximately 25% less wood in advanced frame walls

Insulated headers

Insulated wall intersections

Studs at 24 inches on center

Option: Notch for wiring

Option: Unnecessary cripples eliminated

Size windows and doors to fit framing pattern

Three-stud corners allow insulation

Advanced framing practice reduces the amount and cost of framing lumber and construction time, and improves thermal performance by allowing more space for insulation. Illustration courtesy of E SOURCE (1993), *Space Heating Technology Atlas*, p. 85, Boulder, CO.

√ Insulation

Make sure your insulation contractor is doing a thorough job of installing the insulation. Many contractors hurry through jobs and end up leaving gaps in the insulation, not insulating properly behind or around light fixtures, electrical boxes, window and door frames, rim joists, kneewalls, plumbing penetrations, and so on. If you want a good job done, hire a conscientious contractor to oversee the work, or inspect it yourself daily.

√ Windows

In cold climates, use superwindows with good thermal breaks and low air leakage. In hot climates, use low-e windows with a low shading coefficient for solar gain control. (See the *Windows* chapter for details.)

√ Garage door

Buy a garage door with windows to provide natural lighting and, if facing south, solar heat gain. In cold climates, get an insulated and weatherstripped garage door.

√ Air conditioning

If your climate justifies a central air conditioning system, minimize your home's cooling load first by following the steps above for insulation, air leakage, and high-performance windows. Then buy a small system with a high SEER (Seasonal Energy Efficiency Ratio) rating. Shade the outside unit.

√ Heating system

Buy sealed combustion furnaces and boilers that use outside air (rather than heated inside air) for combustion. Install high-efficiency condensing gas models if possible. Avoid electric resistance heating for all but the most energy-efficient homes in mild climates—it's cheap up front but over its lifetime will cost, in higher energy bills, far more than other options. Consider heat pumps and the other systems discussed in the *Home Heating* chapter.

√ Ducts

Put all forced-air ductwork inside the insulated envelope (*i.e.*, not above the attic insulation or below the basement insulation). Seal all joints and seams and insulate ductwork as you build. Avoid crimping the air flow with tight turns and constricted ducts.

√ Appliances

Install an efficient refrigerator, clothes washer, dryer, and other appliances. Place the refrigerator away from the range and dishwasher and out of direct sunshine. Do not install a clothes dryer in a cold and damp basement. (Make sure you don't *build* a cold and damp basement.)

√ Lighting

Use electronically ballasted, modular fluorescent lamps and efficient fixtures where appropriate. If you are specifying recessed lighting fixtures, be sure to get models rated for insulation contact (IC) to reduce convective heat losses through the fixture. Some manufacturers make fixtures with superior air leakage control. Maximize effective use of daylighting.

√ Plumbing

Install water-efficient toilets (maximum 1.6 gallons per flush), showerheads, and faucet aerators. A compact house design or stacked bathrooms will allow you to minimize the length of pipe runs, which will save water, reduce hot water distribution losses, and get you the hot water quicker. If installing a pool, specify 2" PVC piping to increase circulation efficiency.

√ Water heater

Install a solar or an energy-efficient gas water heater, air- or ground-source heat-pump water heater, or desuperheater. Consider installing whole-house or point-of-use tankless water heaters. If you're buying a conventional storage tank, get a well-insulated one with built-in anti-convection valves, and add a bottom board. Assess whether a solar water heating system makes sense. (See the *Hot Water* chapter for details.)

√ Piping

Insulate all hot water pipes along their entire length. This may not be strictly cost-effective, but it will reduce energy and water waste and keep the hot water warmer in between uses.

√ Siding and roofing

Side and roof with light-colored materials, especially in warm and hot climates, to reduce heat gain. "White" asphalt shingles, however, absorb most of the solar energy hitting them.

After you build

√ Landscaping

Landscape with deciduous trees to the south, west, and east to reduce cooling costs, and with evergreens to the north to block the wind. Deciduous trees can reduce your wintertime solar gain significantly, however, so you may want to consider high-performance windows and proper shading options instead. The best option is to landscape for solar gain control on the east and west, and provide a roof overhang on the south for summertime shading and optimal solar gain in the winter. Revegetate the site with native plants. (See the Appendix for books and organizations that can help you.)

√ Drainage

Drain water runoff from the roof away from the house, prefer-ably into a cistern or garden pond, and certainly away from the foundation.

√ Then what?

Move in and enjoy your comfortable and resource-efficient home. Spread the word about your success, and encourage others in the community to learn from your example. Pass this book on to friends, neighbors, and colleagues who'd use it.

A rammed earth home in Old Snowmass, Colorado

This passive solar, super-insulated, rammed earth house was designed and built by the author and his family. Illustration by David Gross, Public Image, Boulder, CO.

A Colorado passive solar home

The author's 4,000 ft^2 owner-built superinsulated passive solar home was completed in 1993 near Rocky Mountain Institute in Old Snowmass, Colorado. The family wanted to gain some experience with the ideas discussed in this book as well as live in their handiwork. The 24-inch sculpted and plastered rammed earth walls are made of compressed local dirt and act as the home's thermal mass, storing the solar heat gain and moderating daily and seasonal temperature swings. They are insulated twice as well as local building codes require. Superwindows cut heat loss while permitting lots of solar gain and controlling overheating during the summer.

The home is comfortable year-round with very little fossil energy input, and the yearly energy bills are about a dime per ft^2—one-eighth of what other homeowners in the area pay. Electric bills average $16 per month and space and water heating about $45 per month during the cold season. (This will drop to near zero when the solar collectors are hooked up.) The passive solar design captures nearly all of the wintertime heat needed. The solar thermal collectors will pick up most of the rest by pumping their warm fluid through the radiant floors. They have a small, efficient propane boiler as a back-up system for those long and cloudy periods that occasionally occur here at 7,500 feet in the Rockies.

This southwestern style home makes good use of daylighting and uses off-the-shelf efficient lighting and appliances. Rain and snowmelt is diverted and stored in two small ponds, and water-saving fixtures are installed throughout. Cork floor tiles and other sustainably harvested materials are also used. Most remarkable of all is that the home was built for a fraction of prevailing construction costs in the area: $35 per ft^2 (which doesn't include family labor and ingenuity).

Where to find

information on efficient construction

Builder's Booksource, 1817 4th Street, Berkeley, CA 94710, (800) 843-2028. Order their free *Builder's Booksource Newsletter*.

Builders' Field Guide to Energy Efficient Construction, by Super Good Cents, Southern Electric International (1991), 64 Perimeter Center East, Atlanta, GA 30346, (404) 668-3445.

Climatic Building Design: Energy-Efficient Building Principles and Practice, by Donald Watson and K. Labs (1992), McGraw-Hill, Blue Ridge Summit, PA 17294, (800) 262- 4729.

The Efficient House Sourcebook, 3rd edition, by Rocky Mountain Institute (1992), is an annotated listing of books and organizations that will help you design for energy efficiency.

Energy Source Directory: A Guide to Products Used in Energy-Efficient Residential Buildings, by Iris Communications, 258 East 10th Avenue, Suite E, Eugene, OR 97401-3284, (800) 346-0104.

Guide to Resource Efficient Building Elements, by Steve Loken (1993), Center for Resourceful Building Technology, PO Box 3866, Missoula, MT 59806, (406) 549-7678.

Healthy House Building: A Design and Construction Guide, John Bower (1993), Healthy House Institute, 7471 North Shiloh Road, Unionville, IN 47468, (812) 332-5073.

Passive Solar Energy: The Homeowners' Guide to Natural Heating and Cooling, Bruce Anderson and Malcolm Wells, Brick House Publishing Co., PO Box 256, Amherst, NH 03031, (800) 446-8642.

A Primer on Sustainable Building, by Dianna Lopez Barnett and William D. Browning, Rocky Mountain Institute (1995), is a basic handbook on sustainable design and construction, with information on siting, orientation, house shape, building materials, designing for community, renewable energy, revegetation, etc.

Residential Building Design and Construction Workbook, 2nd edition, by
Ned Nisson, 1988, Cutter Information, 37 Broadway, Arlington,
MA 02174, (800) 964-5118 or (617) 641-5118.

Sourcebook for Sustainable Design, Boston Society of Architects, 52
Broad Street, Boston, MA 02109, (617) 951-1433, $28.

Superinsulated Design and Construction: A Guide to Building Energy-Ef-
ficient Homes, by Lenchek, Mattock, & Raabe, 1987, Van Nostrand
Reinhold, 115 Fifth Ave., New York, NY 10023, (800) 842-3636.

Additional books on energy- and water-saving house design are listed in the book section of the *Appendix.* You'll also find there books on
healthy, non-toxic building materials and passive solar design, plus
several government and private organizations that can help you in
your search for a house that's healthy to live in, friendly to the environment, and easy on your pocketbook. Some utilities offer financial
incentives or free technical advice to help you build a more efficient
home. State energy office phone numbers are listed in the *Appendix,*
which also lists Demonstration Centers and Owner-Builder Schools.

organizations

Energy Efficient Building Association, 1829 Portland Avenue, Minneapolis, MN 55404-1898, (612) 871-0413, has numerous publications and videos on energy-efficient design.

National Association of Home Builders, 1201 15th Street NW,
Washington, D.C. 20005, (202) 822-0200.

Northeast Sustainable Energy Association, 23 Ames Street, Green-
field, MA 01301, (413) 774-6051.

Northwest Ecobuilding Guild, 217 Ninth Avenue, Seattle, WA,
98109, (206) 634-3702.

Passive Solar Industries Council, 1511 K Street NW, Suite 600,
Washington, D.C. 20003, (202) 628-7400, has workbooks and software packages on passive solar design.

U.S. Green Building Council, 1615 L Street NW, Suite 1200, Washington, D.C. 20036-6300, (202) 466-6300.

Appendix

For More Information

. . . the truth lies somewhere, if we knew but where.
—William Cowper

Throughout this book we have referred to books, organizations, state energy offices, utilities, mail-order houses, and Federal sources of information. This Appendix lists all of these sources and more, in separate sections, to facilitate your search for information on what to do, when and where, which technologies to use, and why.

In your quest for information, ask for help. Contact your local utility. Most of the nation's utility companies have "demand-side management" programs that promote the efficient use of electricity, though many are cutting back. Some utilities have public resource centers that demonstrate efficient lighting and appliances and discuss design tips and ideas on how to button up your house. Most state energy offices provide free information too, and we have listed their telephone numbers in this Appendix. You will also find several regional non-profit energy centers eager to help you.

State Energy Offices

State energy offices may be your best source of free energy-efficiency information. Most state energy offices have detailed "how-to" booklets on insulation, weatherization, heating and cooling, appliances, and so on. Particularly useful might be local references, leads to financial assistance, and climate-specific information. Regrettably, some states have feeble energy service and public education programs, in which case we hope the rest of this Appendix proves useful to you in your search for information.

	In-state WATS number	Direct dial number
Puerto Rico		(809) 721-0809
Alabama	(800) 452-5901	(205) 348-4523
Alaska	(800) 478-3744	(907) 563-6749
Arizona	(800) 352-5499	(602) 280-1402
Arkansas		(501) 682-1370
California	(800) 772-3300	(916) 654-5106
Colorado	(800) 632-6662	(303) 620-4292
Connecticut		(203) 566-5898
Delaware	(800) 282-8616	(302) 739-5644
District of Columbia		(202) 727-1800
Florida		(904) 488-6764
Georgia		(404) 656-5176
Hawaii		(808) 587-3800
Idaho	(800) 334-7283	(208) 327-7870
Illinois	(800) 252-8955	(217) 785-5222
Indiana	(800) 382-4631	(317) 232-8940
Iowa		(515) 281-4739
Kansas	(800) 752-4422	(913) 296-2686
Kentucky	(800) 282-0868	(502) 564-7192
Louisiana		(504) 342-1399

Maine		(207) 624-6800
Maryland	(800) 723-6374	(410) 974-3751
Massachusetts		(617) 727-4732
Michigan		(517) 334-6261
Minnesota	(800) 657-3710	(612) 296-5175
Mississippi	(800) 222-8311	(601) 359-6600
Missouri	(800) 334-6946	(314) 751-7056
Montana		(406) 444-6697
Nebraska		(402) 471-2867
Nevada		(702) 687-4909
New Hampshire	(800) 852-3466	(603) 271-2611
New Jersey	(800) 492-4242	(201) 648-7265
New Mexico	(800) 451-2541	(505) 827-5900
New York	(800) 423-7283	(518) 473-4377
North Carolina	(800) 662-7131	(919) 733-2230
North Dakota		(701) 238-2094
Ohio	(800) 848-1300	(614) 466-6797
Oklahoma	(800) 879-6552	(405) 843-9770
Oregon	(800) 221-8035	(503) 378-4040
Pennsylvania	(800) 692-7312	(717) 783-9981
Rhode Island		(401) 277-6920
South Carolina	(800) 851-8899	(803) 737-8030
South Dakota	(800) 872-6190	(605) 773-5032
Tennessee	(800) 342-1340	(615) 741-2994
Texas		(512) 463-1931
Utah	(800) 662-3633	(801) 538-8690
Vermont	(800) 828-4069	(802) 828-2393
Virginia		(804) 692-3220
Washington	(800) 962-9731	(206) 296-5640
West Virginia		(304) 293-2636
Wisconsin		(608) 266-8234
Wyoming		(307) 777-7284

Federal Information Sources

Your tax dollars support these worthwhile programs. Get your money's worth. Give 'em a call.

**Energy Efficiency and
Renewable Energy
Clearinghouse**
PO Box 3048
Merrifield, VA 22116
(800) 363-3732 (DOE-EREC)
(800) 523-2929
Start with EREC for basic information on the full spectrum of renewable energy technologies and household energy- and water-efficiency opportunities. EREC provides free consumer information, materials, and technical advice, and is funded by the U.S. Department of Energy. They also have a computer bulletin board, and can refer you to manufacturers of resource-efficient equipment.

**Environmental Protection
Agency**
Public Information Center
401 M Street SW
Washington, D.C. 20460
(202) 260-2080
The EPA provides an information service with referrals to various EPA hotlines and programs: radon, indoor air quality, asbestos, drinking water, hazardous materials, efficient commercial lighting, computers, and buildings.

**Housing and Urban
Development**
HUD USER
PO Box 6091
Rockville, MD 20850
(800) 245-2691
HUD USER maintains information on subjects that include public and assisted housing, building technology, community development, residential energy conservation, fairness in housing, housing rehabilitation, and state weatherization assistance programs for low-income families.

**Lawrence Berkeley
Laboratory**
1 Cyclotron Road
Building 90, Room 4000
Berkeley, CA 94720
(510) 486-7489
LBL is a national research laboratory that does work on building energy analysis, building science, modeling software, high-performance windows, lighting, etc. Call for a list of publications and research papers.

National Energy Information Center

U.S. Department of Energy
1F-048 Forrestal Building
1000 Independence Avenue SW
Washington, D.C. 20585
(202) 586-8800

The NEIC disseminates energy statistics to Federal, state, and local agencies, the academic community, industrial and commercial organizations, and the public. Information provided at no charge over the phone includes data on energy extraction, electricity generation, imports, consumption by sectors, detailed residential energy consumption statistics, etc.

National Institute of Building Sciences

Building Environment and
Thermal Envelope Council
1201 L Street NW, Suite 400
Washington, D.C. 20005
(202) 289-7800

The Institute coordinates research and promotes publications relating to building, thermal envelope performance, and new technologies and construction techniques.

National Renewable Energy Laboratory

1617 Cole Boulevard
Golden, CO 80401
(303) 275-4099

NREL is the nation's principal research, demonstration, and development laboratory of solar, wind, and other promising renewable energy technologies. The laboratory publishes numerous technical and popular reports on residential, commercial, utility, indus-

trial, and transportation uses of renewable energy. The number listed is for the public education office.

National Technical Information Service

5285 Port Royal Road
Springfield, VA 22161
(703) 487-4650

NTIS provides access to information from the Federally funded research laboratories and government departments. They can provide research papers on specific topics of interest, usually at relatively low cost.

Oak Ridge National Laboratory

Building Technologies Center
PO Box 2008
Oak Ridge, TN 37831-6070
(615) 574-1945

Conducts research and publishes papers on energy-efficient buildings, building science, insulation, moisture, heating & cooling equipment, indoor air quality, ventilation, and renewable energy topics.

U.S. Government Printing Office

732 North Capitol Street NW
Washington, D.C. 20401
(202) 512-0000

The GPO sells thousands of government reports, most at reasonable prices, and many helpful to consumers and homeowners. You may want to check your phone book first for regional GPO offices. If you have the exact title and document number, call the sales office at (202) 512-1800.

Selected Nonprofit Groups

Many national and regional energy groups have been created to help you find the right energy solutions and technologies for your housing type and climate. All of the organizations below publish papers on home energy, efficient residential design, building energy codes, and related issues. Most cannot answer detailed or site-specific questions, but can refer you to another helpful organization.

Alliance to Save Energy
1725 K Street NW, Suite 914
Washington, D.C. 20006-1401
(202) 857-0666
The Alliance provides materials on home energy rating systems, building codes, and efficient new construction and design.

American Council for an Energy-Efficient Economy
1001 Connecticut Ave. NW, #801
Washington, D.C. 20036
(202) 429-8873
ACEEE publishes books and papers on industrial, commercial, and residential energy efficiency (including the *Consumer Guide to Home Energy Savings*). The Council sponsors a bi-annual conference on efficient buildings.

American Solar Energy Society
2400 Central Avenue, Suite G-1
Boulder, CO 80301
(303) 443-3130
ASES researches practical uses of solar heating and electricity, so-lar buildings, and other renewables. Call them for a list of regional solar energy associations.

Building Research Council
School of Architecture
University of Illinois at Champaign-Urbana
One East St. Mary's Road
Champaign, IL 61820
(217) 333-1801
The Council publishes research papers on home energy, building science, design, construction, retrofitting, and lighting.

Center for Resourceful Building Technology
PO Box 3866
Missoula, MT 59806
(406) 549-7678
CRBT's emphasis is on innovative building materials and technologies that reduce stress on regional and global resources. They have published the *Guide to Resource Efficient Building Elements* and other materials on recycled building materials and waste minimization.

Energy Ideas Clearinghouse

Washington State Energy Office
PO Box 43171
Olympia, WA 98504-3171
(206) 586-8588

EIC has a bulletin board with design ideas, technical information, resources, and helpful organizations. Emphasis is currently on commercial and industrial energy savings, but a residential line is expected to open in 1995. Log-on numbers: Northwestern states: (800) 762-3319; other western states: (800) 797-7584; rest of U.S.: (206) 956-2212.

Energy Crafted Home

Conservation Services Group
441 Stuart Street
Boston, MA 02116
(617) 236-1500

This group offers nationwide technical assistance on home energy, green design, and affordable residential construction.

Energy Efficient Building Association

1829 Portland Avenue
Minneapolis, MN 55404-1898
(612) 871-0413

EEBA members are experts on building performance, efficient design and construction, superinsulation, moisture problems, and indoor air quality. Call for a list of publications and videos.

Energy Outreach Center

503 West Fourth Ave
Olympia, WA 98501
(206) 943-4595

The EOC provides information on a variety of topics, including efficient building design and construction, renewable energy, and transportation planning.

Florida Solar Energy Center

Public Information Office
300 State Road 401
Cape Canaveral, FL 32920-4099
(407) 783-0300

FSEC offers a wealth of information on helping homes work in concert with the sun for heating, cooling, hot water, and electricity. Technical publications and solar house plans are available.

Green Seal

1730 Rhode Island Avenue NW
Suite 1050
Washington, D.C. 20036-3101
(202) 331-7337

Provides free consumer information on the environmental impact of various types of appliances, lighting, and other consumer goods. Products that meet their environmental criteria are awarded the Green Seal label. Their Environmental Partners Program encourages and assists businesses to purchase recycled or resource-efficient office products and equipment.

Mass-Save

200 5th Avenue
Waltham, MA 02154
(617) 890-7788

Mass-Save is committed to providing long-term value to clients through cost-effective, quality energy conservation services. Mass-Save designs, delivers, and manages energy-efficient and environmental products and services.

National Association of Energy-Efficient Mortgage Service Companies
3121 David Avenue
Palo Alto, CA 94303
(415) 858-0890
This association runs the Energy-Efficient Mortgage Program and promotes policies to make it easier for homeowners to finance energy-efficiency improvements.

North Carolina Alternative Energy Corporation
PO Box 12699
Research Triangle Park, NC 27709
(919) 361-8000
The NCAEC specializes in electric efficiency measures for the residential, commercial, and industrial sectors. The center promotes efficient cooling, heating, and air-handling systems.

Oregon State University Energy Extension Program
800 NE Oregon Street, MS #10
Portland, OR 97232
(800) 457-9394
OSU has publications and videos available for home construction, weatherization, home energy retrofits, and low-income housing.

Passive Solar Industries Council
1511 K Street NW, Suite 600
Washington, D.C. 20005
(202) 628-7400
PSIC provides information on solar building design and retrofit issues, daylighting, insulation, and windows. Excellent publications, software, and videos.

Rocky Mountain Institute
1739 Snowmass Creek Road
Snowmass, CO 81654-9199
(303) 927-3851; area code changes to (970) on 2 April 1995
RMI carries out research and education to foster the efficient and sustainable use of resources. RMI has seven focus areas: energy, water, agriculture, transportation, green development, global security, and economic renewal. Call for an information packet and a list of RMI's publications on energy, climate, and resource policy, electric utility regulatory reform, water efficiency, super-efficient technologies and products, green building design, "hypercars," and home energy topics.

Southface Energy Institute
PO Box 5506
Atlanta, GA 30307
(404) 525-7657
Southface specializes in energy-efficient construction techniques for the southern climate. The institute has a demonstration building at 158 Moreland Avenue and also offers a home-building school and energy audit and duct-sealing services.

Underground Space Center
500 Pillsbury Drive SE
Minneapolis, MN 55455
(612) 624-0066
This research center provides public information on moisture protection, foundation insulation and design, and underground building for residential, commercial, industrial, and transportation purposes.

Magazines

Most of the following specialty magazines are not available in local bookstores or libraries, so you may need to call the publishers.

Energy Design Update
Cutter Information
37 Broadway
Arlington, D.C. 02174
(617) 648-8700
Reports on new energy products, materials, techniques, building science research, and field results: indispensable for technically-minded architects and builders.

Environmental Building News
RR1, Box 161
Brattleboro, VT 05301
(802) 257-7300
Covers environmental aspects of buildings and materials. A must-read for architects and builders dedicated to creating healthy and environmentally friendly buildings.

Fine Homebuilding
Taunton Press
PO Box 5506
Newtown, CT 06470-5506
(800) 283-7252
Articles on innovative home designs, materials, and construction techniques for architects, builders, owner-builders, carpenters, craftsmen, and other aficionados of beautifully crafted buildings.

Home Energy
2124 Kittredge, #95
Berkeley, CA 94704
(510) 524-5405
Excellent articles on energy retrofits, state and utility programs, and new products and techniques for saving energy.

Home Power
PO Box 520
Ashland, OR 97520
(916) 475-3179
Magazine on independent energy systems, photovoltaics, and renewable electricity options.

Journal of Light Construction
RR2, Box 146
Richmond, VT 05477
(802) 434-4747
Construction management, building techniques, contractors' problem-solving, and energy issues.

Solar Today
American Solar Energy Society
2400 Central Avenue, Suite G-1
Boulder, CO 80301
(303) 443-3130
Innovative passive and active solar house designs, solar technologies, building performance, cost-effective designs, case studies, etc.

Books

Most of the following are available at local libraries and book-stores. If not, give the publisher a call. For help in finding out-of-print books, you may want to contact a book-search company; search fees vary. One such company is Book Look, Inc., 51 Maple Avenue, Warwick, NY 10990, (800) 223-0540.

We first list books available in three categories—**home energy retrofits, new design and construction,** and **renewable energy**—then those available from Rocky Mountain Institute.

Home energy retrofits

Book of Light
Real Goods Trading Corporation
966 Mazzoni Street
Ukiah, CA 95482
(800) 762-7323
A well-illustrated compendium demonstrating why today's advanced lighting products work better, last longer, save money, and provide the best possible light for your home. $5.

Consumer Guide to Home Energy Savings
Alex Wilson and John Morrill
American Council for an Energy Efficient Economy
2140 Shattuck Avenue, #202
Berkeley, CA 94704
(510) 549-9914
The numbers book on energy efficiency. A must for anyone who wants to know just how much can be saved by using energy-efficient products, who manufactures them, and how to install them. Also lists performance ratings for the most efficient refrigerators, appliances, water heaters, and heating and air conditioning equipment. $8.95.

Eco-Renovation
Edward Harland
Chelsea Green Publishing
Post Mills, VT 05058-0130
(800) 639-4099
An ecological home improvement guide covering living space, energy, health, and renovation materials. $16.95.

Energy: 101 Practical Tips for Home and Work
Susan Hassol and Beth Richman
Windstar Foundation
2317 Snowmass Creek Road
Snowmass, CO 81654
(303) 927-4777
Well-documented book on what individuals can do to reduce energy waste at home, at work, and in transportation. Also books on household chemicals and recycling. $4 each.

Energy Efficient Windows
Ted Haskell
Oregon State University
Extension Service
Administrative Services A422
Corvallis, OR 97331-2119
(503) 737-3311

Selecting and installing efficient windows, plus window energy-efficiency ratings. $1.50.

Home Insulation
Harry Yost
Storey Communications, Inc.
Schoolhouse Road
Pownal, VT 05261
(800) 827-8673

All about insulation: what to use, why, where, and how. $11.95.

Household EcoTeam Workbook
David Gershon & Robert Gilman
Global Action Plan
84 Yerry Hill Road
Woodstock, NY 12498
(914) 679-4830

A step-by-step program for groups or individuals who want to have a positive impact on the environment, starting with their own households and neighborhood or community groups. $14.95.

The Lighting Pattern Book for Homes
Lighting Research Center
Rensselaer Polytechnic Institute
Troy, NY 12180-3590
(518) 276-8716

This book discusses practical designs to help you see well and save money, and contains details on energy-efficient bulbs, fixtures, and controls. It has specific effi-

cient lighting plans for rooms and houses of various sizes. $50.

Making Your Mobile Home Energy Efficient
North Carolina Alternative
Energy Corporation
AEC Publications, PO Box 12699
Research Triangle Park, NC 27709
(919) 361-8000

This step-by-step guide helps owners of mobile homes save energy and increase their comfort. The book covers topics such as attic insulation, air sealing, and heating and cooling strategies. $5.

Mechanical System Retrofit Manual: A Guide for Residential Design
Paul A. Knight
Van Nostrand Reinhold Co.
115 Fifth Ave.
New York, NY 10023
(800) 842-3636

Introduces all types of residential heating systems including furnaces, boilers, electric resistance, and heat pumps. Key retrofit decisions, installation procedures, and safety checks noted. $46.95.

The New Woodburners Handbook: A Guide to Safe, Healthy and Efficient Woodburning
Storey Communications
PO Box 445
Pownal, VT 05261
(800) 827-8673

Information on stove selection, operation, proper wood selection, safety, maintenance, and installation. $12.95.

Passive Solar Remodeling Guidelines
Passive Solar Industries Council
1090 Vermont Avenue NW, #1200
Washington, D.C. 20005
(202) 628-7400
Allows remodelers and home-owners to make informed decisions about improving the energy-efficiency of passive solar remodeling projects. $50.

New Complete Do-it-yourself Manual (1991)
The Reader's Digest Association
Reader's Digest Road
Pleasantville, NY 10570
(914) 241-5786
Shows do-it-yourselfers how to draw plans, buy materials, estimate costs, get approvals, and complete the job. It also describes what's involved when hiring a contractor. Good chapters on weatherization, insulation, and solar applications. $28.

Renovating Old Houses
George Nash
Taunton Press
63 South Main St., Box 5506
Newtown, CT 06470-5506
(800) 283-7252
Focuses on renovation aspects, but also describes weatherization, infiltration, and home heating systems. $37.95.

The Residential Energy Audit Manual
Dale Schueman (ed)
Fairmont Press
700 Indian Trail
Lilburn, GA 30247
(404) 925-9388

Intended for aspiring house doctors and auditors. Full of conservation and solar tips, step-by-step procedures, and descriptions of weatherization materials. Also appropriate for the dedicated do-it-yourselfer. $58.

Retrofit Right: How to Make Your Old House Energy Efficient
City of Oakland
1330 Broadway, Suite 310
Oakland, CA 94612
(510) 238-3941
A little dated (1983) and written for California housing types and climate regions (including mountain areas), but still one of the best weatherization and retrofit books available. Includes lists of priorities for 16 climate regions. Great illustrations. $11.20.

Solid Fuels Encyclopedia
Jay Shelton
Storey Communications
Pownal, VT 05261
(800) 827-8673
A comprehensive and easy-to-understand account of all the solid fuel heating options. Provides information on wood and coal, catalytic afterburners, heat exchangers, and air dilution devices on the market. $12.95.

Sustaining the Earth: Choosing Consumer Products that are Safe for You, Your Family, and the Earth
William Morrow & Company
1350 Avenue of the Americas
New York, NY 10019
(212) 261-6500

Evaluates hundreds of consumer products and whether their production and use is environmentally sustainable. Includes appliances, insulation, food, personal, and household products. $15.

The Water Heater Workbook
Larry and Suzanne Weingarten
Elemental Enterprises
PO Box 928
Monterey, CA 93942
(408) 394-7077

Explains how water heaters work, why they fail, and how to prevent them from failing. Also details water heater upgrades and how to reduce energy use. $9.75.

Your Mobile Home Energy and Repair Guide, *and* Your Home Cooling Energy Guide
John T. Krigger
Saturn Resource Management
324 Fuller Avenue, Suite S-8
Helena, MT 59601
(800) 735-0577

These two books discuss energy retrofits of mobile homes and reducing cooling costs and improving comfort in site-built homes during hot weather. $15.95 and $12.50, respectively.

New home design and construction

Alternative Housebuilding
Mike McClintock
Sterling Publishing Company
387 Park Avenue South
New York, NY 10016
(212) 532-7160

A good overview of non-traditional construction materials and building techniques: log, timberframe, cordwood, stone, earth masonry, and earth-sheltered houses. Now out of print.

Builders' Field Guide to Energy Efficient Construction
Southern Electric International
64 Perimeter Center East
Atlanta, GA 30346
(404) 668-3445

This book is an excellent source of tips and information on superior construction techniques, although it is focused on Northwest building codes and conditions. Contains an excellent chapter on air and moisture barriers, sealing techniques, and ventilation. Numerous drawings. Very useful for architects, builders, and homeowners. Free while supplies last.

Climatic Building Design: Energy-Efficient Building Principles and Practice
Donald Watson & Kenneth Labs
McGraw-Hill Book Company
Blue Ridge Summit, PA 17294
(800) 262-4729

Interesting, technical, and amply illustrated book on solar gain, infiltration and ventilation, climate control, comfort issues, and design strategies. $32.95.

Energy-Smart Building
Philip Russell with Joe Hemmer
Home Builder Press
National Association of Home Builders
1201 15th Street, NW
Washington, DC 20005-2800
(800) 223-2665

Offers unrealistically low estimates for the energy saving potential of energy-efficient new construction. Some good tips, but not the most useful of references. $20.

Environmental by Design
Kim Leclair and David Rousseau
Professional Edition
PO Box 95016
South Vancouver C.S.C.
Vancouver B.C. V6P 6V4 Canada
(604) 378-8189

Compares the environmental impacts of interior building materials from insulation to furniture. A 14-symbol legend is used to evaluate the production process, packaging, installation, and resource recovery. It comes in a binder with two updates. $40. A bound version for $19.95 is available from Hartley & Marks Publishing, (206) 945-2017.

Environmental Resource Guide
American Institute of Architects
PO Box 60
Williston, VT 05495-0060
(800) 365-2724

A comprehensive guide that discusses the embodied energy of building materials and the environmental aspects of their extraction, manufacture, use, and disposal. $165.

Healthy House Building: A Design and Construction Guide
John Bower
Healthy House Institute
7471 North Shiloh Road
Unionville, IN 47468
(812) 332-5073

Comprehensive book on construction materials and building practices that may affect your health, plus a listing of less toxic alternatives. $21.95.

Massachusetts Audubon Society publications
Educational Resources Office
208 South Great Road
Lincoln, MA 01773
(617) 259-9500

Publishes a series of very helpful little books: *All About Insulation; Building an Environmentally Friendly House; Contractor's Guide to Finding & Sealing Hidden Air Leaks; Financing Home Energy Improvements; Home Heating with Wood & Coal; Oil & Gas Heating Systems: Maintenance & Improvement; Solar Ideas for Your Home or Apartment;* and *Weatherize Your Home or Apartment.* $3.75 each.

The Natural House Book
David Pearson
Simon & Schuster
1230 Avenue of the Americas
New York, NY 10020
(201) 767-5937

Beautifully produced book on natural building and decorating materials, energy and resource issues, sunlighting, and ideas for feeling good in your home. $19.95.

The New Solar Home Book
Bruce Anderson with Michael Riordan
Brick House Publishing Co.
P.O. Box 256
Amherst, NH 03031
(800) 446-8642

The most recent edition of a huge best-seller of the 1970s, offering lively and readable coverage of all the important aspects of passive and active solar energy systems and uses. $16.95.

Passive Solar Design Strategies: A Guidebook for Designing Passive-Solar Structures

Passive Solar Industries Council
1090 Vermont Avenue NW
Suite 1200
Washington, DC 20005
(202) 628-7400

Users get the basics of passive solar, sun-tempering, direct gain, thermal storage mass walls, sunspaces, and natural cooling strategies. Contains site-specific information for 220 locations ($50). **BuilderGuide** is a companion software program ($100).

Passive Solar Energy

Bruce Anderson and Malcolm Wells
Brick House Publishing Co.
P.O. Box 256
Amherst, NH 03031
(800) 446-8642

A 1994 update of a classic treatment of the topic, enhanced by Wells' entertaining and clearly informative drawings. $24.95.

The Passive Solar Energy Book

Edward Mazria
Rodale Press
Emmaus, PA 18098-0099
(215) 967-5171

One of the best passive solar books around, now out of print.

Residential Building Design and Construction Workbook

Ned Nisson
Cutter Information Corporation
37 Broadway
Arlington, MA 02174-5539
(800) 888-8939

A how-to workbook for building a comfortable and energy-efficient home, written by the editor of *Energy Design Update*. Discusses superinsulation, energy dynamics, and moisture control. Also discusses the interrelationships between roofs, ceilings, walls, windows, foundations, heating, cooling, ventilation, and indoor air quality. $95.

Superinsulated Design and Construction: A Guide to Building Energy-Efficient Homes

T. Lenchek, C. Mattock, and J. Raabe
Van Nostrand Reinhold
115 Fifth Ave.
New York, NY 10023
(800) 842-3636

A good in-depth look at efficient building design. Now out of print.

Superinsulated Houses and Air-to-Air Heat Exchangers

William A. Shurcliff
Brick House Publishing Co.
P.O. Box 256
Amherst NH 03031
(800) 446-8642

Written by a Harvard University research physicist, this is a classic work on superinsulated home construction and how to handle the resulting problems with air and radon. $19.95.

Renewable energy

All of the following books are available from Real Goods Trading Co., 966 Mazzoni St., Ukiah, CA 95482, (800) 762-7323.

The Independent Home
Michael Potts

A compendium of ideas and inspiration for anyone who dreams of a sustainable lifestyle. $17.95.

The New Solar Electric Home
Joel Davidson

Gives you all the information you need to set up a PV system, whether it be a remote site, grid connected, marine, stand-alone, or auxiliary. $19.

The Solar Electric House
Steven J. Strong

Helps you determine your electricity requirements, designing a solar electric house, system options and economics, stand-alone and utility-interactive systems. $21.95.

Solar Living Sourcebook

A how-to and where-to-get-it guide in one. A "comprehensive collection of the finest energy-sensible technologies." 400 pages of information and products for renewable energy systems. $23.

Wind Power for Home and Business
Paul Gipe

A comprehensive guide to modern wind machines for people who want to know how to design, evaluate, install, and operate a small wind power system. $35.

Rocky Mountain Institute publications

You can order any of the following publications with the form at the end of this book. RMI's address is 1739 Snowmass Creek Road, Dept. E Pubs, Snowmass, CO 81654, (303) 927-3851. Area code (970) after 2 April 1995.

A Primer on Sustainable Building
Dianna Lopez Barnett and William D. Browning

This green builder guidebook for architects and developers discusses sustainability as it applies to individual buildings and small-scale residential and commercial developments. It gives reasons for "going green," and ideas on site selection, landscaping, how to save energy and water, and building ecology. $16.95.

The Community Energy Workbook
Alice Hubbard and Clay Fong

This detailed workbook is a one-stop source for anyone wanting to improve their local economy and the environment. A step-by-step framework helps users calculate their community's energy bill and its economic implications, organize an Energy Town Meeting, and involve the entire community in creating and implementing an energy action plan. $16.95.

The Efficient House Sourcebook
Robert Sardinsky

An annotated bibliography for anyone building, designing, or retrofitting a house. Lists state, Federal, and other sources of information, and reviews dozens of books and trade magazines on energy-saving home design and construction. 3rd edition. $13.95.

The Energy Directory: A Guide to Energy Efficient Products and Services
Richard Heede & Linda Baynham
The printed and electronic versions of this book are templates—first developed for RMI's own local community—written to be readily adapted by other communities. Covers home energy retrofits, equipment, materials, and professional services. Comes with a guidebook for local utilities, chambers of commerce, grassroots organizations, and other groups

to develop a directory suiting their climate and region. Available in 1995.

Home Energy Briefs
A series of informative briefs on residential equipment and materials for consumers and homeowners. Titles include: *Water Heating*; *Windows*; *Refrigerators & Freezers*; *Cooking Appliances & Dishwashers*; *Washers, Dryers, & Miscellaneous Appliances*; *Home Office Equipment*; and *Lighting*. The series can be re-packaged for utilities and organizations. $2 each.

Water Efficiency for Your Home
A useful brochure featuring products and advice that save water, energy, and money. $1.

Videos

Arizona Dept. of Commerce
Phoenix, AZ (602) 280-1402
Video of three photovoltaic installations.

Energy Efficient Building Association
Minneapolis, MN (612) 871-0413
Videos on building science, construction practice, envelope design, ventilation, weatherization, and air barriers.

Iris Communications
Eugene, OR (800) 346-0104
Several training videos on how to do weatherization, leak detection, insulation, etc. Iris also produces

The Energy Source Directory: A Guide to Products Used in Energy Efficient Buildings, and *Window Design Decisions*.

New Mexico Energy Extension Service
Las Cruces, NM (505) 646-3425
Video on mobile-home energy retrofits and passive solar.

Oregon State University Extension Energy Program
Portland, OR (503) 737-2513
Many helpful how-to videos and publications on energy retrofits, weatherization, insulation, blower-door testing, and related topics.

Owner-Builder Schools

Building Education Center
812 Page Street
Berkeley, CA 94710
(510) 525-7610
Classes on specific topics (*e.g.*, plumbing) to comprehensive design and construction courses.

Cedar Valley Workshops
215 East Muskegon Street
Cedar Springs, MI 49319
(616) 696-0603
Short, intensive courses on energy-efficient construction and renewable energy technologies.

Earthwood Building School
366 Murtagh Hill Road
West Chazy, NY 12992
(518) 493-7744
Classes in cordwood, masonry, and earth-sheltered housing.

Florida Solar Energy Center
Public Information Office
300 State Road 401
Cape Canaveral, FL 32920-4099
(407) 783-0300
Classes for architects, contractors, and owner-builders on designing and building for Florida's hot climate. Solar water heating, passive cooling, and renewables.

Heartwood
Johnson Hill Road
Washington, MA 01235
(413) 623- 623-6677
Classes on conventional and timberframe construction.

Institute for Independent Living
Real Goods Trading Corporation
966 Mazzoni Street
Ukiah, CA 95482-3471
(800) 762-7325
Dedicated to the study of all aspects of self-sufficient and sustainable lifestyles. Courses on planning and building a renewable home energy system.

Natural House Building Center
RR1, Box 115F
Fairfield, IA 52556
(515) 472-7775
Workshops on straw and clay design and construction. Emphasis on using local materials.

Natural Spaces
37955 Bridge Road
North Branch, MN 55056
(612) 674-4292
The dome-building and design people. Hands-on classes. Tours.

North Carolina Alternative Energy Corporation
PO Box 12699
Research Triangle Park, NC 27709
(919) 361-8000
The NCAEC offers training materials on how to build your home, have one built, and how to work with your contractor. Also workshops on heat pumps and other energy technologies.

Out On Bale
1037 East Linden Street
Tucson, AZ 85719
(602) 624-1673
Workshops on the fundamentals
of strawbale construction. Offers
hands-on experience in raising
and finishing strawbale walls.

Owner-Builder Center
Houston Community College
4141 Costa Rica
Houston, TX 77092
(713) 956-1178
Design and construction classes.

Shelter Institute
38 Center Street
Bath, ME 04530
(207) 442-7938
The Institute's 90-hour class covers the design and construction of
efficient new homes and retrofits.

Solar/Adobe Associates
847 East Palace Avenue
Santa Fe, NM 87501
(505) 984-0077
Workshops on all aspects of designing and building energy-efficient solar adobe homes.

Solar Energy International
PO Box 715
Carbondale, CO 81623
(303) 963-8855
SEI's renewable energy program
teaches the practical use of solar,
wind, and water power. Hands-
on workshops show how to design, install, and maintain renewable electric systems. SEI also
offers classes on designing and
building state-of-the-art solar

homes that are efficient and earth-
friendly.

Solar Survivor Architecture
PO Box 1041
Taos, NM 87571
(505) 758-9870
Hands-on design and construction
workshops on Reynold's "Earth-
ship" rammed earth tire homes.

Southface Energy Institute
PO Box 5506
Atlanta, GA 30307
(404) 525-7657
Southface's building school helps
those interested in contracting or
building their own home learn energy-efficient construction. Covers passive solar design, electrical, plumbing, managing subcon-
tractors, materials, and financing.

**Southwest Solar Adobe
School**
PO Box 153
Bosque, NM 87006
(505) 898-8829
Teaches owner-builders and professionals techniques for passive-
solar, environmentally conscious,
and resource-efficient earth construction. Hands-on experience
for *adoberos* and rammed earth en-
thusiasts. Publishes the excellent
Earthbuilders Encyclopedia ($20).

Yestermorrow School
RR 1, Box 97-5
Warren, VT 05674
(802) 496-5545
Courses on timberframe and
strawbale construction, co-housing, landscaping, solar design, etc.

Technology and Design Demonstration Centers

These are just a few of dozens of public energy technology and design demonstration centers around the country.

Center for Resourceful Building Technology
PO Box 3866
Missoula, MT 59806
(406) 549-7678

Customer Technology Application Center
Southern California Edison
6090 N. Irwindale Avenue
Irwindale, CA 91702
(818) 812-7500

Desert House
Desert Botanical Garden
1201 North Galvin
Phoenix, AZ 85012
(602) 941-1225

The Energy Outlet
61 West 34th
Eugene, OR 9740
(503) 683-5060

Energy Resource Center
Portland General Electric
410 SW Oak Street
Portland, OR 97214
(503) 464-7501

Florida House Foundation
4600 Beneva Road
Sarasota, FL 34233
(813) 927-2020

Florida Solar Energy Center
300 State Road 401
Cape Canaveral, FL 32920
(407) 783-0300

Lighting Design Laboratory
Seattle City Light
400 East Pine
Seattle, WA 98101
(206) 325-9695

National Association of Home Builders
400 Prince George's Boulevard
Upper Marlboro, MD 20772
(301) 249-4000

National Renewable Energy Laboratory
1617 Cole Boulevard
Golden, CO 80401
(303) 275-4099

Ontario Energy Home
368 Phillip Street
Waterloo, Ontario N2L 5J1
(519) 844-6421

PG&E Energy Center
Pacific Gas & Electric
851 Howard Street
San Francisco, CA 94103
(415) 973-7206

Rocky Mountain Institute
1739 Snowmass Creek Road
Snowmass, CO 81654-9199
(303) 927-3851; (970) April '95.

Southface Energy Institute
PO Box 5506
Atlanta, GA 30307
(404) 525-7657

Mail-Order Services

Listed below are a few mail-order houses that specialize in energy- and water-saving equipment or other environmental goods.

Alternative Energy Engineering
PO Box 339
Redway, CA 95560
(800) 777-6609
Renewable power and efficient energy technologies for off-grid, self-sufficient living.

Applied Energy Products
3920 State Street NW
Canton, OH 44720
(800) 255-7996
Carries a line of weatherization materials such as caulk, insulation, air-tight vents, and water-heater wraps.

Eco-Source
9051 Mill Station Road, #E
Sebastopol, CA 95472
(707) 829-7562
Environmental and bio-degradable products, recycled paper, recycling systems, efficient lighting, air and water purification equipment, and non-toxic materials.

Energy Answers
PO Box 24
Lake Bluff, IL 60044
(708) 234-2515
Compact fluorescents, showerheads, aerators, water heater wraps and timers, tankless water heaters, solar attic fans, etc.

Energy Federation
14 Tech Circle
Natick, MA 01760
(800) 876-0660
Specializes in resource-efficient products. An excellent selection of compact fluorescents, as well as water-efficient showerheads, a non-CFC insulating foam, rope caulk, door sweeps, setback thermostats, high-temperature duct tape, mastic, radiator reflector material, heat-recovery ventilators, and water heater wraps.

Environmental Store
125 Pompton Plains Crossroad
Wayne, NJ 07470
(201) 616-0220
"Clean and green" household products for washing and personal care. Ecologically friendly testing and packaging.

Fowler Solar Electric
PO Box 435
Worthington, MA 01098
(413) 238-5974
Efficient lighting, photovoltaic equipment, refrigerators, and helpful publications.

Jade Mountain
PO Box 4616
Boulder, CO 80306
(800) 442-1972

Efficient lighting, appliances (propane and electric refrigerators, cookstoves), water heater wraps, other energy-saving products, water purification, and renewable energy equipment.

Photocomm
7681 East Gray Road
Scottsdale, AZ 85260
(800) 223-9580
A design guide and catalog for solar electric power systems. Also carries the CFC-free Danish Vestfrost 10.6 ft^3 efficient refrigerator.

Real Goods Trading Company
966 Mazzoni Street
Ukiah, CA 95482
(800) 762-7325
Publishes the *Solar Living Sourcebook*, an annual catalog chock full of information on photovoltaic cells, twelve-volt light fixtures, inverters, and various other devices for those wishing to escape from the utility grid. Their quarterly catalog also offers a diverse line of environmentally friendly household and yard items. Several renewable energy and home energy efficiency books are listed.

Resource Conservation Technology
2633 N. Calvert Street
Baltimore, MD 21218
(410) 366-1146
Manufactures and distributes state-of-the-art building materials for contractors and technical professionals. Air-sealing gaskets, high-quality weatherization materials, pond liners, roofing materials, and more for new construction and large remodeling jobs.

S&H Alternative Energy
RD 3, Box 312
Putney, VT 05346
(802) 722-3704
Efficient lighting supplies (AC and DC), lighting kits for PV systems.

Seventh Generation
49 Hercules Drive
Colchester, VT 05446
(800) 456-1177
Publishes a free catalog with many items for energy and water savings, including water-efficient showerheads, programmable thermostats, caulks, compact fluorescent lighting, radon test kits, etc.

How Energy Is Measured

As you examine how much energy your home uses, you will come across units such as kWh and Mcf. For the curious, here's an explanation of energy measurement units.

Measuring electricity

"Watts" describe the rate at which energy is being consumed or produced. Watts describe, for example, the power output of a generating plant or the amount of electricity a light bulb requires at any given moment.

1 kilowatt (kW) = 1,000 watts

This is the power it takes to light ten bright 100-watt incandescent bulbs. You can get the same amount of light with 10 efficient compact fluorescent bulbs, using about 270 watts.

"Watt-hours" measure the total amount of energy used or produced over a period of time. This total is determined by the power consumption rate and how long the power is used. For example, when a 100-watt bulb is on for one hour it uses 100 watt-hours. Since electricity is used over periods of time, measurement of electricity consumption is always in watt-hours. The difference between watts and watt-hours is like the difference between miles per hour and miles traveled.

1 kilowatt-hour (kWh) =
1,000 watt-hours

How much would it cost to run ten 100-watt light bulbs continuously for one year? There are 8,760 hours in one year. Therefore, the total energy consumed would be 1,000 watts multiplied by 8,760 hours, which is equal to 8,760,000 watt-hours, or 8,760 kilowatt-hours.

The average residential rate for electricity in the U.S. is 8.3 cents per kilowatt-hour (although rates range from about 4.5 to 16 cents/kWh). The total cost of running those ten 100-watt light bulbs for a full year would be 8,760 kWh times 8.3 cents per kWh, or a whopping $727!

A typical U.S. household consumes about 10,000 kWh of electricity per year, costing homeowners an average of $830 annually, but this varies widely by region of the country, house size, income, whether electric heating or air conditioning is used, etc.

Measuring heat

One Btu (British thermal unit) is defined as the energy required to raise one pound of water (about a pint) by one degree Fahrenheit—roughly equivalent to burning one kitchen match. A typical home consumes a total of 180 million Btu per year (including the energy lost in the generation and transmission of electricity). Of this total, roughly one-half is for space heating, and the remainder is for appliances, water heating, air conditioning, lighting, etc. This "consumption" of 180 million matches would fill one-third of the volume of the average home. (Related factoids: The average refrigerator consumes its volume of coal every year, whereas a car typically consumes its weight in gasoline annually.)

Measuring natural gas

Natural gas is usually measured by volume at a specific temperature and pressure, since gas can expand or contract depending on temperature and pressure. The standard unit of measurement for natural gas is a cubic foot at room temperature and sea-level pressure. Since a cubic foot of gas is not really very much, natural gas companies usually measure gas by the hundreds (Ccf) or thousands (Mcf) of cubic feet.

Some gas companies measure natural gas in terms of heat content, because that is what determines its usefulness. Rather than cubic feet, these companies use "therms," which is defined as 100,000 Btu. One hundred cubic feet of natural gas is roughly equivalent to one therm. Natural gas can vary in its heat content, depending on where it comes from.

Btu content of various fuels

One gallon of home heating oil	139,000 Btu
One gallon of gasoline	125,000 Btu
One gallon of propane	91,100 Btu
One kWh (heat yield at home)	3,412 Btu
One kWh (heat lost at the powerplant)	6,688 Btu
One cubic foot of natural gas	1,031 Btu
One pound of automobile tires	13,000 Btu
One pound of coal	11,560 Btu
One pound of wood (dry hardwood)	8,600 Btu
One cord of wood (Aspen)	16.2 million Btu
One cord of wood (Elm, maple)	21.4 million Btu
One cord of wood (White oak))	29.2 million Btu

ORDER FORM

Rocky Mountain Institute
1739 Snowmass Creek Road
Snowmass, CO 81654-9199
(303) 927-3851 / FAX (303) 927-3420
After 2 April 1995 use area code 970

Please send me the following RMI publications:

D95-2	*A Primer on Sustainable Building*	_____	$16.95
E95-3	*Homemade Money: How to Save Energy and Dollars in Your Home*	_____	$14.95
E92-9	*The Efficient House Sourcebook*	_____	$13.95
ER95-4	*The Community Energy Workbook*	_____	$16.95
W92-16	"Water Efficiency for Your Home"	_____	$ 1.00

Home Energy Briefs *(circle titles ordered)*

  • Lighting • Refrigerators and Freezers • Windows •

  • Water Heating • Cooking Appliances and Dishwashers •

  • Washers, Dryers, and Miscellaneous Appliances •

• Home Office Equipment •	_____	$ 2.00 each
RMI *Newsletter* (three issues, one year)	_____	$10.00 *
RMI Information Packet and Publications List	_____	Free

*requested minimum donation

subtotal:	
+ 20% shipping/handling:	
+ 3% tax if shipped to Colorado	
total enclosed:	

We normally ship by U.S. Mail or UPS; for faster delivery, please call.

☐ *My check or money order is enclosed*

☐ *Please charge my:* ☐ *Visa* ☐ *Mastercard* *Signature:* _____

Card #: _____ *Exp. date:* _____

Please send the publications to: (please print or type)

Name: _____

Address: _____

Town/City: _____ *State:* _____

ZIP/Postal code: _____ *Country:* _____

Telephone: _____

QUESTIONNAIRE

Where did you hear about the book?

Did you find it useful?

Well organized?

What information is the book missing?

How many measures did you implement as a result of reading this book?

Which ones?

Did you find the measures as cost-effective and as easy as we suggested?

Can you estimate how much you will save on your monthly energy bills?

Did you find the book motivating?

Other comments:

A PRIMER ON SUSTAINABLE BUILDING

Few realize that buildings use more than a third of this country's energy. Their construction profoundly affects our environment, from the materials used to the site chosen. **A Primer on Sustainable Building** is written for architects, developers, general contractors, landscapers, homeowners, and others who are interested in improving the economics, marketability, performance and aesthetics of buildings while at the same time enhancing their environment. The *Primer* provides important insights on how integrating "green design" processes can result in buildings that are far superior to traditional design and construction. *125 pp., $16.95.*

THE PRIMER DISCUSSES THESE ISSUES:

- How sustainable building design affects market performance, resource consumption, and affordability;
- Reducing environmental impact through site selection, site development, transportation planning, building placement, open space design, and landscaping;
- Enhancing efficiency through a building's shape, interior layout, size, and solar orientation;
- Using building materials, appliances, heating, cooling, lighting, and water systems that save cost and improve air quality.

*"**The Primer** is a must for those who wish to positively affect the lives of future generations by the way that they choose to build and develop throughout this land. The principles and ideas presented are both easily understood and of immense value to professionals in the building industry as well as interested individuals."*

—Susan Maxman
1993 President, American Institute of Architects

THE COMMUNITY ENERGY WORKBOOK

Introducing a new sourcebook that will make it easy for your community to explore the economic benefits of improved energy use and develop a plan to make tangible improvements in the community. **The Community Energy Workbook** outlines a simple yet complete process for actively involving citizens, businesses and government in increasing energy efficiency and the use of renewable energy. *265 pp., $16.95.*

THE WORKBOOK WILL HELP YOU TO:

- Calculate your community's total energy bill, including the environmental costs of current energy use;

- Demonstrate to your community that economic and job-creation opportunities can be realized through increased energy efficiency and use of renewable energy;

- Organize a media and public outreach campaign to put energy efficiency as an economic development tool on your community's agenda;

- Hold an Energy Town Meeting to involve citizens in developing a community energy action plan.

WHAT THEY'RE SAYING ABOUT THE WORKBOOK

"We could forge no better energy policy than to put copies of **The Community Energy Workbook** *on the desk of every local official and active citizen in the country."*

—David Orr
Professor and activist, Oberlin College